I0126720

Double Edge
The Intersections of Transgender and BDSM

Raven Kaldera

DOUBLE EDGE

The Intersections of
Transgender and BDSM

Raven Kaldera

Alfred Press
Hubbardston, Massachusetts

Alfred Press
12 Simond Hill Road
Hubbardston, MA 01452

Double Edge:
The Intersections of Transgender and BDSM
© 2009 Raven Kaldera
ISBN 978-0-9828794-0-5

All rights reserved.
No part of this book may be reproduced in any
form or by any means without the permission of
the author.

Printed in cooperation with
Lulu Enterprises, Inc.
860 Aviation Parkway, Suite 300
Morrisville, NC 27560

*Dedicated to my slaveboy Joshua who serves me
with such amazing commitment,
my bitch Ruth who stands by me loyally,
all my kinky trans lovers past and present,
and my wife Bella who puts up with me in spite
of everything.*

Contents

Foreword
Patrick Califia

Double-Edge: The Intersection of Transgender and BDSM is a smart book that tackles difficult, fascinating, controversial subjects with panache and compassion. It's the latest public service from the fierce and tender pagan priest, activist, farmer, community organizer, oracle, nightmare of those devoted to the normal and ordinary, and all-around role model Raven Kaldera, whose complex identity gives him a rather comprehensive perspective on the topics of kinky sex, alternative relationships, and gender variance. As he says:

> Somewhere along the line, the fact that I have an alternative sexuality and live in alternative relationships became just as defining as the fact that I have an alternative gender (not to mention my alternative spirituality or all my other non-mainstream choices). It's all tied up in me, but not in a tangle because I spent years combing out those strands and making them lie together. They complement each other now. Each taught me things that helped me to see the others more realistically. I'd say that rather than a tangle, they're tied up in a package. Take one and you get all the others as well. I am a self-made work.

Kaldera is a prolific author whose previous works include *Hermaphrodeities*, a unique exposition on transgendered spirituality and deification, and *Dear Raven and Joshua: Questions and Answers About Master/Slave Relationships*. I can't overstate how much I appreciate Kaldera's intelligence and all of the good things he has done for our community. He shows a level of respect for diversity and sensitivity toward intimate, potentially hurtful topics that challenges the rest of us to come up to his standard. This book consciously takes a "big tent" approach to the issue of what the term "transgender" means when we are discussing the experience of gender-variant people in the BDSM community. Kaldera's description of the folks who potentially fall into this category is a model of care and understanding. He "gets" the subtleties that elude many so-called gender specialists who have academic degrees but no personal experience with fighting gender stereotyping and mislabeling upon and within their own bodies.

Of course, in order to be understood, Kaldera has to make use of the terms that are currently popular, deemed to be politically acceptable and respectful. As transgender people become more visible, as we continue to dialogue with one another, our self-understanding and the discourse about us will change. Paradigms and jargon and identities themselves will evolve in step with these changes. I think this book will weather those sea changes much better than most. It is an excellent compilation of the contested yet relatively safe place of trans people in the BDSM community, and the problems and rewards that result from that involvement, and as far as I know, the only work of its kind.

If I didn't know better (hey, I saw that movie too—yes, *that* one!), I would suspect Kaldera of being a big old softy. He exhibits such a tender heart toward our struggles and victories. Like many a good Daddy and Master, he knows how to be "cruel to be kind", reminding us of things that make us uncomfortable, stuff we don't know, or mistakes we have made, without shaming or invalidating us. It takes a lot of courage to tackle a topic that many would see as being too specific, too minority-oriented, without a large enough readership. It takes an even braver reader to wade into the complicated threads of this work, and begin to examine what it implies for people who may never have met a transgendered man or woman or someone who is gender-queer, as well as us kids in the in group.

Kaldera is not just asking how trans people can have better lives. He is asking big questions about gender socialization and how it affects our whole society, the state regulation of sexual expression and how to confront it, connections and disconnections between intimacy and pleasure, how to find wisdom in ordeals and rites of passage, conflicting ideals of what constitutes a good relationship, the nature of boundaries and how they are drawn, and a hundred other topics that concern everyone. I deeply, deeply wish I could get "outsiders" to absorb the material that Kaldera lays out in *Double Edge*. I often feel, when I read a cogent queer book, that it deserves a much bigger audience. Well, books go in some odd directions. *Macho Sluts* made it into Saudi Arabia and China, if I can trust my fan mail. Who knows where these ideas will float, like a letter in a bottle thrown into the ocean?

As Kaldera emphasizes in multiple ways, transgender people and BDSM practitioners are *people*. Perhaps this is the hardest thing for the larger world to grasp. We are part of the whole world. What affects us, what hurts us, will also hurt the rest of our species. Properly understood, the things that make us joyful or empowered are also good for the larger society. We are not just strangers to be ignored, vilified, or tolerated. We have lessons to teach, art and poetry to promulgate, love to share. Turn your back on us at your peril. Not because we are scary thugs who will bring the whole world down upon your ears, but because of the things we have seen and the forbidden things we have experienced. We know things that I believe all human beings need to understand if our troubled world is going to survive and become a more just and decent place. Kaldera points out:

> I've said before, many times, that what we repress just migrates to our crotches and ends up coming out there. It's the one place where our subconscious can best force us to face things that are troubling or difficult for us. ... I've always believed that sexual urges were a force that could be used for social change, not simply ignored and repressed if it didn't match one's politics. There's also that kink and sexual pleasure do not need to be justified by personal evolution. They are beneficial in and of themselves, and any positive side effects—like courage, understanding social patterns, or fully experiencing the whole range of gendered energy in one's self—are just icing on the cake.

Like the author, I had my first experiences with violating gender taboos in the BDSM community. As a child, I believed myself to be a boy. It would be hard to say which element of my core sense of myself caused more trouble—the knowledge I was a boy or my tingling fascination with images of bondage and corporal punishment. I was shocked and traumatized when adults ridiculed me and insisted I had to be a girl. It took a lot of verbal abuse and physical violence to make me stop talking about being a boy. The fantasies I would eventually come to label BDSM frightened me. Did I want somebody to hurt me or kill me? Did I want to hurt somebody else? I didn't understand the difference between fantasy, role-playing, and nonconsensual reality.

In order to survive, I had to hide these feelings in a very deep place. But they never went away. By the time I was 17, I knew that sex was problematic for me. It was hard to have an orgasm with a partner. I desperately wanted to be touched, but when someone put their hands or mouth on me, I left my body. It was hard to stay present in my actual flesh, with the secondary sex characteristics that puberty had used to brand and scar me. Sadistic and masochistic fantasies were widely condemned in lesbian-feminist culture during the 1970s and 1980s. Not having an orgasm with a female partner was enough to call my fragile lesbian identity into question. Women were supposed to be able to automatically please one another better than any man could hope to do; that way, we could simultaneously prove we were superior to brainwashed heterosexual women and also avoid talking about our naughty bits, the rude demands of cunts and clits striving for liberty.

I kept looking for reasons why I felt so bad about my body and nauseated by sex. Seeking solutions to these problems, I got involved with the sex education movement, sex-positive feminism, and anything else I could think of that might ease the pain. I changed my public image from feminine to butch and back again. I forced myself to take risks, hoping that if I found the right combination of drugs and willing flesh, I would come home to myself. The repeated failures were depressing, to say the least.

I won't claim that I never had any fun, or that I never experienced love or desire or physical gratification. I did. I'm not supposed to acknowledge that, because transsexuals are supposed to hate their bodies so much that they are virtually asexual. I think that is an old stereotype that needs to be discarded. Just as many transwomen engage in ultra-macho activities, becoming Marines and fighter pilots, cops and bounty hunters, in a desperate attempt to make a male identity work, some of us feel that if we address our shame about sexuality and root it out, we will not be transgendered any more. (Besides, some of us have very strong libidos.) If we have managed to glean any pleasure from our besieged bodies and psyches, and if that helps us to hang on and live to fight another day, we deserve kudos for discovering a coping mechanism.

I don't think an active or a kinky sex life prior to transition should invalidate a person's transgendered identity. One of the things Kaldera doesn't address is the fact that a diagnosis of Sexual Masochism can be used to deny a trans person access to hormones or surgery. The desire to alter the body is seen as just another expression of a desire to inflict pain upon oneself. This is one of the reasons why getting Sexual Masochism and Sexual Sadism out of the Diagnostic and Statistical Manual is an important plank in any activist agenda.

I took lovers, organized sex parties, flogged relative strangers, studied different bondage techniques, and read obsessively about sexuality. But it was never enough to get down to the root of my problems. I was like an alien, studying human beings, trying to imitate them so they would not realize just how different I was. I anticipated, with dread, being excommunicated or obliterated. Until I went to my first FTM conference, I never looked at a group of people and felt they were my people, and I was home. If this is you, stop for a moment and allow yourself complete honesty. What did you bury, hidden even from yourself, when you were a child? What have you been protecting all of your life, hoping no one else would guess that it was a part of you? Being buried alive is no way to live. Find courage, and become your whole self.

It's ironic that it was a lesbian community that gave me my first taste of operating a hard cock. I had a lover who had a lot of rape fantasies and a shy desire to be a gay man. I was also having sex with a bisexual man who liked to get fucked. The first time I saw a pair of leather shorts with a cock ring, I had to have them. Then I started making my own dildo harnesses, with interchangeable rings so I could wear a cock of any size. It was so exciting to see somebody else's hand or mouth on my cock, or to watch my erection slide in and out of a (hopefully) ecstatic body. It was a thrill that went right to my broken mind/body connection and started to heal it.

But this was a double-edged sword. My cock was real inasmuch as it pleasured others, and once in a while I had an orgasm from pressure at the base of the dildo, but it wasn't hooked up to my central nervous system. I couldn't feel myself getting hard or sliding into a wet mouth. It got harder and harder to ignore the fact that I wanted those experiences. This didn't seem appropriate for a lesbian. Or a woman. Confronting the right-wing morality I'd learned in church or being a better feminist, eliminating internalized misogyny, wasn't going to make this go away. So sometimes the best fucks would make me feel absolutely awful as soon as they were over. I would imagine how that might have felt if I had a completely male body. If my partner wanted to pleasure me, I was often unable to allow them to do it. I felt like an animated sex toy who got other people off without being able to ejaculate myself. Talk about blue balls! But can you even claim to have blue balls when the tissue that should have been a scrotum is empty, two structures on either side of the vulva, flat outer lips?

I endured this for longer than many transsexuals or other gender-variant people. I heard from Lou Sullivan when he founded his FTM support group, and I subscribed to the newsletter. Years later, I watched as leather dyke friends left that identity behind to become FTMs. But it wasn't until my forties that I finally started looking for a doctor who would allow me to take testosterone. I wanted to see what being a man outside of the bedroom or dungeon was like. Sexual fantasies no longer took the edge off.

I've chronicled my transition elsewhere, chiefly in *Sex Changes: The Politics of Transgenderism* (second edition) and *Speaking Sex to Power*. I will always be grateful to the leather community for being a place where I could delve into, accept, and develop two long-repressed identities. How often does that happen? It's like getting blue stamps at the gas station. The men and women I met there had all faced their own struggles when they came out as kinky people. The little boy I once was found a rough and ready group of midwives in their play rooms, dungeons, and demonstrations.

Kaldera is taking a big risk by suggesting that a higher percentage of differently-gendered people may be involved in BDSM than cisgendered men and women. As a therapist and a long-time observer of the kinky community, I have to agree with this perception. Like Kaldera, I have heard questions about this from other trans people and members of the helping professions. Maybe someday the funding will exist to do research that will prove or disprove these anecdotal assessments.

But not everybody in the transgender community is at ease with BDSM. In fact, there are many people who are so hostile toward it, they want us to just go away. I've read scathing slander online that rivals anything the feminist anti-porn movement had to say about us. I've also encountered intense homophobia. There are large numbers of heterosexually-identified trans people who believe that any deviation from that standard will invalidate their hard-won ability to live as men or women. (There are also heterosexual trans people who are kinky themselves or allies of queer or kinky people, of course.) This book may face a lot of distortion and unfair criticism from people who want their own civil rights, but cringe at the thought of extending the same understanding or protection to people further out on the edge.

Anti-BDSM sentiment is still a virulent force in the larger society. Right-wing groups are still targeting our community events, threatening to boycott hotels that host them, and infiltrating workshops so they can publish distorted accounts of them. For a long time now, lesbians and gay men have had to cope with Christian fundamentalist attempts to paint little black leather costumes on them all—because, of course, such perverted and mentally ill and dangerous people don't deserve equal rights. Many trans people are afraid that the same thing will happen to our fledgling organizations as they bravely demand guarantees that our physical safety will be protected, and that we won't be shut out from equal access to decent jobs and housing and medical care.

But I suspect that even if our public image was not a political issue, there would be a host of trans people calling for Kaldera's head on a spike for writing this book. It seems axiomatic that in minorities, anybody who dares to actually do anything instead of just complain about what we don't have will be trashed. And second of all, because (as Kaldera points out), the trans community is far from being a universally sexually enlightened place.

Nevertheless, the publication of *Double Edge* is an important event that in the long run will do a great deal of good and very little, if any, harm. The bigots who use BDSM as an insult or epithet to smear gay or trans people would just find another rock to throw at us if that one were not available. This text defines and defends the existence of gender-variant people. It documents our participation in BDSM organizations, clubs, play spaces, and conferences. It offers helpful information to kinky BDSM trans people that might ease someone's way into that world and strengthen them when they are not respected, so they can demand appropriate treatment. There's a lot of educational material for groups that would like to be more welcoming toward trans people, or are being torn by conflict over the issue of what to do with men and women with nonstandard equipment or people who don't pass (or may not wish to pass) as men or women. As far as I know, this is the first work to assert that kinky transpeople exist, which also makes it clear that being transgendered is not necessarily a fetish—that our identities don't go back into a suitcase at the end of the evening.

Unfortunately, I can't report the generally positive experience that Kaldera has had with cisgendered BDSM people. The kinky world seems to be a place where gender is both fluid and incredibly rigid and traditional. Cross-dressed submissives may be welcome at a dominatrix's formal afternoon tea party. A pansexual party or a fetish club open to the public may admit all kinds of trans people, who may or may not find allies and a genuine welcome there. But the BDSM world is fractured along lines of gender and sexual orientation. There are homophobic and transphobic male dominants who would never consider a transwoman as a potential partner. There are lesbian organizations that are absolutely closed to transwomen, FTMs, and anybody without a legal female ID who won't sign an oath that they are women-born-women. And there are many, many gay men's bike clubs, leather organizations, and public gatherings where a growing awareness of gay and bisexual FTMs has simply resulted in a dick check at the door, so we can be excluded.

I feel ambivalent about these policies in spaces that are intended to nurture and liberate sexual energy. If someone's desire flows only toward cisgendered people, do I have a right to tell them that they have to open their doors to less narrowly defined spirits? In a world that still discriminates against all lesbians, much less those who enjoy bondage and flogging, is it actually progressive to include people who will ruin everybody's good time at a sapphic whip fest? I am similarly queasy about disrupting a gay men's leather bar or play party. I want there to be more homosexual lust in the world, not less. If a man needs to grab hold of another man's hard cock to feel it is safe to let his cum fly, do I have any right to tell him he should be on his knees next to a boy whose dick is not big enough to take out of his fly? I know there are trans people who want to confront any event that is based on binary gender, but I personally don't want to ruin anybody's good time. I hate the fact that there have been such bitter and divisive battles over who counts as a man or a woman.

Certainly, we can't alter certain forms of sexual expression or desire. There are people (some of them trans) who will never eroticize the bodies of trans people. But that doesn't have to mean they can invalidate our identities. No matter how horny you are, if you are a straight woman, you don't want to have sex with every straight man you meet. If an FTM is at a club and you don't want to interact with him, there are plenty of other choices to focus on, so move on to a man who will make you clench your thighs. Cisgendered people usually seem to have an intense need to believe that they can always spot the tranny. But you only notice the trans people who don't pass. Given how many of us there are, you can assume that you've passed by a transman or woman who didn't set off your gender radar.

As many queer theorists have pointed out, we rarely base our assumptions about other people's gender on their genitals anyway. We are reading the cues sent by their masculinity or femininity; we rarely glimpse what's in their underwear. There are cisgendered men whose erect penises are not large enough to comfortably penetrate their partners. There are transgendered penises and vulvas and vaginas that are very nicely done. But people (and their gender) should not be reduced to genitalia. I look forward to a day when good manners will dictate that you first determine how someone defines their gender, and the terms they prefer to use for that identity, then take them at face value.

The fact that some people are initially taken aback or (let's be honest) revolted or frightened by transpeople doesn't mean that they remain in that unhappy state for the rest of their lives. Lesbians who thought they hated men, all men, forever and ever, sometimes realize they are turned on to FTMs (or an FTM) and that the sex with him is hot, hot, hot. The same thing can happen to that proverbial straight male dominant who couldn't be bothered with transwomen—until he meets one who makes his cock get hard. Sometimes the lack of acceptance or interest in sex with trans people is just the result of ignorance and lack of experience. While books like this one can take the edge off some of that prejudice, the bulk of the hard work of changing it has to be done one-on-one by kinky trans people. These determined activists often take an unbelievable amount of crap before they see any evidence of progress. A friend of mine who is a leather dyke and a trans woman waited twenty years before the women in her city were comfortable enough with her to include her at their events. And they still tried to exclude her woman friends who were not born female.

Stories like this make me feel tired and sad. But then I remember that The Fifteen Association in San Francisco invites me and my boy to their parties. A certain old-guard club in Chicago may continue to exclude FTMs from their annual party, but we have cisgendered advocates from coast to coast like the brave and sweet Peter Fiske. San Francisco's Eros Center, a sex club for men who have sex with other men, takes a lot of guff from a few of their patrons, but continues to admit transguys. And I can report a major victory like the recent election of Tyler McCormick, Mr. Rio Grande Leather, as International Mr. Leather (IML) 2010.

McCormick's victory is the result of years of work by out-of-the-closet, kinky transmen. Chief among them is Billy Lane, then-Seattle Mr. Leather, who ran for IML in 1998 and placed as a semifinalist.

Civil disobedience, lobbying our elected officials, teaching classes, and writing books do a hell of a lot of good when it comes to creating a safer and more respectful world for all sexual minorities. But I still believe the longest-lasting change is done by one-to-one contact between those of us who can somehow survive if we are publicly identified as very, very different. Going about our daily lives, doing ordinary things as visibly different people, makes change. If you are a fair-minded, kind, rational person who doesn't believe in a hateful god, it is very difficult to sustain prejudice when you actually know somebody who wears one of those scary labels like "pervert," "homo," "transexual," "cross-dresser," "queer," etc. *Double Edge* is a good resource for us and the people who might be trying to understand what we are really like. Kaldera gives us the language we need to feel pride and stand strong.

So if you don't agree with everything in this book (I certainly don't), perhaps you should write an article or book or blog of your own. But for heaven's sake, have some class about it. Let's not treat each other the way starving wolves would treat the carcass of a dead elk. Respect begins with self-esteem and compassion toward each other. This text will be accessed in college classrooms, workshops, and other educational efforts. It will hopefully also be used by tons of kinky transpeople looking for help coming out, greater self-awareness, support coping with social or political problems, and allies who want to want to stretch their horizons.

Double Edge isn't the last word on its subject. Rather, it's the first of many. That is an important part of how Kaldera writes and lives. There is room for every voice, he seems to be saying, and all of our stories are legendary. Instead of supporting an outmoded notion of what gender dysphoria is or a single path to easing one's discomfort, he looks forward to a world in which we have the space and freedom to make that experience our own. Being differently gendered can be an ordeal in a spiritual sense, a strenuous and challenging experience that leads to a new phase of life and a deeper understanding of the human condition. Gender has as many faces as love itself, as many names as Eros can assume. By being honest, by seeking authenticity, each of us can become a hero in the face of adversity. And heroes are very, very sexy people.

Introduction:
Bridges Into Forbidden Territory

For me, at least, the BDSM came first. Or perhaps the transgender feelings had come first and I'd just done such a good job of repressing them that I didn't really notice them until I was older. The BDSM, though … while my parents made it clear that they both found sex in general a bit distasteful, or at least not a high priority, they hadn't specifically told me anything about what I was supposed to be aroused over. Maybe that's why those images of people being tied up and tortured, beaten and humiliated, or raped and enslaved all filtered into my thirteen-year-old mind. Those images were there from the very beginning, from my first fumbling attempts at masturbation. I never jerked off to anything vanilla. By the time it occurred to me that most people were probably beating off to much tamer fantasies, it was too late. My sexual arousal was set in stone.

Years later, I would find myself ensconced in a feminist political space, hanging out with people whose politics (much of it, anyway) I admired, and they would make it very clear to me that the fact that my sexual urges were bound up with pain and power was evidence that there was something very wrong with me. At the time, I wasn't acting on any of those urges; in fact, I had never met anyone who actually wanted that sort of thing and I was very careful to be gentle and egalitarian with my lovers, because that was what they wanted and it was the only thing I knew. Still, the rhetoric of my political colleagues terrified me. I feared that an uncontrollable predator lurked inside my lumpy, nerdish exterior, and might burst out at random if I didn't expel it completely. So for months, even years, I worked at eroticizing egalitarian vanilla sex, masturbated only to safe, romantic fantasies, and tried to keep myself from going away into my "special" fantasies while I was pursuing orgasm with my partners.

It was probably the most sexually boring and frustrating time of my life, and mostly it succeeded in ruining sex for me entirely, until I gave up with a guilty sigh of relief and went back to my "evil" thoughts. I gave up on trying to change myself, and resolved only to keep it a deep, dark secret ... until the Universe suddenly dropped a lover in my lap who enjoyed kinky sex. At first we just played games of rope and slap and tickle, but then I ended up with her at my first play party and felt like I'd come home. Here were people who did the things I dreamed about, and none of them seemed like psychopaths. (Most of them seemed just as nerdy as me, actually; the party was held at a science fiction convention.) I watched several "scenes", and then topped in a few for the first time. I'd never done it before, but it felt like I'd done it a thousand times. After that, there was no looking back. The tie-dyed hippie clothes gave way to my first leather jacket, the Birkenstocks to my first pair of badass boots.

However, no sooner had I gotten used to the gorilla that had pushed its way into my living room than the Tyrannosaurus Rex I'd buried even deeper pushed its way in right behind the whip-wielding gorilla. Once I let myself go no-holds-barred on my fantasies, once I'd started to act some of them out (the safe ones), the "camera" in my mind turned around. Up until that time, my masturbatory fantasies had been like a movie; I watched, but wasn't physically involved myself. (Yes, I was pretty dissociative. Gender dysphoria will do that to you.) Suddenly I was taking part in the fantasies, incorporating my own mental sensations ... and my body was male. I had a cock, and I knew how to use it. Those fantasies were just as forbidden to a former radical-cultural feminist, and even more horrifying to me because I had a sinking feeling that they presaged something more serious than installing an eyebolt in the ceiling of the bedroom and investing in some cool toys.

To make matters worse, my new lover was transgendered. No, that was no accident; I believe that the twin demons of my basement deliberately picked someone out who would model their faces for me every night in my bed. Later, when she became my MTF wife, we'd kid about "tranny cooties", those mental bugs that crawl across the bed from the openly transgendered lover to the repressed one, infecting them and forcing their secret issues out into the open. Jokes aside, I can tell you this: If you are repressing transgender urges, it is damn near impossible to lie in bed every night next to a transsexual body and not have those urges storm your mental gates and demand voting rights … and perhaps even declare a coup.

My lover compounded the problem by making me a strap-on dildo and asking me to fuck her with it. Oh boy, did that do a number on my head. It was even more intense than my coming-home experience at that first play party, but at least the whipping had been entirely real, the welts of the bottom hot and red under the flesh of my hand. I both desperately wanted to keep fucking with that rubber cock, and desperately wanted to curl up in a ball and cry because it wasn't attached to me, wasn't my own flesh and never would be no matter how much I drove it into a willing, panting orifice. The dysphoria I'd repressed welled up in me like a tsunami, pouring through the opening made by kinky, fulfilling sex. I ended up becoming stone for years, my genitals only accessed via friction against a rubber cock. (This was actually just fine with my femme lover, who was admittedly something of a do-me queen, but it left me feeling empty afterwards.)

Eventually I made the jump to changing my body and transitioning, although my psyche is still somewhere in the middle and always will be. I looked like a man in short order, except for my genitalia which became enhanced by testosterone into something … between the two. I did get a double mastectomy, but have decided to take a pass on genital surgery (a decision that different FTMs work out in different ways). Testosterone set me free from my stone prison; once the libidinous urges got strong enough, they overrode the dysphoria and I just started fucking, and fucking, and fucking. There was so much kinky sex to be had, and even in the midst of whips and chains I'd been starving myself. With every bodily change, I was more comfortable with myself and more able to be present in my own flesh, to be that guy in the movie rather than just watching.

I'm also polyamorous, and live with my two partners. I went through a series of butch, genderqueer, and FTM "boys" over the years until I met the one who was realio-trulio willing to be my full-time, live-in slave. After eight years, this relationship produced our coauthored book *Dear Raven and Joshua: Questions and Answers About Master/Slave Relationships*. Somewhere along the line, the fact that I have an alternative sexuality and live in alternative relationships became just as defining as the fact that I have an alternative gender (not to mention my alternative spirituality or all my other non-mainstream choices). It's all tied up in me, but not in a tangle because I spent years combing out those strands and making them lie together. They complement each other now. Each taught me things that helped me to see the others more realistically. I'd say that rather than a tangle, they're tied up in a package. Take one and you get all the others as well. I am a self-made work.

About two decades ago, my wife was briefly the co-chair of a local kink organization, and I was a roving "reporter" for their newsletter. As one of my assignments, I interviewed a psychiatrist about the psychiatric community's attitude towards BDSM. Since he was my wife's shrink (that's how I got in to see him), he was also familiar with transgendered people's issues, and indeed had many transgendered clients. A gay man himself, he was vanilla, but not unsympathetic to people getting what they needed sexually so long as it didn't impair their self-esteem or general functioning.

We talked for a time about how the mental health community's attitude towards homosexuality had changed after comprehensive studies were done that showed that gay folk weren't any more nuts than straight folk, and how BDSM practitioners were just going to have to come up with some similar studies. Afterwards, as I was packing up my notebooks and tape recorder, he asked if he could ask me a question. "Why are so many of my trans patients into BDSM?" he asked. "Not all of them, certainly, but a significantly higher percentage than a non-trans population, even a gay population." It wasn't just his sample set, either; he'd talked to other shrinks who worked with transfolk, and they had also commented on this odd fact. It was, he suggested gently, one reason why mental health researchers were having a hard time separating gender dysphoria from paraphilias. If a third to a half of your trans clients are big ol' pervs, that looks statistically suspicious to a mental health researcher, above and beyond any other biases they might have.

At the time, I had no answer for him. Most of my trans friends were into BDSM because it was BDSM that had opened me up to my own transgendered nature, and I'd met my trans friends at play parties or fetish-event fundraisers. It made me think, though, and I began to ask the transfolk I'd meet in clubs how they got there, and what the appeal was. Their reasons tended to be:

A) They were just big ol' pervs, and always had been. Several speculated that they didn't develop a "normal" sexual-object focus because the gender dysphoria got in the way; if you can't eroticize having genital sex in your own body with anyone else, you might shift the erotic focus to activities-once-removed that didn't call attention to your fleshly configuration. That actually made a lot of sense, given my own proclivities.

B) They weren't much into SM, but they had a fetish for cross-dressing, and people in the BDSM community were tolerant, wouldn't bat an eye at their lacy panties, and might even play with them. Obviously, there were a lot of cross-dressers and former cross-dressers in this category. Some cross-dressing "subs" admitted that they weren't really submissive at all, but they wanted someone to dress them up and help them get over their guilt, and being dominated as a "sissy slave" was the only way that they could get that kind of interaction.

C) They hadn't been much into SM in the beginning, but there was an instant appeal to a venue where one could get hours of erotic activity without having to get naked or deal with one's genitals, and they eventually eroticized mild (or not so mild) levels of SM play as a result. Unlike swinging or sex clubs, the BDSM subculture has created a space where nongenital (and sometimes even nonsexual) physical interactions are completely acceptable—and sometimes mandatory, as some clubs and play parties have legal or aesthetic issues with anything that looks like "traditional" sex and is thus bustable by police, or might get them confused with a swinger's club.

All this added up to a population with a much higher percentage of kinksters than most others, even if one didn't include the population of people who considered themselves normally gendered but had a cross-dressing fetish. Actually, there were a lot of border wars in many small trans groups about whether those people counted as transgendered at all. Some transsexuals argued that their issues were different; fetishists could disappear back into a closet and didn't really understand what it was like to live it as an identity instead of a hobby. Other transsexuals pointed out their own history with fetishistic cross-dressing, which in some cases had gone on for decades as their repressed urges had nowhere to exit except for their genitals. Some genderqueers felt that the "parody" many cross-dressers made of gender expression wasn't politically savvy, while others felt that anyone playing with gender, even a little, was better than never questioning it in any way. Some trans activists wryly posited a hierarchy of respect within trans support communities, with the guy who secretly wears his absent wife's panties resigned to the very bottom of the stack.

As for the cross-dressers themselves, some tried hard to get into trans groups, some tried and went away shamefacedly, and some laughed at trans groups from their place of closeted privilege. Some downplayed the sexual aspect of their kink and showcased the political transgression in order to be accepted in trans groups. It's still a sensitive subject on both sides, and not entirely resolved.

On the BDSM side, transgender in all its forms was—for some decades, anyway—considered to be just another sexual kink. One example of this was the first book to come out as a mainstream-oriented survey of BDSM—the 1996 edition of *Different Loving*. It contained an entire section on transgender topics, including transsexualism, which disturbed many non-kinky transfolk. While the book acknowledged that many transfolk weren't kinky, the way that the material was presented made it easy to mentally class sex changes with water sports, whipping, and latex. From being in a BDSM community at the time, I can also vouch for the fact that most non-trans kinksters saw transgender issues as just another fetish category. Many still do. The first FTMs I ever met in person were doing a workshop on transsexuality for the local leather group. They were aware of the assumed "kinkifying" of their lifestyle choices by speaking in this venue, but felt that it was better to speak out anywhere they could, because, as one said to me, "…there's always someone in the back row who gets That Look on their face, and they either bolt out of the room or come up to us afterwards for more information, and saving their life is the reason we're there." Being as that time I was one of those someones, I was grateful.

Transfolk who speak to BDSM groups about their conditions (and I've been one of those, too, many times, for the same reason already articulated) also get asked questions about kink that don't get asked by a workshop for, say, a hospital or high school class. Sometimes those questions even moved beyond stupid ones ("…are you sure that this isn't just a cross-dressing hobby that just got out of hand?") to intelligent, thoughtful ones about how people who'd been both genders saw sex and moved differently through kink communities. These were the questions that I wanted to hear answered by articulate transfolk other than myself, and the ones that I tried to ask when I sent out questionnaires for this book. There may be a lot of us in the kink demographic, but how do we see things differently? What's it like to live at the intersection of two very unacceptable lines? What kind of outsider perspective does that give us, and what can we learn and teach from living there?

This book is first and foremost by us and for us, an exploration of who we are. It is secondarily aimed at nontrans people in the BDSM demographic who are interested in what we think and how we experience the BDSM community. I am reminded of a particular style of discussion group that has recently come into fashion called the "fishbowl". It was developed for outsiders who wanted to hear an in-group talk among themselves about things important to them, while the in-group didn't want the outsiders to make comments. It works by one group of people sitting in the middle and talking to each other, and an outside circle of people who can watch but not speak. This book is a fishbowl, with transfolk and our partners in the center, and the rest of you watching from the edges. This is what we say when you're not around to hear it. Who knows, you might find it interesting.

My interview sample is not comprehensive by any means. I advertised on the Internet, and while I got over a hundred questionnaires back during the period I was writing, I am aware that the Internet is an elitist playground and leaves out many valuable people. Far more FTMs than MTFs responded to my interviews, even when I deliberately sought out more MTFs. I have no idea why this was. While my respondents were from 7 different countries, I did not attempt to create parity in racial or class or ethnic samplings. I did see some very interesting trends when I compared people's answers, but I don't pretend that this small sample is an adequate picture of a multinational transgendered demographic. This book is not meant to be an academic study. It's meant to be a book that makes people think and question, laugh and cry, see themselves and their lovers and friends, see other ways of being and experiencing. It's a stepping-off point. Where you go from here is up to you.

Most answered sincerely but briefly, giving me demographic information but not necessarily quotable material. Some answered at length and said great things, and their words make up a large portion of this book. A few were eloquent enough—and gave me pictures of themselves and their activities—that I showcased their interviews periodically throughout the book. I think it's important that we are seen as real people with real faces and bodies and sexualities, and I am grateful to those who gave of themselves in this way. (For the record, every photo in this book is a donated picture of an interviewee.)

Definitional Hell

Definitions, in the transgender demographic, are controversial and debated and generally a mess. There are no perfectly accepted words for anything, no matter what some people might tell you. My job of defining terms is made particularly difficult by the fact that this is a book of interviews, and the various contributors all make different choices about terminology, some of those choices contradicting those of others. Some are Americans, some Europeans, and there is a different understanding of English and its terms. Some even created their own special definitions. I chose not to change people's preferred terminology, out of respect. That means that throughout the hundreds of quotes in this book, the terminology may jump back and forth, and that's just another example of how diverse we are. Try to be patient with it.

What I will do, as best I can, is to define all the terms people have chosen in the book, and hope that the reader understands that the choice of one term over another is more personal preference and style than correctness at this point. Where individuals have created their own terminology, I've allowed them to define it in their own words.

For the purposes of this book, the word *transgender* is being used as an umbrella term for people who do not fit into the categories of people born male or female who identify and stay that way. I realize that this is a definition about what we're not rather than what we are, but it seems to be the only fair assumption: most of the people in the world are born with normally-sexed male or female bodies, are happy with the gender of those bodies and with being seen publicly as that gender, and never intend to change them. We aren't those people. (Some use the contraction TG as shorthand for transgender; some simply shorten it to "trans". I use "transfolk" as my own favorite affectionate term for my people.)

The word *transsexual* is used a little more specifically to refer to people who have significantly altered the gender of their bodies via medical means—generally exogenous hormones and possibly surgery—and legally adopted the opposite gender. Some have identities that are firmly on the male or female ends of the spectrum; some have more fluid third-gender identities even as they change their bodies and pass partly or fully as the sex opposite their birth gender.

"FTM" or "transman" or "trans man" are loose terms that describe someone who was raised female and moved towards the male end of the gender spectrum; similarly, "MTF" or "transwoman" or "trans woman" describe someone who was raised male and moved towards the female end of the spectrum.

"Transmasculine" and "transfeminine" are also sometimes used. "Tranny" is another affectionate term that some of us use, and I assure those who may squirm at it that it is always meant with love.

"Genderqueer" is a recent term used by people who do not consider themselves either male or female and consciously live and dress in ways that show this identity, often as a political as well as a personal act. Originally the term referred specifically to individuals who chose not to change their bodies but instead focused on living openly with androgynous and/or genderfuck presentations. More recently it has been used by some transfolk who have changed their bodies but still retain an androgynous presentation or even just feel that way inside. (In almost all cases, the post-transition individuals who identify as genderqueer started out as the first variety, and didn't want to give up their term when they changed their bodies.)

Terminology for the rest of the population varies from person to person and culture to culture. Some transfolk simply use the term "nontrans". Some use the term "biomale" or "biofemale". Some use the Internet-geek term "cis", as in "cismale", "cisfemale", and in some cases "cissexual". Again, the choice is mostly made via personal preference and comfort, and in some cases the comfort of friends who fit into that category and would prefer to choose their own labels, just as we would prefer to choose ours.

Every one of these terms are objected to by someone, in or out of the trans spectrum. In fact, I'm sure that every one of the definitions I've given above will be objected to someone, in or out of the trans spectrum. That's life; you can't please everyone, especially in this highly diverse and often squabbling demographic ... who are all, every last annoying one of them, my people. This book is my gift to those of my people who are also citizens in the World of Fire and Darkness, the land of whips and chains and harsh truths, the world where comfort is put aside for intensity, where propriety is tossed away in search of the deeper experience. Our dual citizenship in these countries can make people who only own one of these citizenships very uncomfortable with us, and to those who own neither ... we may well look like their worst nightmares.

This book has an entire long chapter on the difficulties that transfolk have in BDSM communities. However, since not all or even most transfolk are kinky, those of us who are out about our sexual proclivities tend to upset our vanilla trans brothers and sisters. They fear that we'll make them look bad, that people (from gatekeeping doctors to potential sex partners) will assume that everyone in the tribe is just a pervert looking for kinky sex, and this whole gender thing is just part of one big fetish. We are a threat to their attempts to prove to the world that they're just normal women and men. Some of us dual-citizen types have been ostracized over that issue.

Outside of both groups, those of us who are out about both "axes of offense" have it even worse. We are transgressors of two very large and frightening boundaries—gender, and how people "should" have sex—and we may scare people who don't like to think about either of those boundaries as being as fluid as they are. Several of us have seen a good deal of discrimination in our religious communities, and other communities as well. Either being trans or being into BDSM is an excuse for the state to take away children you may have custody of; to have both is practically a death knell. Ditto for issues of housing and keeping jobs. That's why most are in the closet, for their own safety It's also why I tended to get most of my correspondence from people who are out in their local communities, because even with pseudonyms—which most people chose to use—it isn't necessarily safe. The scared couple who do their activities home alone and never talk to anyone else are living that life for a reason.

But I've long believed that education makes things safer, over time, through the process of desensitization. So this book is also my offering to anyone who wants to learn, to expand their horizons, to get those questions answered before you buttonhole that poor trans individual and ask them things that they don't want to go into one more time. Maybe it can also be a way to show that we are also sexy, hot, fascinating, imaginative, and worth the trouble.

Identities:
Crossing Spectrums

The transgendered demographic is highly varied in its identities, more so than even most of the people in that demographic are aware of in many cases. While I can't compare a cross-section of kinky transfolk to non-kinky transfolk (and as I've said in the introduction, this is not meant to be a scientific survey), my interviews did seem to mirror the diversity I've seen in the trans demographic as a whole, traveling and speaking in different parts of the US. The borders of who's in and who's out depend on location and age of the participants, for the most part—the greatest difference in transgender variance seems to be between younger and older age-groups, in many cases—but in the cross-section that overlaps with BDSM practices, anything goes.

Like my pool of transgendered friends, my interviewees ranged from transsexuals to intersexuals to cross-dressers to genderqueers to those who identified as no more specific than simply transgendered. Some had changed their bodies to one degree or another; some preferred (or were resigned to) staying with the bodily conformation of their birth gender. Some passed as their chosen gender; some could not due to the difficulties of genetics; some chose not to. Some were solid in their identities and some were fluid, up to and including being extremely fluid. Their ages ranged from eighteen to seventy. All of them practiced some form of BDSM.

One of the first questions that I asked my participants was about identity: how do you label your gender? Some were clear that they had a strong and single identity; it was just their bodies that needed to be modified to match it.

> I am a post-op MtF woman, but I regard myself simply as a woman. My identity hasn't really changed much except that at a certain point I was able to stop wishing I was a woman and start being that woman.
> – Ashley Lynch

My gender identity, once I became aware of it, has stayed female. There were a number of years, until I was about 22 or so, it was an incredibly strong feeling of alienation and had no idea to the source of it. A friend at the time mentioned the possibility to me that I was transsexual and it was like everything clicked into place.
– Brianna Ahava Morrigan

I identify as a woman, pretty squarely within a binary, actually—I have always identified on the female side of the gender spectrum, though early in transition I tried on dual gendered and genderqueer type identities. They did not fit. I find identifying squarely as a woman with fluctuating gender presentation (from femme to butch and in between) seems to be most me. – Siobhan Phoenix

My gender is Male, always has been Male. Regardless of the female anatomy my self-identity has been consistent. – BEAR A-M Rodgers

I was a very mannish dyke! And somehow I convinced myself that that was good enough for a very long time. I always did the hard jobs; on some level I was trying to prove something. As a dyke I was an Amazon! Outstanding in every way, tall, wide shoulders, narrow hips. As a man, I'm pretty average—5' 10", broad-shouldered, narrow hips. Maybe more narrow due to testosterone and the redistribution of body fat. I guess, other than presentation, it really hasn't changed. I've always been a guy, now I just look more accurately male to the rest of the world. And I don't get ridiculed when going into a public restroom. – Cole R.

My gender identity is male. I'm not someone who knew I was male from a very early age, although I did have some anxiety back in elementary school that I might be a "man trapped in a woman's body" after I saw a sitcom with a (ridiculed) trans woman character. I decided to suppress those feelings/fears and did not give my gender identity additional conscious thought for many years. I first met trans people when I was 20, before my last year of college, which was an intense experience for me. I started asking myself questions and soon realized that I did not identify as a woman. At first I was not sure how I did identify and thought I might be genderqueer. Eventually, over time and after I began transitioning, I came to develop/realize a very strong internal sense of myself as simply male. I have never considered myself terribly masculine (or terribly feminine) in terms of gender expression—there are certainly stereotypes for men and for women that I have never matched. Lately I have become comfortable doing some role-play—both in terms of gaming and in terms of BDSM—in the role of a woman, but I continue to identify my core gender as male. – Micah

Some of my interviewees had a fairly stable gender as male or female, but saw and respected aspects of themselves that they had brought with them from their originally assigned gender. Lord Tom explains:

Growing up, I did not feel a distinct gender gap. My dual nature allowed me to see that I fit both male and female roles comfortably. I was fortunate to have parents who let me choose toys and activities for myself. I was just as happy playing with dolls as I was with race cars and action figures. The difference between each gender became far too clear to me when puberty hit. My female body caused me severe distress. I would much rather have remained androgynous than experience these confusing and often horrifying changes to my body. I shut down for a few years and barely spoke to anyone, falling into a deep depression. I never gave up hope, though, thinking that if there was a way out, I would find it. I had to. My first year of college finally allowed me the freedom to express myself again.

I came to the slow realization that I had always related to men more than women. I was more inclined to fantasize about being the hero in the epic, the villain; any strong male character was one I secretly longed to emulate. I began to let that side of me out to "try on" male identities, and found it so natural that the people around me began to read the masculine energy I put forth, even though my physical appearance had not yet changed. That was the true beginning of my transformation, when I projected my male essence into the world.

Today I see my gender identity as mostly male. I tell people I am a man, but I also embrace the feminine in me, too. I strive for balance. I think people have both feminine and masculine sides to them, and that gender can be more fluid than people like to believe. Officially, I prefer to be known as a transgender man.

Many of us admit that when the body isn't right, it's tempting to overdo the behavioral traits in order to push the balance. Conversely, when the body is a better fit, it's easier to be more relaxed about behavior. TransPunk writes about how he transitioned to male in order to be able to own his own feminine traits more comfortably:

> Growing up, I thought I was a boy with a different body than my younger brother. At very young age, I thought I would grow up to become a man. I was not uncomfortable in my body though as it was until puberty. I simply played and acted like a boy and my parents let me, as my dad was a professional coach, my parents were of working-class background, and being an athletic tomboy and playing a bit rough was fine with them. Puberty was somewhat traumatic, I didn't like the changes of my body. After a while I accepted I was supposed to be a female and tried to adjust. I never really succeeded. I did succeed in finding male partners, but stayed tomboyish, was teased for not being feminine enough, and my best friends mostly were boys.
>
> When I moved to Hamburg to study and became part of the anarchist scene there, I was a really hardcore feminist separatist for a while and attributed my body issues to the impact of patriarchal beauty ideals. I tried to be a lesbian, assuming my body issues had to do with sexual identity. Then I realized it was my own body that was the "problem", not my partner's bodies. I started out my trans ID as a lesbian fag, relating to male lovers as male and to female lovers as a butch dyke. It was always through my sexuality that I got in touch with my body and my gender identity, that I negotiated my gender identity. I worked a lot on redefining my female body as male and was quite successful in this for a while—e.g. my slave and I referred to my cunt as ass-cunt, a term used by gay men in Germany for their assholes. I never packed and I never bound my chest except as part of sexual play occasionally, as it did not make me feel better and I felt I did not have to make it easier for others. After a while I realized my body dysphoria was getting worse. I started not having any sex which involved my cunt or breasts. That worked quite well, since I had become an exclusive top by then. That way I was in control of how I got touched and it fit well with my role not to be naked.

But in the end I realized that I had been shutting out all my feminine traits in order to feel male enough. So I felt I had to make my body more male in order to become whole as a human being. I started with T and felt much better immediately. After chest surgery I felt at home in my body. And after getting my womb and ovaries out, I felt very right. Since, I am constantly on a day-to-day-basis feeling unambiguously male and third gender at the same time without any contradiction. I feel most myself in my shamanic practices and the dreaming reality. A little while ago I got a tattoo of my oldest spirit guide, a ram, on my chest and this has shifted my body image some more. I now feel much more in my body. So these days I usually call myself a transman, since being male is very taken for granted for me these days, but the trans history and being in between is also a big part of my identity. By now I do enjoy the luxury of being able to pass and not always make it an issue. But on the whole, I am very out about it and I don't feel comfortable with having to pass. I want my friends to know all of me, and I am proud to be a polyamorous gay FTM Top.

Some of the post-transition individuals in my survey had initially embraced a solid identity, but had slowly come around to something more fluid. Jonathan remarked: "I spent my first two years on testosterone trying to make up for everything female that had been forced on me. Fortunately for my own sanity and the patience of my friends, I got over it and loosened up. Now I see myself as a feminine man, instead of a masculine woman. Once in a while I revert to a more feminine-feeling affect for a few hours or a day. Fortunately my partner thinks I'm cute on the rare day when I'm a bit of a girl again." Similarly, Finn and Jackkinrowan both came to a more fluid place later in their lives, while Blaise Garber-Paul considers himself to be extremely fluid:

> I was born female, and was a tomboy in childhood, refusing to wear feminine clothing. From my teenage years to early twenties, being largely ignorant of, or intimidated by, the concept of transgenderism, I lived uncomfortably as an androgynous female. In my mid-twenties, after a lot of contemplation and research, I changed my name, began taking testosterone, and took advantage of my luck in quickly 'passing' to live as a 'stealth' heterosexual man. Almost two years later, I feel fully cognizant of my gender identity for the first time, and I am overjoyed to be able to live openly as a genderqueer transboy. – Finn

> I was assigned female at birth, and while that never felt correct, that's how I identified (what else?) until I found there were other options. I saw myself as a tomboy, somewhat masculine female, but unfortunately stuck in a female body. When I learned about butches, I thought maybe that was it, but I didn't see myself as particularly butch, although I did identify with the masculinity, so I kept looking. When I read about FTMs, I knew immediately that that was me. Today I live my life as male. I often use genderqueer or queer as well because I really dislike boxes, even if I live mine in the M one at this point (but for example, I can't totally because I can't change all my documents, don't have standard male genitals, etc). I am fairly out as trans/FTM because I believe in honoring the many years I lived as female. As painful as they often were, they brought me to this point, and pretending they didn't exist is disrespectful to me and also perpetuates the invisibility of FTMs. – Jackkinrowan

> I currently live as a passing queer man. Unless I assert my transgender identity I am assumed to be a cisgendered man. Most people easily pick up that I'm not straight. I identify as a queer transgendered person, meaning that my gender and sexuality do not exist along

binary spectrums and are most identifiable by their perpetual mutability.

My sense of my own gender, and my relationship to categories like masculinity and femininity, man-ness or woman-ness is complicated. Often I experience my gender as almost an absence, something that fluctuates and flows internally without a solid socially legible center. I'm most aware of my gender when other people reflect it back to me. My gender also seems to be interpersonal or situational—people might see me as having a specific gender because their personal energy or the social space we are inhabiting encourages a specific set of consistently gendered behaviors from me. Different leather spaces elicit different kinds of masculinity from me, for example, and Radical Faerie spaces reveal more and more complicated kinds of genderfuck and femininity. What might appear as a static gender is, in fact, only one aspect of a multifaceted self.

I've gone through many gender identities—I started as a straight goddess-worshiping feminist. I moved into bisexuality, then bi-dyke, then stone butch, then then trannyboi, then genderqueer, then trannyfag, before settling on the most recent terms explained above ... Many of the labels overlapped at times, as I used the one that best seemed to convey who I felt like I was in that given moment. – Blaise Garber-Paul

"Genderqueer" is a difficult and debatable term, in that it began as a way to differentiate transsexuals who chose to live as (and ideally pass as) the gender opposite to their birth assignment from nontranssexuals who strove to present a deliberately gender-ambiguous image. There was a strong assumption that genderqueers did not modify their bodies with hormones or surgery, and even some heated debate over the political merits of the passing transsexual versus the genderqueer who kept their assigned body but presented it in a nonstandard way. However, as time has gone on, some fully transitioned individuals have decided to identify as genderqueer as well. E. Nelly explains his gender journey at length in this way:

My gender identity has had four major changes over time. First, I came out as a lesbian in 1998 (I was 16 at the time) and began a long journey to my current identity as a genderqueer trans man. My first understanding of lesbian gender was an understanding that there are butches and there are femmes. I examined myself and felt that I was more aligned with femme at that time based on my clothes choices, body shape, hair style, personality, and other factors. At that time my girlfriend certainly took on the butch role. In my young mind I didn't think it was possible for two butches to be together so I happily took the femme role. Then, when I was 18 I begin to explore my gender identity again. This is when I first began identifying as a butch dyke and began slowly phasing out women's clothes for men's clothes (and masculine-coded clothes). I maintained a very short haircut, hid my curves, and engaged in more masculine mannerisms.

Again, in 2002 I began exploring more. I started school and was first introduced to trans people. I dated a trans guy briefly and began to understand that transition was inevitable because I knew it would be the fullest expression of my identity. I dabbled in drag a bit and playing with gender during sex and for social events. I continued to progress towards a more traditionally masculine presentation.

In 2005 I began the official medical, spiritual and therapeutic process to transition. I had been a butch dyke and very publicly allied with the trans community. Finally beginning the process of transition was challenging for my relationship at the time, my political understanding of myself and my role in the community. I started taking hormones in December of 2005. During the first six months of hormone therapy I was thoroughly convinced with every shot that I was getting more and more feminine in so many internal ways while my body was becoming more and more masculine in external biological ways. While I am fairly confident that my gender will not remain totally static, I know that femme, genderqueer, and trans man labels make sense right now. I am not traditionally masculine and am continually frustrated that men's clothes have so few options, especially for bigger guys.

Lizzie, a MTF who transitioned but ceased to bother with passing and female identity, speaks for several of my respondents when she says: "Consciously my gender identity has been atypical since about 2001 when I was confronted with the lifestyles of other trans people; but my gender really has always been in a sort of flux. Not so much that it is fluid; more that it vibrates at its own frequency. I started out my trans life trying to cling to binary gender, and I went through the motions of trying to be female rather than male, but ultimately that had the same amount of problems. My current gender views are hard to describe, but I essentially feel like I am all genders. Every gender has a place in me, and not just the binary ones. I tend to feel that gender-wise, the fact is that I am just me. I don't complain about pronoun use, but really, any description of my gender that limits itself to one idea is incorrect."

Genderqueer and Kinky

About a third of my respondents were outright non-transitioning genderqueers, and this formed the core of their identity. As one might imagine, the descriptions of their identities are a rainbow of diversity. Some add the term "trans" to their labels in some way; some don't bother. They seemed to be evenly divided between the ones who were proud to be gender-ambiguous and those who struggled with wanting to be seen more easily as their non-assigned gender. The latter group often lamented the difficulty of getting people in their local BDSM community to see them as any gender other than their assigned birth designation. Mik, Netdancer, Sejay, and Del were a few that I chose to describe the experience of living this courageous contradiction.

I currently identify as a genderqueer trans man, although this often translates into me being read as a feminine gay man. As a young child I identified as a tomboy, however I disliked getting dirty or doing any kind of rough or violent play. I suppose I wanted to be seen as a girl who could take care of herself and was independent and I equated that with masculinity and being male. In college I began exploring my gender more—wearing alternately cowboy hats and Carhartts, ties and suspenders, and halter tops. Around my sophomore year I began to identify as genderqueer and started pursuing what that might mean in terms of my physical body and how I wanted to live legally. By my senior year I had sorted out the difference between sex and gender, at least as it applied to me. I realized that I identified as male and wanted to have "he" as my pronoun but that I didn't equate being male as being masculine. For a long time I had to sort out how to live as someone feminine and male, I had to decide when and if I would wear pink again, how I would apply eyeliner and whether I would insist on taking over "masculine" duties with my partners. I'm still figuring all of that stuff out. – Mik Kinkead

The way I view myself has changed a great deal over time. At age 10, I was very androgynous with male leanings; by the time I was 13 I was aware that I was more male then female, and I was desperately trying to act more female and fit in as one. That went on until my 20's, when I became more neuter again due to just not feeling as if I fit anywhere. In my late 20's I started aggressively identifying as trans and began to accept myself as a man. After a somewhat embarrassing period of being more macho than macho, I settled much more comfortably into my skin. I am non-surgical/no hormones for health and financial reasons. – Netdancer

I just started publicly identifying as genderqueer in the past year or so. I was female-assigned at birth, but never really liked being "girly" (I played with marbles as my imaginary characters instead of dolls or action figures, felt really uncomfortable in pink/heels/dresses, and was often "mistaken" as a boy although I didn't think that was bad in and of itself). I didn't really have a language for understanding gender identity and expression until college, and soon after began to look at my own. Moving far away from my parents after college, I started playing with gender and exploring what felt good sexually and fashion-wise (wearing binders, "men's" clothing, performing/playing in drag, etc.) over the past two years. I still have somewhat effeminate facial features and an hourglass figure, so it's sometimes difficult to express the way I'd like to be perceived. Although it's constantly fluctuating, I've found the most comfort with my masculine side, and lately have considered transitioning to male, though I still feel connected to my feminine side and strongly identify as genderqueer. – Sejay

My mother claims that when she got the amniocentesis, they told her she was having a boy. At least, my parents teased me about it a lot; however, they were both known for making up stories just to mess with me, so I don't know if that's true or not. I believed it, because I was ever so much a tomboy growing up. I never dressed feminine, although I was forced to wear my hair long because it was so pretty (being a natural redhead). I always felt strange when I tried to conform to the concept of "girl" or "woman"—at first I thought it was about my sexual orientation, but even after coming out as a lesbian, I still felt strange. I always had male best friends, and hated when I was excluded from things like bachelor parties and poker nights because I was a woman. (And the gender-appropriate activities, like bridal showers and sleepovers, made me feel awkward and out of place.)

So I shunned the whole concept of gender, and ignored it for years. I didn't feel comfortable as a woman, but in no way did I feel the right to try to claim any sort of masculine identity, either. For many years, I lived a very gender-free existence, other than avoiding the ob/gyn due to it triggering a feeling of "wrongness".

It was only in the last two years that I really started demanding honesty from myself, and exploring the concept of gender as how it relates to me. I felt spiritually as though I were lying if I didn't face up to the fact that when I imagined myself, I saw myself as being hermaphroditic, some sort of fantasy human that could shapechange their own genitals. But I also came to realize that if I didn't at least begin to ask people to recognize the masculine spirit, I would go through life dissatisfied with how I was treated due to my gender—so I tentatively started calling myself a genderqueer person. But even that wasn't enough, because "genderqueer" is like "bisexual" in the 1980's—it's typically regarded as someone who either isn't honest enough to begin transition, or who wants to hide behind the privilege of being able to present as their birth gender when it suits them, but to claim male privilege when that's a better deal. Between all of that nonsense, and wanting to explore my own masculinity, I finally started calling myself "trans". I have no plans on surgically or hormonally changing my body, and for me "trans" is as much short for "transgressive" as it is for "transgender". – Del

There And Back Again

A transwoman friend of mine who became a Buddhist nun once described her entrance into the monastery. She explained her transition to the Tibetan abbot, and he nodded genially. Surprised, she asked if this was something he might find theologically inappropriate. He informed her that his lineage saw such things as gender transitions in a relaxed way; one was allowed up to three of them. Three? She was taken aback. Yes, he told her; once to try it, once to see if one had made a mistake, and once to change back it the first choice had been correct. More than that, he reassured her, was considered excessive.

It's a dirty secret in the transgender demographic that a very small percentage of people who cross over to live as the other gender, and might even take hormones and get surgery, eventually decide to transition back to their original gender. Their reasons are variable, but none of them (surprisingly) that I've known seemed to feel that their first transition was a terrible mistake. Most are glad to have done it, if only to have known what it was like. They talk about how it was fulfilling for a while, and then it ceased to be so for personal reasons. Three of my correspondents fell into this category to one extent or another. One, a biological male who later withdrew his interview due to his partner's objections, spent about five years presenting as female, but went back to living as male due to difficulty finding work and female partners. Two others reported:

For me, gender has always been about the journey and not the destination. Gender is something that I started playing with at 17 when I was kicked out for being queer, and it's something that I've never stopped exploring. I've lived my life as a butch dyke, a transgender man, and now for the past several years as a genderqueer high femme. Over the course of my years of gender conscious living, my identities have shifted a lot and so has my body. I started injecting testosterone right before my 19th birthday. I remained on T for about a year, quit for six months, went back on for another two years before finally quitting completely. – Sassafras Lowrey

I first started questioning and experimenting with my gender identity at around 16, I went from a feminine appearance with long hair, to cutting it very short. I started dressing and acting a bit more androgynous, playing with boyishness, as I never felt like a "man", nor a "woman". I adopted a boyish nickname in high school, and it became clear to family and friends that these were probably not just temporary changes.

As I read about FTMs in detail and learned about the possibility, I realized it was something I wanted to do. I lived for several years as a FTM/genderfucker not on hormones, until I finally took several steps, all in the course of the same year: changed my name and gender legally, began taking testosterone, and paid for chest surgery from my own savings. A few years later, I wanted to genderbend in the opposite direction. I began expressing an effeminate male/androgynous identity, and also stopped taking hormones. I eventually started passing as female again, and grew my hair longer. At present, you could say I am a FTMTF, at heart always a genderfucker, and I'm not done playing with my identity yet!

I'm currently in a live-in relationship with my "Daddy"; in fact I moved to Germany just to be with him. We met through a website and chatted about our fantasies of him modifying me through "sissification" and "bimbofication". We both took a big risk, and as luck would have it, everything worked out! – Dax

People who transition back to their originally assigned gender have a rough time of it in the transgender demographic, especially among transsexuals. *It's hard enough to convince medical professionals to let us transition, the logic goes, that the ones who give it up after all that work are giving us all a bad name.* (The same goes for the ones who claim an intermediate identity even after transition, or don't act according to socially acceptable gender cues, or bear or sire children after partial physical transition.) *After all, if the medical professionals got wind of them, they might hold it against the rest of us who would never dream of doing anything like that!* Generally, formerly transitioned transfolks quietly leave the demographic and don't look back for fear of being stoned. If they're at all kinky, however, they do tend to end up in the BDSM demographic, where being unusually gendered in one way may not be seen as that different as being unusually gendered in any other.

The Sacred Third

Intersexuality makes the dance of identity and gender even harder than that of transfolk; you have some kind of physical "proof" of your difference, but it's generally treated with even more horror and sometimes drastic medical repression. Some intersexuals

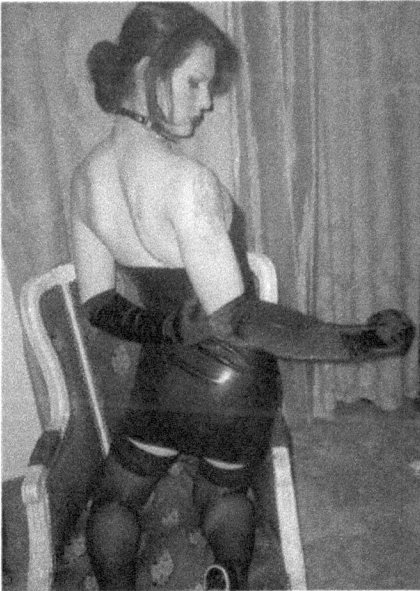

adapt to the gender that they are assigned (usually female) but many suffer from gender dysphoria as severely as transsexuals. Of these, a certain percentage see themselves fairly traditionally as members of the sex opposite to their birth assignments; VioletErotica from Italy says: "I had feminine hormone levels in a genetically male body from 6 to 15 years old. In the meantime, I expressed to myself the desire to be a woman at 11 years old. During my puberty I clearly felt that I was in the wrong body. At the age of 16 I had a crush on a female professor teaching Italian in other class. At that moment I discovered myself to be lesbian. Finally, at the age of 20 I began to transition."

On the other hand, my own experience of being intersexed (I have congenital adrenal hyperplasia, the most common IS condition) was a major factor in my feeling of being somewhere in the middle ground of gender rather than at one side or the other. The clear example of my in-between body reinforced my mind's view that I was just meant to be in-between; after all, I'd been made that way, hadn't I? Instead of seeing myself as "stopped halfway to male and prevented from reaching it", I internalized myself as dual-gendered, and thus able to choose whatever part of the continuum worked best for me physically, so long as I wasn't on the uncomfortable and inappropriate-feeling far end of either female or male. I finally settled on "male of center" for both the point where I felt most authentic physically and mentally, as opposed to "female of center", which was where I'd lived for the first 28 years of my life. For me, that meant transition and chest surgery, but no genital surgery.

One of the milestones that helped me to accept my intermediate identity as being acceptable (including among transgendered individuals, who were mostly set on being seen as entirely male or female in the era of my transition) was the fact that I eroticized being physically hermaphroditic. The revulsion of my parents (and especially my mother) at my body's attempts to masculinize somehow didn't find a place to root in my own self-image, and what blocked them out was one of my own particular sexual perversions. I just couldn't convince myself that my body, and my desire to let it keep changing (and even encourage it) was wrong ... because it seemed so sexy to me. I wasn't exactly a classic mythical hermaphrodite with breasts and a large phallus—and I think that I could have borne having breasts a lot better if I had an equally big schlong—but I was something, and it was vaguely, indefinably hot. How could it be wrong? My libido won over my social programming on that point. It wouldn't be the last time that happened, either. I have a lot to thank my libido for when it comes to keeping me sane and with reasonable self-esteem.

The upshot of this chapter is that when someone in the BDSM demographic runs across someone who calls themselves transgendered, they are actually getting a lot less useful information from that term than they might hope. The identity of someone under that umbrella group could fall into any one of a number of categories with regard to their preferred pronoun, their level of comfort with their body, and what gender they might want to be referred to and/or treated as. All it means is that they experience gender very differently from the average woman or man, and this will need to be taken into account when dealing with them.

One nontrans partner who responded to my survey wrote wryly, "I've learned that the label 'transgendered' or something like that only means: Warning! This is someone who may be a minefield of issues around physical and social gender, any of which is likely to give them offense if you accidentally hit a sore spot, and you'd better question them thoroughly in order to find out how not to offend them, even though questioning them is likely to give offense. I'm *dating* two of them and I'm saying this!"

While it may make transfolk wince, it's something to think about. How can we learn to discuss our most painful issues without jumping at every well-meaning but ignorant twinge? One key is to keep in mind that most people honestly do want to do the correct thing socially and are discomfited when they don't know what that is, but conversely many are more likely to resist following a new rule when it is explained to them in a way that makes them feel belittled. Not everyone wants to turn every play party or munch into an educational session, but if people don't know what's appropriate for the situation—and with our vast diversity, it's dangerous to assume that what is appropriate for one of us works for another—they won't be able to come through. Sometimes one has to sigh and educate anyway. Informational pamphlets, handed over with a friendly smile (not a glare or snarl or roll of the eyes) when someone asks a difficult question can be a way to educate without wasting recreational time.

Our existence is a monkey wrench thrown into the cobbled-together gears of binary human gender. We show the cracks in the system. We *are* the cracks in the system ... just as BDSM practitioners are the cracks in the "normal" sexuality system. We have a lot in common, although some of it is fear, worry, defensiveness, shame, longing for acceptance, searching for understanding partners and community, and struggling with being public or closeted. We're more alike than we think ... and there are enough of us who live in both these worlds that alliances are in order.

In fact, there are enough transgendered people who are also BDSM practitioners that we have a stronger presence in those communities, percentage-wise, than in much of the rest of the world. The average nontrans and non-kinky average Joe or Jane who has never knowingly met and interacted with a real live transsexual (even for a few minutes) is depressingly high. Of those few who have, the overwhelming majority have only interacted with one, perhaps a lone friend or family member. On the other hand, I would bet that the majority of nontrans people who are active in the BDSM scene have interacted (usually fairly positively, or at least neutrally) with more than one openly transgendered person. While I know that demographics vary from area to area, I base that bet on having talked to a lot of kinksters in many different places. It's not that there are no transphobic BDSM practitioners, but to the majority of people in many if not most BDSM communities, we are not faraway and fearsome monstrosities only ever seen on talk shows. We're fellow kinksters who wore that cool outfit or had that neat scene or were also drooling over the glass buttplugs in the dealer's room. We're fellow transgressors in the sexual arena, in our different ways. Familiarity is the first step to eventual acceptance, and in the BDSM demographic we have a chance to do some pretty serious "familiarity activism" (meaning "Hi, I'm Jean, and I'm a real person who has things in common with you and my trans status is not that big a deal in this interaction") without the attendant danger of being beaten to death.

But this means that we have to breathe a lot, go slow, and keep being brave about ourselves and our stories. A freak show who can look you in the eye, shake your hand, tell you their name and talk calmly about a mutual interest can send you home not thinking of them as a freak show any more. What is familiar is harder to think of as alien, and in the dark and chain-hung halls of this subculture, we are slowly becoming just another part of the ordinary landscape.

The Double-Barreled Shotgun: Growing Up A Trans Pervert

It's bad enough to grow up knowing that you're differently gendered. There are the nights spent lying awake, sure that they'll find out that you're a monster, and then all hell will break loose. It's even worse when you know that your sexuality isn't even "normal" for the opposite gender that so appeals to you. Some kinky transsexuals have admitted that part of what held them back from exploring their gender identity was actually their perversions; either they worried that their gender dysphoria was just another sort of sick glitch in their sexuality, or they understood its separateness from their sexuality but felt that they oughtn't to take that step if they wouldn't ever have a normal sexuality in any gender.

On the other hand, for many (including myself and my partners) kink was an encouragement to transition. After all, if you're already socially abnormal in one way, it's sometimes easier to go ahead and be socially abnormal in other ways. One may as well be hanged for a flock as for a lamb, as it were. Some came into their understanding of themselves as sexually different, or as desiring control or bring controlled in their interactions with others, at the same time or before they understood their gender configuration. Lord Tom reminisces: "I have been doing BDSM since I was as young as four years old, though I did not associate it with sex until I was a teenager. I enjoyed the control, and the responsibilities that came with that control even then. Other children would come to me and ask me to be the leader role in our games. They would tell me they wanted me to tie them up, or be the doctor to their patient, the parent to their infant, the bad guy who captured them and left them to struggle until the hero arrived to save them. When I wasn't playing pretend, I enjoyed expressing my creativity using what others offered. I helped other children lie down while I drew on them with magic markers, colored their arms, legs, painted their fingernails, and covered their skin with glitter. I even cut their hair on occasion (though this activity was usually reserved for my sibling). The kids enjoyed the process of being my canvas."

For some respondents, gender exploration and BDSM jointly filled their early childhood fantasies. Cordelia Wynn Shea recounts: "I started by tying up my action figures as a young boy. They would interrogate and torture each other, and I would switch off in my head being the horrible villain and the sacrificing hero. Then the villain started humiliating the hero and dressing him in women's clothing ... which meant that I had to steal my sister's Barbie clothes and wrap them around GI Joe the best I could. Sometimes the hero would escape and call the posse on the villain, who would then dress up as an elegant woman and escape pursuit in disguise. Eventually this turned into me cross-dressing myself in stolen clothing and bits of Halloween costumes, playing either part at my whim—including tying myself up—and then the game began to include masturbation. At some point I was discovered in self-bondage in a dress, and it all went downhill from there."

Lee Harrington also ambivalently remembers starting young: "I decided I was into kink at the age of 6 or 7, when I read a magazine (Penthouse Forum) story that talked about a girl's 21st birthday at a local kink community gathering. I wanted friends who would help me make my dreams come true, and at the time, kink is the word I had for it. It still is, and I have those friends now. I started tying myself up around that period, and tying up other people not long after. By 13 I was in service to my first Master, who was a NAMBLA (North American Man-Boy Love Association) boy, who trained me. At 15 I ended up getting involved with the public BDSM community under a fake ID, and I am glad for it as I discovered things like slaves had the right to say no, that sharing blades in knife play can lead to HIV, etc. I would likely be dead because of how heavy I was playing back then if I had not gotten into the public community."

Similarly, Siobhan Phoenix started out with young peers who had limited community involvement and knowledge of safety:

> Early on, I had little to no education about any dangers. Blood play with one partner was common (we loved the idea of drinking each other's blood). A few years later, fast forward—after a traumatic period where my parents had me locked up for being transsexual (at 19

years old until I was almost 21), I started exploring things from a more organized point of view in the Goth/Fetish scene. The primary appeal to me was that all the things I found hot (blood, pain, etc.) were accepted as "normal" in that subculture, and I loved it. The fact I wanted to be a woman was also well accepted within the fetish communities.

Genderqueer Sassafras Lowrey leaped into the pool at the deep end as well, into power exchange and gender-bending at once: "All of my serious relationships have included explicit D/s aspects as key components, specifically Daddy/boy. I started doing BDSM in my first real relationship. I had just turned eighteen and moved cross-country to be with my first trans-butch lover. The leather aspect of our relationship started sort of accidentally, without much negotiation or forethought (not how I would recommend anyone else start, but I was really lucky). Essentially I was on the floor deep-throating his cock and he called me his boy and told me to call him Daddy. I was disconcerted and aroused all at the same time. I was raised female, and at this point in my life was really just starting to explore my own masculinity and gender. Leather gave me an opportunity to allow my gender to shapeshift outside of "male" or "female" and gave me a chance exist in ways I hadn't even imagined."

On the other hand, BDSM created a safe space for some respondents. BEAR A-M Rodgers contrasts with: "I began formal BDSM education in 1981. It was part of my education while thriving in a Leather family. Being properly trained made me safer, and provided a means of income when I was an emancipated minor in California."

Joshua wrote about his early experiences with kink, gender, and community as a teen at the Rocky Horror Picture Show:

> I'm a third-gender FTM. I transitioned from female to male, hormonally and socially, 9 years ago when I was 22. I was a fairly dorky androgynous girl prior to transition, but I didn't have any strong feelings about my gender identity for most of my youth. I wouldn't have said my mother was a feminist, but she raised her kids in a very gender-neutral way without ever making a big deal about it. She never

gave me any hassles about my gender presentation or encouraged me to have "gender-appropriate" interests. When we talked about my future it was always in gender-neutral terms about professional goals and education, not about being a wife and mother.

I never put much thought into my gender presentation until I got involved in a Rocky Horror production at 14. So my first experience of intentionally presenting myself in a very female way was in fetish clothing—corsets and latex and thigh-high boots. It was also my first experience of an intentionally sexual social role, and it was very exciting for me. I became much more self-confident, and I was able to see my difficulty fitting in with social groups in school as an issue of social incompatibility rather than of me being fundamentally flawed. I also learned about kink and fetish at Rocky, where teens routinely handcuffed each other while making out in the restrooms after performances, so the issues of sexual expression, gender, and kink all came out together for me.

BDSM was the forum where I played out my burgeoning gender issues. I cross-dressed for what started out as fetish reasons, but became more than just sexual. I vividly remember my boyfriend of the time tying me up with belts in such a way that my breasts were pressed flat and scratching "BOY SLUT" into my chest. I transitioned while being actively involved in the BDSM scene. The club I eventually went to was a perfect example of "East Coast Pansexual" play space, which means the club organizers think it would be really great if some queers would show up, but aside from some bi-curious women, they almost never do. (On the West Coast, the pansexual play spaces supposedly have a good number of queers.) I never got any problems about my gender presentation from folks there, but many were entirely clueless about transgendered people. Some thought I was a male-to-female crossdresser who had previously been coming to the club in drag. At that point I had started hormones and passed as male. I hadn't had chest surgery yet, and I did take my shirt off on occasion. Many folks didn't quite know what to make of that, but they never suspected I had been born female. Most seemed to suspect that my breasts were due to some kind of kinky "gay thing" that as middle aged suburban heterosexuals they weren't hip enough to be familiar with.

Both transgender and kink are difficult things to cope with at a young age, when sexual identity is forming and there may be a lot of shame around being too different or flawed. For some respondents, fantasizing might have been somewhat acceptable during the formative years, but doing anything about it seemed too wrong. Drik from Germany sums up the difficulty: "I started playing with age, gender and humiliation in my early teens. I was introduced to the scene by a play partner and friend of mine. We did one scene, and I was really scared. Then I spent 4 months thinking, exploring, reading and learning to accept. I think that the scene we did scared me so much because I finally got what I was looking for. I had a lot of prejudice about kinky people, and it was hard for me to accept that I belong in that community."

To grow up and be sexual as a transgendered youth generally means having to rely on one's imagination a great deal in order to be sexually functional. The "ordinary" sexual stories don't work for you, and that can include the gay or lesbian stories as well. Creativity can be the key to making it happen at all when your self-image finds no sexual role models. Simon Strikeback recounts: "I started doing BDSM when I was 19 or 20. I just got with someone where that was the only way we knew how to fuck. Some of the most creative amazing play I did was with her because we didn't have any language to talk about it, but we were both deeply queer and feminist. It was also right before I came out as trans and she really helped me through that sexually and emotionally. The appeal was about our bodies and consent and trust and making up stories and bodies to go with those stories."

In some cases, the stresses of adolescent gender identity crisis—on top of all the other emotional stressors that are possible in any given life—can create a need for intense emotional sensations that bring the distressed individual back to some kind of center. BDSM became that center for some transfolk, in ways that might take vanilla folk aback, but that did the trick to bring them into feeling alive again. Dax Constantine tells us:

> I've experienced bondage, masochism, heavy verbal abuse and humiliation, exhibitionism, sissification, feminization, submission; being used and degraded seems

to be the key activity for me. My first sexual fantasies were very hot, degrading, and kinky, so it was never a question that I would end up doing it someday. At a young age I met a handsome "sugar daddy", with whom I felt submissive, and was extremely turned on by the imbalance of power. When I moved to San Francisco, young and naïve, I constantly searched for a dominant sex partner ... The main bond between us was our sexual experiences; they were never a stable or serious relationship, and always without a strong level of trust. I was playing with fire, embodied in a dreamy dominant stud, and learned my lessons well. Some of these "relationships" were abusive, but drawing the line between BDSM and abuse was difficult for me at the time.

The internet and Craigslist were useful tools for me, I don't know how I would've realized my sexual fantasies without it. The main appeal for me was the escape from reality and general anxiety, the emptiness of daily existence, something that hit me right in the center of being and took over, made me feel passionately alive, even in pain.

Hurting

For some, pain and sensation play was the draw. Mistress Cayenne says, "Pain became a positive thing when my borderline personality started developing. The appeal was excitement and release. It lets me know that I am still here." Jackkinrowan comments: "I like the pain, I like the sex with the pain or, more occasionally, making someone else take the pain. Going from pain to pleasure and back to pain for a few rounds was just amazing to me. It was like coming home. Sort of like finding out about FTMs."

Justin tells about his early experiments and where they led him: "As soon as I became aware of my own sexuality in early adolescence, my interest was in BDSM related activities and power exchange fantasies. Beginning at about age 13, I would beat myself with a belt while masturbating and daydreaming long scenarios about being dominated. I finally convinced a girlfriend to paddle me during sex when I was in college, and it definitely lived up to what I had hoped for ... BDSM provides an incredible sense of emotional peace for me as well as physical excitement and release, from those earliest explorations to now. Afterwards, I feel centered, calm and clear-headed. I've also had several mystical experiences while doing BDSM; those insights are also part of the appeal for me."

Finn in Germany writes about how he started with a particular sensation in his own cultural context:

> My primary interest is in spanking, and I am certain that this fetish was encouraged by the prevalence of this activity in child-raising in Ireland, where I grew up, and also in children's media, even that of the mid-1980s; friends of mine would regularly discuss their experiences of spanking, and characters in my childhood comic books would regularly be spanked for misdemeanours, and I was fascinated by this. At the age of around 8-9, I participated in games with my friends within which spanking was used as a penalty, and was always keen to lose so that I would experience this "punishment", but even then I was disappointed by the lack of vigour with which it was inflicted, and was dissatisfied with the jovial atmosphere which surrounded it, although I would never have admitted such to my friends. I decided that I would start to test my own limits and to spank myself whilst fantasizing that I was being punished by some unknown adult; upon reaching puberty, I became very practiced at this and even made a few spanking implements for myself; I had my first orgasm whilst spanking myself with a birch I had made and kept concealed. The Internet revolutionized my understanding of my fetish, since for the first time I had access to videos, pictures and stories which far surpassed my previous resources (such as the dictionary within which I would regularly look up the definition of "spanking"); and I also became aware that my desires were shared by many people.

As some transfolk have explored in the chapter on coping mechanisms, pain could sometimes be a way to create non-genital sexual sensations. Blaise Garber-Paul tells us: "I started doing BDSM from the very beginning of exploring my sexual expression, at 14. My first sexual partner was a someone with a vampire identity. Early into our experimentations he took my arm in his hand & smacked it. He asked me to describe the difference between the sting in my arm and the buzz in my crotch. I couldn't. I started experimenting with pain by myself around the same time, often using it instead of masturbation."

For transsexuals, once we realize what it is that we want and that there's a way to get it, we may have to deal with assumptions by decades of gatekeepers. While I've known many a transsexual who was too dysphoric to use their genitals sexually—and I've been there myself for a time—I've also known a few who read the medical "standards", including the parts about how that reluctance is gatekeeping-touchstone for transsexuality, and stopped using their junk so that no one could question their "realness". Coreyboi poignantly describes how this can affect someone with BDSM proclivities:

> I don't believe that my transgender status is a as big a focus in my sexuality as it used to be. It has definitely changed over the years. While everything is connected in a myriad of ways, I do believe that being trans is a underlying cause of my liking BDSM. Once I became more comfortable with myself and accepting of the fact that my female parts do not make me any less of a man, I was able to settle back and allow myself to enjoy physical sensations of my body. I had spent so many years hating my female body that I did not allow myself to feel the pleasures it could afford me for fear that I would be considered less of a man, or that the "gatekeepers" would not allow me testosterone or surgery if I enjoyed vaginal sex. The only physical sensations I allowed myself were those of pain. I began to enjoy cutting myself, and soon cutting became a sexual release. I could justify touching my breasts and vagina if I did so with a razor. It took a long time, but I got over that. I came to the conclusion that while I want surgery, I may as well enjoy what I have for

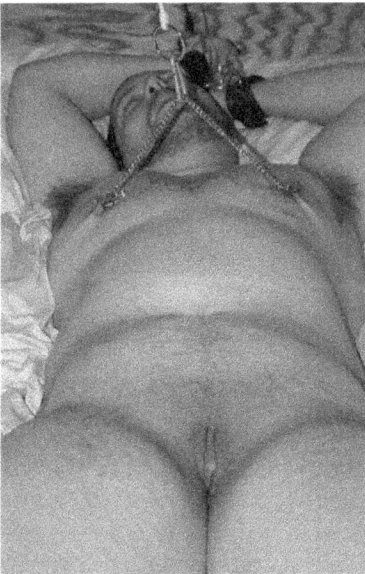

now instead of denying myself pleasure. Now I enjoy both "normal" sexual stimulation and BDSM. – coreyboi

Mind Games

Others in the community were more turned on by the psychological aspects. Ashley Lynch recounts: "I enjoy fetwear, D/s, objectification, collars, leashes, obedience training, Goddess worship ... pretty much anything to do with control. I'm much more into the D/s aspect of kink than I am into BDSM. Pain for pain's sake bores me."

Some of my respondents wrote about their attraction to control and sexual theater:

> I'm a perv. I'm into psychological role-playing and power play. I'm primarily a top but getting more into switching. I don't do pain play much, either giving or receiving. But I play rough in any kind of sex I have. Sex without some kind of consensual power play isn't very interesting to me. – Simon Strikeback

> I like to be submissive, but I'm not too much into pain, besides quite soft spanking. I like it when someone else is in control, I like being verbally abused (I love being called a cocksucker and a slut.), I like my partner to give me orders and get rough. I'm into some role play about the idea of being at someone's mercy, about being forced to submit and enjoying it. Or about being a young, smart-assed and kinky teenage boy who needs to get tamed in order to take the pleasure the way someone more mature and powerful

wants it, not as he wants it. Oh, and I like to get fucked hard. – Jonah

> I am definitely more into mind games than anything else. I tend to eschew any activity that directly involves sexual organs, *especially* mine, and I do not much have the patience for bondage or training. Really, the power dynamic and the sadism are what I get into. I have a feeling that controlling the situation makes it easier to relax into it. – Lizzie

The psychological aspects of BDSM can create the feeling of deep intimacy very quickly, perhaps quicker than in a vanilla situation. That feeling can also be a strong draw, as evidenced by Netdancer who says, "For me the biggest appeal is in contact, in making a deeply and nakedly intimate connection with another person. And in the power granted by such a connection; when someone is wide open to me they are more likely to be amenable to being shored up mentally and emotionally." Similarly, Mik Kinkead mentions the self-exploration that comes with such intense sexual relationships, a self-exploration that is crucially important for transgendered people:

> I believe I began being involved in BDSM as I found it a natural way to explore gender and equality. Holding consensual (or as consensual as it can be) power over another person was a way to figure out how I wanted to interact with the world and a way to regain a lots of control and trust during sex—something I've always had an issue with. I find I enjoy sex acts more when I have an idea of the parameters sex is set within, and when I feel secure about how my body and myself will be treated. I have a friend who defines all kinky sex as sex where there is a conversation about what is wanted and how that want will be achieved—so in a way all the sex my partner and I engage in is kinky to a certain degree, as we talk about almost everything. – Mik Kinkead

And Where We Ended Up...

Transgendered folk, in general, can be found in any area of BDSM that any nontrans person might frequent. Their fetishes are many and varied, as my respondents reported to me. Some of their commentary about BDSM practice is below; I wish that I could include more, but it would fill a book at this point. This is a sample of our diversity.

> I enjoy participating in piercing, flogging, bondage, suspension, pressure points, hunting (me chasing my pet around till I catch her, although getting her to run is harder than you might think; she giggles and blushes and says "I don't want to"). – Cole R.

> I serve my Sir in domestic servitude. I engage in ageplay with my daddy. I enjoy submitting to the desires of my De Sir E, I enjoy engaging in impact play and humiliation play. I love the blood and pain combination. When I do something he doesn't like I get punished, which is a list we came up with together but he decides the severity of the offense. We like to wear costumes and play with roles like Boy Scout/Scoutmaster, clowns, dirty Republican/non-profit director... – boy bailey

> When it comes to play, I'm most known as being a needle/bloodplay top. I also like to punch, kick, and physically abuse people in rough play. I have a toybag full of floggers, paddles, and the like, but almost always I'm just interested in what our bodies can do to each other. I call myself a "clinical sadist", in that I derive sexual and psychological pleasure in someone's discomfort, particularly when that discomfort doesn't make them happy. That is, I actually want my bottoms to suffer, rather than just enjoy, our time together. – Del

> My Owner flogs me, figgs me, binds and plays with me with candlewax, ice, clamps, needles. She forces me to service Her other slave sexually and lends me out for demos. She cages me and plugs me anally. She does whatever She wishes. i cook for Her at times and serve at functions for Her ... i remember reading an article in an old magazine about the book the story of O when i was young and i was fascinated. i was a cutter when i was younger; my cutting evolved from being a psychological crutch to being a sexually arousing act. i enjoy the freedom i feel when i am bound and unable to do anything but be and feel. When i am in service i can concentrate exclusively on the present, on what i am doing and on my Owner's wishes, nothing more. – coreyboi

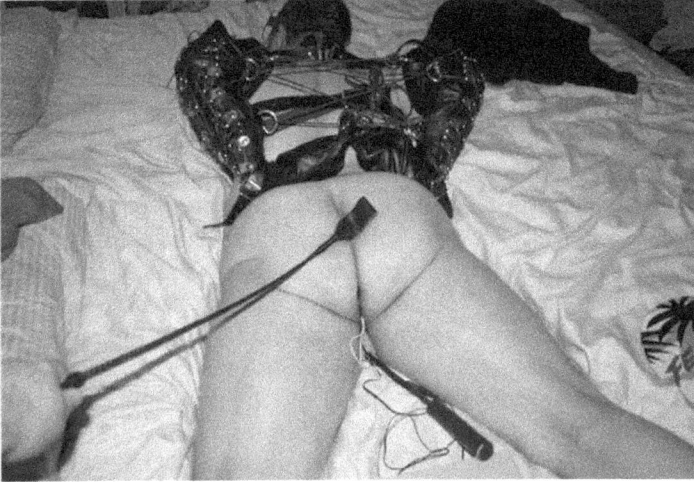

In the beginning of my sexual relationships, I experimented with bottoming during scenes. While I liked and still enjoy sensation play, I found out quickly how very much I need to be in control. I am a dominant, and recently I have become a Master. My D/s and M/s relationships involve myriad BDSM activities, as I keep pushing myself and my partner(s) to try new things. Favorite activities include: Roleplay (ageplay, teacher/student, puppyplay, and all manner of roles we feel like playing at the time), sex magick, sacred sexuality, spiritual rituals to name a few of the activities in which we enter a deeper mental headspace. A lot of sex magic I do is influenced by Egyptian magick, and I use mummification bondage in many of these rites. I use masks and costuming, props during scenes and rites because of their transformative abilities. In most of the scenes my partners and I do, we exchange energy. My slave (who is also my wife) and I are in the process of better establishing a firm Master/slave relationship that we live 24/7, which will include BDSM scenes and elements, but will also be the nature of our service-oriented relationship.

Other specific kinky fetishes and BDSM activities I enjoy as a top are spanking, nipple torture, hot wax, anal play, medical play, caging and confinement, caning, edge play, gas masks, humiliation, sensory deprivation, talking dirty, strap-ons, voyeurism, sadism, masochism, latex, leather, rubber, blood play, chastity, mind fucks, biting, body modification, boot worship, foot worship, electrical play, sensation play, predicament bondage, flogging ...to name a few. – Lord Tom

I'm a switch. I think bloodsports are my core-kink—piercings, cuttings, bleedings, etc. I really enjoy body mod—like permanent piercings, piercing-suspensions and brandings. These acts feel like ritual to me, I often use them to mark or induce important self-transformations. More recreationally, I also like to bottoming to heavy impact play (punching, kicking, stomping, boots, etc.); breath play (choking, rebreathing, gasmasks, etc.); single tails and other whips; rope and leather bondage. In D/s I had a long streak of Daddy/boy and Sir/boy arrangements, generally limited service contracts with negotiated consensual non-consent. I've tried most things people have come up with (caning, feet, puppy play, water sports). I'm always looking for new things that push my edges.

I'm beginning to re-explore myself as a top. I like D/s more than S/M: giving orders that are obeyed willingly; bondage; and imposing personal restraints and control. As a top I tend to be most attracted to femme dykes and faeries. I like resistance as a top, I like when bottoms push against me and resist. I like including my own masochism as an advantage as a top. I've found that I tend to attract bottoms who bite—more than one has told me that I make an excellent chew toy—and I like to remind my bottoms that I could take more than what I give. Inflicting pain or intense sensation is interesting to me as top in a more limited sort of way. I don't usually put bottoms through the same paces I like to be put through, though.

I'm a bootblack. It was one of my first identities within the BDSM scene. I started bootblacking for my first Daddy, then found that it was a skill that gave me a place in the leatherfag community. I've blacked with the New York boys of Leather, the Floating World, Black Rose, MidAtlantic Leather, the New York Leather Pride Night and Folsom Street East. I think bootblacking is more community service and leather tradition than a sexual exchange for me at this moment. I have had very intense energy exchanges from bootblacking though, and I've definitely experienced release from simply touching a special pair on a special person. – Blaise Garber-Paul

At this point, I only top (although that includes activities to me that some people would consider as not dominant, like having my bottoms perform any sexual services I am into) and most of my play is spiritual. I have adopted my shamanic practices to my BDSM, especially when it comes to flogging. I administer them as I do shamanic healings. But I am also into deep D/s. I am mostly interested in the psychological, energetic and spiritual aspects of it, and any practices that fit in are welcome ... Roughly half of the biofags I encounter for play these days are HIV positive. Sero status does not affect me in my choosing of play partners, only responsible behavior around it by all partners involved.

I am trying to keep it real, when it comes to my BDSM relationships, but there is also fun role play, like alien abduction scenes or sailor and whore. I have done quite a lot of Daddy and boy, but that has vanished as I grew up to be a man ... I used to play a lot with gender, but that has ceased as well, as I am living a male gender now and don't need to explore much anymore. But I would be open to my partners playing with gender. I have gotten my slave to impersonate a transvestite sex worker before.

    – TransPunk

I am a masochist. Getting beaten is a real favorite of mine, especially if the beating goes deep with a lot of thud. I particularly favor leather floggers, leather slappers, and fists (particularly if covered in leather gloves). I have also enjoyed being on the receiving end of a range of other types of masochistic fun, including hot wax, ice, electricity (violet wands), knife play, clothespins, biting, pinching, slapping, etc.

I am also submissive. As a sub, I have done a lot of Daddy/boy (and even a little Daddy/girl!) play. Scenes that involve mock rape, verbal humiliation, forced feminization, taking orders, being led on all fours on a leash and collar, licking and kissing feet and boots, getting pissed on, and being photographed naked have all been exceptionally hot for me. I am also a bottom for bondage and fucking. I love getting tied up; I find it very calming. Getting fucked is pleasurable in and of itself and sometimes also gives me a masochistic and/or submissive charge.

Group sex and public sex are also great fun, although not specifically BDSM related. I also enjoy the smell of leather and think that men look hot dressed in leather, although I am not into leather or any other materials/clothing in as deep or intense a way as some fetishists I have known. Submission, masochism, and bottoming do not always all go together for me in a particular scene. Sometimes I really love and even prefer receiving pain without any sort of a strong D/s dynamic happening at the same time. I can also have a very intense

submission/humiliation scene without any pain involved—
although I do think a bit of pain usually adds something to
it.

I didn't actually go to an SM club or play in a heavier
way for the first time until I was 22. It was a revelation.
The first time I got flogged I was utterly ecstatic. I had a
hard time focusing on anything else for many weeks
afterward; every day I couldn't imagine how I would get
through it without getting flogged again. I learned some
patience, but it wasn't easy. – Micah

It was a revelation for me, too. There were people doing the
same things I'd fantasized about doing, and having real relationships
I'd fantasized about having, and they weren't guilty at all, at least
most of the time. While I won't say that the entire scene was free of
guilt, when someone got up and proudly talked about how they
were a slave or liked diapers or piss play or got hung on hooks, it
was not lost on me that I could be at least as proud of being
transgendered as I could of being a pervert—and among the
perverts I could be openly proud of both and no one would bat an
eye. The outside world might think that we were all an
undifferentiated batch of sickness, true. But here were nontrans
people who could, if not understand exactly, at least willingly bond
with me over the things that we were driven by our various urges to
do, and that we wished were socially acceptable to be out and proud
about.

BDSM also gave me a way to be sexual with my lovers when
the body dysphoria got bad enough that I could no longer function
in any "normal" sexual way and went almost entirely stone. This
was the year before my transition, often spoken of as the hardest
year of all in any transsexual's life. If I couldn't do anything else, I
could have a scene with my lovers, and both satisfy them and find
some kind of satisfaction for myself. Until my physical transition got
me into a space where I could be safely in my body for sex, BDSM
was the life raft.

Roleplaying had come early to me—I was a dramatic,
theatrical child—and I fell into it naturally with most of my teenage
lovers, starting at age 14. We played Dungeons and Dragons and

then replayed the "scenes" live with each other, sexualizing them and enacting the "off-camera" parts. I wrote bad porn with characters that were often adult versions of myself and my friends; I inserted myself into the stories in both male and female characters, and of course they were always kinky. I remember a vanilla age-mate with whom I wrote bad science fiction as a hobby; she would always say, "You get to write the abduction and torture scenes—you're so good at it."

The appeal was visceral as well; whenever I had trouble masturbating as a teenager due to those bad feelings about my body, I could go into an internal world where there were bound, tormented slaves and cruel, alluring captors, and I'd always get off. It never failed, and I thank BDSM (even though I didn't know that acronym, nor that there were others who actually agreed to do these practices) for sustaining my sexuality all those many years until I could finally take control of it.

Interview With Sable Twilight

If I separate out things such as my spiritual, sexual, relational and other identities, than most commonly I find myself using genderqueer transsexual woman. Sometimes I will refer to myself as a butch transsexual woman or tranny dyke. There are other times—infrequently—when I use transgender transsexual woman. And once in a great while I like to use the term hot she-male sex goddess. I do point out that I make a distinction between my gender identity—the relation I have with my social role and identity display—and my sexual identity—the relation of my mental/subconscious sex and the physical characteristics of my body. Both are transitional to me. Neither conforms to societal norms or exceptions. My gender identify has evolved greatly over the years. For most of my life I did identify as a guy or male, though it was always an uncomfortable identity for me. Through the late 90s and early 2000s, when I came out as wanting to understand my trans identity, I explored terms such as transgender, Gallae, male-to-femme transgender person or male-to-femme transgender grrl, or trans girl. It was not until 2005 that I accepted the identity of transsexual woman for myself, and even then I soon found myself refining my identity even further. And I fully expect my identity to continue to evolve over time.

My current sexual preference I would describe as queer, with a primary interest in women—cissexual, transsexual and transgender. I date and scene with a number of transsexual women. And much like with cissexual women, we engage in a wide range of roles and play with one another. In some ways I find it easiest to connect with transsexual women, since there is a element of shared experiences, and we both understand the importance of being able to have open and respectful dialog about our bodies with one another. There have been a few male partners in my life, but I would say they are most definitely in the minority. I also have a very strong attraction to energy workers, and in particular vampire-identified individuals, to the point that one of my lovers has labeled me "vamp-sexual".

Like my gender identity, my sexual preferences have changed over time. Even though my first sexual encounter was with another boy, through my teenage years and my 20s, I primarily considered myself heterosexual, or possibly what might be considered today as heteroflexible. That is, I was willing to entertain the idea of fooling around with another slightly effeminate male, but it was not something I ever actually pursued. As I found myself become more comfortable exploring my gender identity, I also found myself become more comfortable with exploring my sexual identity as well. For a brief time I consider myself bisexual, but found the "bi" prefix to be rather limiting. Soon after that period I started using the term "sexual" or "simply sexual" to describe my orientation. However, using that required a bit more explanation than I wanted to deal with on a general basis. I have settled on the terms Queer, since it seems to be truly the more comprehensive and accurate term I have come across thus far. My sexuality is queer. Quite queer indeed.

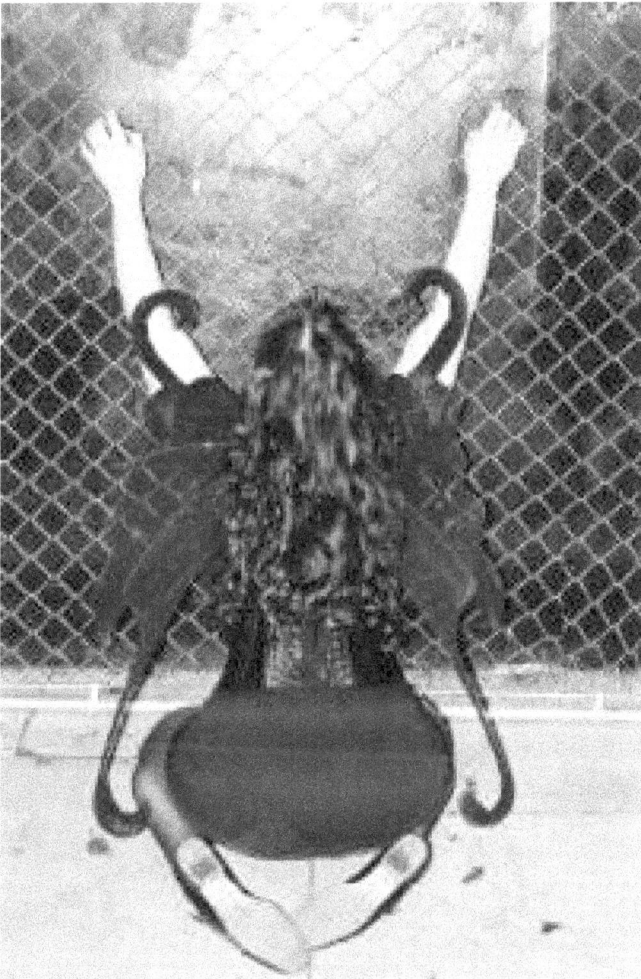

I have a collared live-in pet whom I am own. It might be considered comparable to a Master/slave relationship, but I do not consider it nearly as strict or demanding; mostly I do my best to act as a guide and support for her. We engage in role play and age play, knife play, punching, spanking, and biting. On occasion we will visit one of the local play spaces. I am a girl to a Daddy, though most of our time together more closely resembles conventional dating—going out to movies and such. There are a few other lovers with whom I engage with some bedroom wrestling, rough sex, biting, and energy exchange.

When more active in the scene, I identify as a switch. I have always had both dominant and submissive aspects to myself, and my ideal has always been that of an alpha slave—submissive to a dominant or owner, but dominant over other member of the household. I especially enjoy the role of companion submissive—a strong-willed, confident submissive who serves at the side of a dominant, looking after the dominant's needs, being an extension of the dominant's will, as well as plaything in the dungeon and bedroom. When topping, I enjoy bondage, tease and denial play, spanking, knife play, various forms of sensation

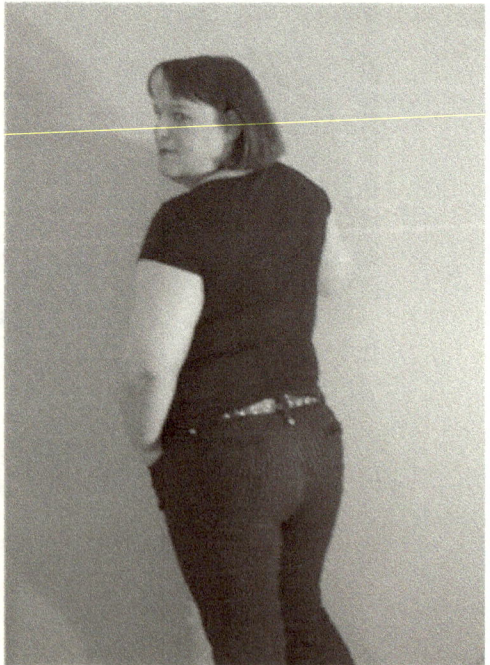

and energy play. As a top, I found I enjoyed the reactions I could bring about in the person I played with. I also find that I enjoyed the ability to positively influence their feelings of self and self-confidence. As bottom, I like the loss of control and the opportunity to simply release into the experience of the moment.

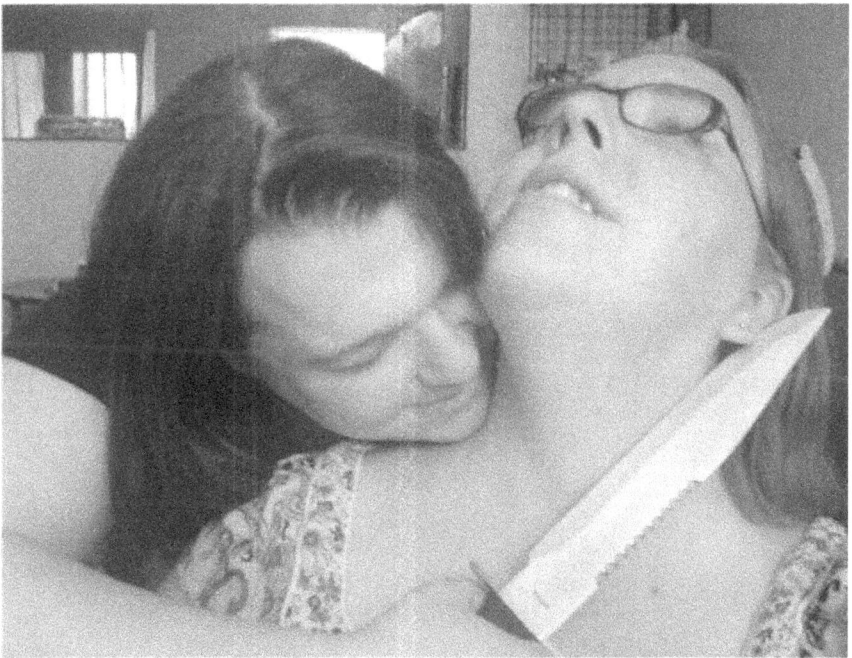

Forbidden Costumes:
Cross-Dressing As Fetish And Identity

A friend of mine calls cross-dressing the "gateway drug of transgenderism". It's true that you can fantasize all you want, you can dress androgynously or get that unigendered haircut, you can take up hobbies and activities of another sex, but it's not until you actually go out of your way to buy those clothes and dress to deliberately give the impression of being that sex that it starts. Then, in so many cases, it's got you. If it becomes (or always was) a sexual thing for you as well, it's damn hard to turn back. Some people will stay in that place comfortably, assuming that they do become comfortable with their own proclivities. Others will take it further, and for some cross-dressing really is the "gateway drug" to sex reassignment.

BDSM communities are one of the few places that people can experiment publicly with cross-dressing and have it be reasonably accepted. (One of the other rare places, oddly enough, is historical recreation groups such as the Society for Creative Anachronism or other living history hobby groups. I've met a surprising number of people who began there as well.) At BDSM clubs, no one ostracizes you for bending gender or showing up in costume and playing a role. In some communities, it's accepted that people have a "fetish persona" and that's all you'll ever see them presenting in fetish venues, while they may be closeted about their ordinary name and life. It's not considered unusual or dishonest for Mistress Tatiana to only be Mistress Tatiana when you see her at the play party or even the munch, while Bob the insurance adjuster whose name is on Mistress Tatiana's driver's license is never seen or referred to.

Of course, many of the people at a BDSM club or party or support group won't be cross-dressing because they are exploring gender or have an identity that isn't wholly male or female. They do it because it's hot. The gender divide is an abyss that one is penalized by society for attempting to cross, and the same social disapproval that gets a transsexual beaten to death in an alley also makes transgressing that forbidden boundary a source of sexual thrills. BDSM practitioners have a long history of playing with social fire, eroticizing and messing with all sorts of socially unacceptable urges. In fact, for many, the more the transgression is reviled, the hotter it is to play with.

Both male-bodied and female-bodied people play with gender in scene, although male-bodied cross-dressers are more numerous and prominent. This is partly because there are just more male-bodied people than female-bodied people openly practicing BDSM. It's also partly because there is a solid and well-documented fetish niche for male-to-female crossdressers, with decades of visual pornography, written erotica, and clubs. Female-bodied people who enjoy cross-dressing don't have the group support, the role models, or the permission of their social upbringing to be strongly concerned with their sexual desires. That doesn't mean that they don't do it. It just means that there is a great deal of shame and secrecy around it.

When I was watching dykes cross-dress in the lesbian leather community, there was a lot of resistance to even using the words "cross-dresser" or "transvestite". *That's not what we are,* I was told, even after watching scenes where a dyke daddy and his dyke boy would plaster on moustaches, play with each other's realistic rubber cocks, and call each other by male titles and pronouns. Why? The only reason seemed to be, "We aren't men, and those labels are for men." The association with male sexuality seemed to give the terms an extra seediness that the female-raised population was quite uncomfortable dealing with. I also heard a lot of "We're doing this to challenge gender norms in society" when it was abundantly clear that wet cunts were the unacknowledged primary reason. No one out there is going to be challenged by two cross-dressed dykes fucking each other as men in their own bedrooms or even in a dyke club, but one can certainly say that it challenges one's own thinking about gender and how it is expressed sexually.

When I interviewed a number of cross-dressers for an article that I wrote many years ago, I also found that age played a factor in the differences between gender. Most of the male-to-female cross-dressers claimed to have come to their interest in women's clothing at a very young age—some even at a presexual age, dressing up in their mother's clothing in first grade or so. In contrast, most of the female-to-male cross-dressers (and all of the ones who did not move on to transsexuality) came to the practice later in life, after they had grown into their sexuality and sorted out what they were told should turn them on from what actually did. A few have spoken of it as a side-effect of their emotional and psychological maturity. One of the women who was interviewed at the time told me that: "I couldn't find my boy side until I unbrainwashed myself. I had to get past all those things that I'd been told I ought to want, and then I could do what I really wanted. That took until I was 25."

Cross-dressing seems to be the "grey area" for male-bodied people that the current category of "genderqueer" is for female-bodied people—a way to create space to be in between genders without the commitment of legal and physical gender reassignment, which may not be right for them personally, or at least not currently right for them. (That's not to say that there aren't male-bodied genderqueers; there are, but they are a minority, just as female cross-dressers are. The reason for this gender divergence may well have something to do with the fact that it is more acceptable for female-bodied people to be androgynous in public than it is for male-bodied people.) They may have identities that sit squarely in their birth gender even when they are in costume and persona, or it may be a way to express a part of an admitted transgendered identity that doesn't get its less visible aspects acknowledged on a regular basis. It's a continuum of grey area, not a bunch of separate stations one travels to, and it can fluctuate over a lifetime.

These subcultures are also a place where individuals can dip toes into the more permanent changes and then back off if they decide that it's not right. Just as I got surveys from female-bodied genderqueers who had tried transsexuality and backed off from living as male, I also got some from male-bodied respondents who tried the same thing and eventually went back to being cross-dressers who lived as male in everyday life.

Panties and Politics

Most kink starts in the privacy of the bedroom, and many never leave that stage. Cross-dressing, for obvious reasons, is often one of those. If a sympathetic partner is found to help, it may never need to see the light of day. "Bizarre Suzanne" sadly recounts: "My second wife participated in dressing with and for me in the bedroom.

She had to drag it out of me that I was a CD/TV with interests in bondage and sex ... but loved the idea of fetish and played with me until her illness prevented her from continuing. She has since passed on and I am again seeking a partner. Unfortunately, no partners yet ... perhaps my shyness and my age—70's now, dammit!"

Nanette, a MTF transsexual who started out as a cross-dresser, writes: "For years, my wife as supportive of my fumbling attempts to cross-dress, even in the bedroom. I couldn't imagine going out that way, or talking to anyone else about it. When our marriage began to break down, I had to do something, and that forced me out into the BDSM community. I never left! I eventually transitioned, and I am a switch with my girlfriend, but I never would have gotten this far if I'd been able to stay in my marriage, which was stale but safe."

The majority of cross-dressers, however, keep it secret until they are brave enough to bring it out into the open ... and if they're into BDSM, that's where they usually take it, sometimes before their partners ever know. They may play with gender in scenes, and they may also add in whatever fetishized activities have gotten stuck into the same "socially unacceptable for my role" closet as dressing up as the opposite sex. Those things tend to stick to each other, and be difficult to pry apart, especially after decades of being crammed together in the dark.

Male-to-female cross-dressing is strongly associated with submission and bondage in the pornography of the genre. One might not quickly see the political and sociological aspects of that fact, but they're not that hard to make out. In our society, for a man to dress as a woman is humiliating and will be seen as a drop in status by women and other men alike. Male adherence to the culturally male code of dress, acting, and sexual identity is the backbone on which the sexist gender binary is built. Women can wear pants and push for equal pay all they want, but until men—the "former superior" gender—break that taboo code all progress is going to be stalled. It's forbidden, and it's punishable in some cases by death, dealt out by one's own peers. Obviously a transgression this huge is going to build up a lot of erotic heat behind it—and, just as obviously, it will build up a lot of shame attached to that erotic heat. It's no wonder that the cross-dressed male figure is forced, bound, and tortured. There's a great deal of internalized phobia there—*this is what will happen to me if I venture into this forbidden area.*

There's also the loss of that continuing pressure to be the One In Charge. The social contract given to men tells them that they must always initiate everything (and that means being the one to risk rejection, every time) and that they must always run the fuck, taking all responsibility for the outcome. They can work their tails off to be a considerate lover, trying hard to guess the thoughts of their partner (who, if she's been raised female, may well have no idea how to express her desires) or they can stop caring and take on the role of the thuggish, clueless brute. This latter archetype isn't even the solace that one might think, though—you can fail at that, by being bothered by your lover's lack of enjoyment. Everywhere you look, it's on you and you can fail, and your only reward for trying and failing is to be mocked by men and women alike.

It's not surprising that people raised male in this culture sometimes just want to lay it all down—not necessarily entirely, or all the time, unless they're naturally the submissive type—and let someone else, someone trustworthy, be In Charge for a change. That's why there are so very many straight male submissives, wandering the clubs and looking wistfully for someone to help them achieve this goal. For those who venture into femaleness as a fetish or as an identity, it's also not surprising that the "freedom" of women to just put down the reins and have someone take care of them is very seductive. Femaleness is associated with passivity in their fantasies because they desperately want both of those states, and they are fetishizing a female privilege. (And if you don't think it's a privilege, think about how acceptable it is for a woman to be a housewife as a lifelong career, as compared with a man being a househusband, and think about how easy it is to find a partner to help achieve the former as opposed to the latter. Women have won more than one role for themselves; men are still stuck with their original meager allotment.)

There is an exception to the rule, of course, and this is the transvestite dominant Lady, also a role in pornography. She is sometimes paired with a cross-dressing male-bodied submissive, and in this case is usually seen as having achieved womanhood in some way that the sub is still attempting to achieve. Her "superior" ability to be feminine gives her the right to be superior in a way that is more often filled by nontrans dominant women. When she is paired with submissive men, she is seen as having "transcended" evil maleness. When she is paired with submissive women, on the other hand, she may be seen as jealous of their biofemale bodies and wanting to punish them for having the flesh she theoretically wants. (There is a subgenre, however, of the transvestite Queen who is worshiped and submitted to by both men and women because she is "exotic" and superior due to her in-between status.)

The point of talking about all this porn is that it's usually how cross-dressers learn to structure their fantasies, and eventually their scenes if they step into BDSM, and their future partners are going to have to confront these mental scenarios sooner or later. Especially with someone who has been creating masturbatory fantasies in isolation since perhaps childhood, there may be reams of cultural assumptions embedded in the mental stories. The cross-dresser in question may or may not be well aware of them—after all, how many of the "classic" BDSM stories that people beat off to and reenact are built entirely of (largely outdated) cultural assumptions? Once we're able to play with them, they are toys. They're hot, and no longer have power over any part of us … expect, perhaps, our crotches, and we can make a playground for that.

The gay drag queen scene is entirely different from the (mostly heterosexual) cross-dressing demographic, and it rarely crosses with any part of the leather scene, at least in the places I've been. The aesthetic of the gay male leather scene is so Tom of Finland musclebound grunting masculinity that drag queens apparently feel out of place and keep to the drag-acceptable bars and clubs. As the gay male leather scene is where the gay context crosses with the larger BDSM scene, that puts drag queens at least one remove, if not further, from the average pansexual leather club—with rare exceptions that choose to move beyond their ordinary circuit. MTF transsexuals who have come out of the gay drag queen scene generally reported a great deal of pressure not to transition, because it "would be a waste of a man". Stefanie recounts, "When I first started going 'out' crossdressed in public I was shocked at how many gay men treated me badly. I thought they would surely be accepting, but some are not, it's human nature."

While gay drag queens often use their drag persona as a way to get beyond restrictive male social conditioning, there's an underlying assumption that when the makeup is off—meaning when sex is going to occur—that they will simply revert to being standard male-acting gay men. In a demographic where male bodies are eroticized, MTF transsexuals during the unsure and experimental transition phase may find no support in drag culture. The ones with BDSM proclivities, however, had an option.

> I cross-dressed in the scene for years before I decided to transition. I started out doing drag in gay bars, but that quickly went down the drain. In a gay bar, a drag queen is a gay man in a dress, not a woman, not even in fantasy. Gay men want men, and so you don't get to experiment with what it's like to be a woman sexually in public. (I don't mean having sex in public, I mean flirting, being looked at with desire, even being catcalled.) I turned to the BDSM scene because I'd always been something of a pervert, and by the time I transitioned I was even more of a pervert! But it was safer there. Yes, some people were jerks, some people didn't get it and continued to use the wrong pronouns and tried to sabotage my experience of being female out of their own fears, but the overwhelming majority were supportive even when I began transition. I know that some just thought it was about sex and they didn't understand that it became my identity, but even they were cool about it, more cool than people in the outside world who just thought that it was wrong.
> – Cordelia Shea Wynn

Just Make Me

> I don't think my identity itself has changed other than how I define it for others. When I was young I knew I wanted to be a girl, I wished I was born a girl, but as I grew older and wiser I delved into other things as I found

out about them, like BDSM. My life choices made it difficult to talk with others about, or show the real me to my friends and family. Over the years as society redefined transgender I always felt the same about who I am. I just used the new definition, from transvestite to crossdresser, to transgendered. I liked the forced-fem stories so I would dress and tie myself up and fantasize about being forced to be a girl. I mostly enjoy the loss of control, I love to wear corsets and that's partly because of the bondage/loss of control aspect; they are hard to move around in, at least the ones I buy. I feel very comfortable in dresses and leather bondage as long as I'm around people that accept it. I am very shy so I don't go where there will be confrontation. I think for me BDSM removes my ability to control the situation, I give the power to the dom and they are responsible for what happens, not me. – Stefanie

One of the most unusual and meaningful scenes I ever did with a female-bodied "boy" was a weekend of forced masculinization. She came to me and asked me, as a transitioned FTM top, to help her with her gender ambivalence. We discussed it in depth, including the psychological dynamite involved and how she wanted it handled. It included stripping her naked and mocking and abusing her female parts, something that took me a little aback but that she was insistent on. That voice was in her head anyway, she told me. Having it outsourced to an actual human being that she trusted would help her to battle it more openly. Afterwards, I bound her breasts flat and went through a cock-granting ceremony with her, and then he was granted a male name and pronoun, cross-dressed, and treated as a boy for the duration of the weekend.

Doing that ritual really brought the body shame that we deal with into perspective for me. If someone who didn't have gender dysphoria had that level of shame about their gendered body, it would be because of some terrible wound that had been inflicted on them, probably in childhood, with messages about how their gender was degrading—not just their own personal gender, but the entirety of that gender and everyone else in it. For us, it's intensely personal. It's not that being female or male is wrong in and of itself—and we may well truly love people who fall comfortably into those categories—but the one that we ended up with is so wrong for us that we feel shame about it, a deeply personal shame that can masquerade as the "general" wound to an oblivious mental health practitioner. Then, when it doesn't respond to the course of treatment for the general wound around body gender, everyone is frustrated and the transgendered person feels even more broken. Since women are more likely to feel that their gender is degrading due to social messages, it's not surprising that female-bodied people who want forced masculinization are loath to ask for it for fear of it being misconstrued into something political. The boy that I helped repeated several times during our negotiations that this wasn't about the social view of femaleness; he was politically aware and had thought about that for a long time.

Forced feminization, on the other hand, is a submissive fantasy so frequent that it's practically a cliché. While all the female-bodied people I've met who went the forced-gender route were working out their own gender issues, that's not always the case with forced-femme. Some are doing just that, of course; the "nonconsensual" element helps with the guilt and shame around being a gender freak. If the mistress is making you do it, then you're not responsible, and you can explore it without that particular monkey on your back, on top of all the existing monkeys.

Another motivation is the thrill of being controlled, pure and simple. In this case, being forced to put on a dress and panties is in the same category as being forced to drink piss or scrub the kitchen floor or sexually service a guest. It's just one more thing that you would never choose for yourself, but that your dominant can make you do by force of will, and that control is a big turn-on. It can be humiliating, but it's just one in a line of other humiliations, most of which have nothing to do with gender.

Sometimes the dress is about humiliation, however. Many women have complained about forced feminization for this reason—why, they ask, should they be complicit in a context which suggests that it would be degrading for a man to take on female traits? Doesn't that suggest, in essence, that femaleness itself is degrading? The answer is actually more complicated than that.

From talking to many male-bodied and male-identified men who crave forced-femme, it seems that that humiliating part isn't so much becoming female as becoming not-male. Gabriel/le, a cross-dresser who enjoys this kind of play, explains that:

> I think that most women don't understand the huge pressure on men to be Men, and that if you don't do it right—according to a very stringent set of rules—you become a Not-Man. That's not the same as a woman. The men who set these social rules seem to have separate unconscious categories in their heads for women, men, and not-men. To fail at being a man is the ultimate failure, and the ultimate terror. And if you're standing there dressed in frilly panties and a ruffled dress and a big old bow in your hair, you've totally failed as a man. You're certainly not a woman, but you're about as much a not-man as it's possible to get ... and you're still alive. You have survived it. Every time you do that, it gets a little less scary. But you have to go all the way with it, verbal humiliation and mocking and all. After a while, you can get to a point where the threat of failing as a man has no power over you, but it will take some time and repetition to get there.

I've said before, many times, that what we repress just migrates to our crotches and ends up coming out there. It's the one place where our subconscious can best force us to face things that are troubling or difficult for us. The idea of forced feminization as being an unconscious groping by men for a way to work themselves out of years of male programming may seem odd from the outside, but I've always believed that sexual urges were a force that could be used for social change, not simply ignored and repressed if it didn't match one's politics. There's also that kink and sexual pleasure do not need to be justified by personal evolution. They are beneficial in and of themselves, and any positive side effects—like courage, understanding social patterns, or fully experiencing the whole range of gendered energy in one's self—are just icing on the cake.

Sea Changes:
Transitioning On Many Levels

Not all transgendered people transition physically, with hormones and/or surgery. However, those who do physically transition will find themselves riding a roller-coaster of shapeshifting that most other human beings will never experience. There's really no other experience like it. Hormones affect your body—how you see it, and how it's seen by others, and thus your reaction to their reactions—and your mind as well, bringing on new feelings and making others fade further back. Surgery, for those who choose it, is an ordeal of pain and triumph and then adapting to the results, which can go many directions. Even with the best results, we live with bodies that aren't factory standard for any gender, and that affects how we look at the world. It certainly affects how we court others and have sex.

The first level to look at, when it comes to our changes affecting our sex life, is hormonal libido. Here, many male-to-female transsexuals bemoaned estrogen's dampening effects, even as they praised its other gifts. Mistress Cayenne says flatly, "Since going on hormones sex has gone south. I have pretty much taken it for granted that I will not have normal sex. But I do love anal sex. I have also taught my slave to take anal sex so that I can do him with a strap-on." Cordelia Shea Wynn admits that:

> Sex drive is a real problem. It's the knot in the middle of my struggle with being transsexual. It's why I haven't had any lower surgery—I hate my testicles, I want them gone, they give me terrible dysphoria. I can't do yoga in tight pants because of them. But if they're gone, I'll have no sex drive. As it is, the estrogen makes me feel better mentally, but it kills my libido. I have a little card on my wall saying, "Remember that you *like* sex! It's good for you!" When I realize I've gone a month or so not even thinking about sex, not caring that I'm not thinking about it, not caring that it exists, I'll look at that card and remember. Then I'll go off my hormones for a couple of days. I have to watch myself rage-wise, but I'll want sex again. That lasts for a while after I go back on the estrogen. So I live with my testicles even though I hate them,

because otherwise it's the end of sex. BDSM helps me to put off those moments, because sometimes it's sexy enough and perverted enough that it gets my flagging libido to appear unassisted by testosterone, if only for a little while.

On the other hand, some have found it to be a relief rather than a loss. Slave Anneke writes: "In a way the estrogen has set me free. I used to obsess about sexual things all the time, things I couldn't have and masturbating was a way of having them for a few minutes. But it got to me after a while. It made me crazy. I did too much wanking off. I couldn't stop. My sexual needs ruled my life. Now after estrogen, the penis doesn't work anyway, and sex isn't as important. I don't worry all the time about having my sex needs met. I can focus on making my Mistress happy. She doesn't keep me in chastity anymore, because it's kind of irrelevant. The person that I was when testosterone was rushing through me, he would have hated that. He needed that chastity to hold back the uncontrolled sex drive. I love that now I can just be. It isn't a big deal anymore and that's such a relief."

Several transwomen also raved about estrogen's creation of a new erogenous zone—breasts with both enhanced nipple sensation and the sensation of touching the breast itself. Softer skin, which makes SM play—or even just caressing—more intense, was also mentioned frequently. A few had to scale back their BDSM activities due to their new sensitivity.

Female-to-male transsexuals often (though not always) find that the opposite problem occurs. The addition of testosterone can create a spike in libido that can be disconcerting, especially when the transman has the kind of female upbringing that teaches them to ignore sexual needs or consider them to be relatively unimportant. Being faced with random erections whenever another bit of testosterone hits the bloodstream and touches off the spinal ganglia—on the bus, on the toilet, while taking out the trash—can be awfully disconcerting. Boys learn to face it at puberty, but facing it as an adult with set ideas about sexual responses can be an eye-opening experience. "I found myself, one day early in transition, desperately wanting to hump the arm of the couch," Joshua says laconically.

Other FTMs spoke of the testosterone side effect that isn't talked about. Jonathan described his newfound libido as being "frighteningly malleable. Anything I jerked off thinking about became a new fetish, and any new fetish that I ran across on the Internet might suddenly become sexually interesting to me. As a woman, it took me a while to get into anything new sexually. As soon as I started shooting up testosterone, I became a complete pervert. In fact it was the new hormones that got me into BDSM. I'd been vanilla before. I also noticed that my new sexual obsessions were things that my former libido would have rejected as raunchy, gross, humiliating, messy, disgusting. Male hormones turned me into a filthy pig."

Transition can bring on other changes as well. Transgendered folk who were dedicated to one side of the D/s dynamic—entirely dominant or entirely submissive—may suddenly find themselves strongly attracted to the other side. (This is discussed in more detail in the chapter on D/s.) Fetish activities that were once the core of one's sexual practices may become much less interesting—for example, forced feminization may not work once you're that gender for breakfast every day (and the occasional transsexual has even admitted to switching over to fantasies about being forced to be their "original" gender, now that's it's no longer a possibility). As anatomy changes, existing nerve endings may become less useful, or new ones more prominent. Some of my recipients mentioned having to learn how to masturbate all over again in different ways.

Transposing Preferences

One of the most striking changes that transition brings can be a change in the gender that one is attracted to. This is one of those changes that makes mental health gatekeepers throw up their hands; why, they fret, would changing role change sexual object? Of course, some transsexuals never swerve in their orientation, as many of my respondents showed:

I'm more into guys now than I used to be, so instead of bi-curious I feel like I'm definitely bi now. – Ms. Jen

I've always preferred women, I can appreciate the male form more freely and openly now, but I still prefer women! Although the women I like now are feminine whereas when I was a dyke I liked the more butch variety. Don't get me wrong, I still really enjoy the look and attitude of a butch woman, I just happen to have married a femme. – Cole R.

I'm a lesbian. That hasn't really changed either. I was into women before and I'm into women now. They just smell better. Even before I knew I was trans, I used to joke with friends that I was a lesbian at heart. I tried being bisexual for awhile, mostly because I have a lot of guys that are attracted to me, but I just couldn't do it. – Ashley Lynch

I have always been bisexual but prefer men for sex and ladies for relationships. – Double-Edge

I have always been attracted to men. I am homosexual. I denied it for many many years. – coreyboi

I've always preferred women and other transexual women, I love them esthetically and intellectually.
    – VioletErotica Ita

As much as my gender may have shifted at different points of my life, for the most part my sexual preference has remained pretty much unchanged. I am with very few exceptions attracted to transgressive masculinity on individuals who were socialized female. I partner nearly exclusively with transgender butches and consider myself stone-sexual as I feel very connected to individuals who identify their own sexuality as being "stone." – Sassafras Lowrey

My partners are usually clever, sensitive, arty, intellectual guys of my age, and punks at heart. There is a sexiness that comes from intellect, and I would not like to abstain from that. When it's not playtime, I give a lot on equality. My partners need to have a strong mind, because so have I. I like men who are slightly androgynous and a little bit cocky in a good way. They need to be open-minded and playful. It seems to help when they are bisexual, to get along with the way my body looks like. Sadly it occurred that I couldn't be bisexual, because I'm just too much of a fag and not interested in women's bodies and/or images/perceptions of women. I still believe that in a fair world I would be bisexual. But in this world I am not. – Jonah

One reason that transition tended to change or expand sexual preferences was that some transfolk, during their pre-transition phase, stuck to relationships that they were told they ought to have due to their gender ambiguity. They might also have been given messages that members of other genders would not be interested in them. (I don't know how many masculine women have told me that they can get all the girls they want, but men simply aren't interested in butches.) Once they were solidly set in their new gender, they felt confident enough to strike out in new directions.

I have always been interested in multiple genders. However, I did not feel safe in expressing my interest in masculine cisgender males until I had undergone enough medical intervention (transition) to appear to be a cisgender male. So for years I chose female partners while only scening with males without intimacy. Beginning in 1998 I stepped fully into my pansexual orientation on a personal level. – BEAR A-M Rodgers

My sexual preference has definitely changed over time. There was a time when I was so uncomfortable with my body, and so sexually repressed having been raised in a strict Southern Baptist society, that I thought I would be celibate forever. I had a fear of sexual intimacy that was not easily assuaged when I eventually became sexually active around age 19. I thought, at first, that I was a heterosexual woman, but I kept noticing I was attracted to females in addition to males. Each gender stirred arousal in me in different ways. I did not know what to make of it. I discovered I was bisexual, but could not figure out why I could not bring myself to relate to anyone as a woman until later. My sexuality is now pansexual, and to me BDSM falls in its own sexual orientation category.
– Lord Tom

I am primarily lesbian (with the occasional FtM boyfriend as well), though I have, over the past few years become more attracted to men. Not sure whether it's because I am more secure in my skin, and how I am living, or hormones. – Siobhan Phoenix

I've always been attracted to a range of differently-bodied people. I've used different words for it, starting with bisexual, then polysexual (when I embraced a multiplicity of genders), then simply queer. I like queer best, and have used it for the better part of the last decade to explain my sexual preference for individuals who have liberated themselves from strictly binary gender thinking. I am polyamorous. I find I have different kinds of relationships with different kinds of folk. I tend to have more long term deeply emotional connections with people who are similarly bodied to myself. Prior to taking hormones and having top surgery I had intense relationships with female-bodied folk. As I began to transform I had deeper connections with genderqueer folk, then transmen. Currently, the man that I am most seriously involved with (and hope to be with for a long, long time) is a transman with a solidly fag-masculine identity. As I'm reaching a plateau in my transformation I'm finding new doors are opening to more complicated kinds of intergender connections, particularly with queer cisgendered men and transwomen.

I slept with dykes, transguys and straight men before I started passing full time. As I started passing I started playing with more gay-identified men, though those experiences have often been more tense than with any of the other three categories. I felt like I was missing something essential to perform those sexual rites, and I caught myself feeling the need to apologize frequently. I stopped hooking up for a while to focus on building a primary relationship, and in that time found that really I needed to look for queer men rather than gay men—men who were interested in genderfuck, who didn't see me as lacking, and who could recognize and sexualize my body for what it is. Also, I realized I only wanted to find men who had a sense for real interpersonal connection even in limited and non-traditional sexual exchanges. – Blaise Garber-Paul

Growing up, I was usually attracted to boys. I later experimented with dykes and for a while I identified as queer, in terms of being into masculinity of all kinds, regardless of the body involved. So I was playing and having sex with biofags, transmen, butch dykes, off and on also with a queer high femme. This has shifted over time. I now joke that I have become a boring gay man. All my current lovers and play partners are biofags and I have become part of the regular gay male BDSM community more and more. I am still open to being involved with other transguys, no matter in what kind of body, it just hasn't come up lately. I guess I also enjoy transness not being so much of a constant issue after it was so prominent for such a long time ... I usually call myself *schwul* (a German term for gay male), and sometimes *queer schwul*, to point out that my usage of that term slightly differs from the common usage, as it includes all gay/queer masculine expressions, regardless of biomale anatomy. In general, I am very particular about who I have sex with or play with. These days it is weird, as I am only having sexual encounters with "regular" gay men, and I'm always the first FTM they encounter. I feel they make me really regular and non-queer, while I am the queer twist in their biography. Interesting "contradiction" to this experience. – TransPunk

I do feel a much stronger draw towards genetic males now. I find that I am more comfortable with "gender benders", as I do not feel as different when I am with them; but there is still a lot of draw to the "purely masculine". I have a feeling the latter is because of my trans changes. As I am a very big person, most women I have been with have sort of used me as a shield or a big teddy bear. I feel that if I were with a large masculine male, I could switch the roles and feel protected and allow myself to feel weaker. – Lizzie

For other transfolk, the preference changes of transition come out of nowhere and are somewhat mysterious. Some wonder about hormones, some fall in love with sexual subcultures, some fall in love with the one right person that drives them to make the exception they never thought they'd make, and some just shake their heads in bewilderment and go with it. It may be that these individuals have very fluid preferences, and perhaps didn't realize how fluid they were until the earthquake of transition shook the bottle, as it were.

Not unlike my gender identity, there have been a few major changes over time in my sexual preferences. I started having sex at a very early age of 11. While my first sex act was not consensual there were sex acts which followed very closely behind which were definitely consensual. I never really thought of myself as heterosexual and had been having persistent desires for women since I was very young. I had an ongoing sexual relationship my best friend from the age of 11 until 16.

While, I did have one boyfriend as a teenager, I did not think of myself as straight and ultimately knew I would explore beyond what that relationship could give me. I mostly considered myself to be bisexual at that time. Following the first and what I thought would be the last boyfriend, I exclusively dated women and considered myself to a dyke and mostly a separatist. Even as I moved into transition I was unclear what to call my sexual desires. It took a year or so to finally settle on queer. I was very firm in not seeing myself as straight though I mostly had attraction to women. I felt like bisexual implied a binary of which I did not feel a part of.

After I began transition I started to have strong and persistent desires for cismen. I could not explain these desires since I had not felt much of anything sexual for men for many years. In recent years I have thought of myself as queer and have dated/fucked/loved cisguys, ciswomen, and transguys. Currently I find myself intrigued by the people in between man and woman—the gender queers, gender benders, butch women, femme guys, and

all the folks who exist outside of conventional gender
norms and binary. – E. Nelly

Currently I consider myself queer, or sometimes I'll
say gay. My sexual orientation has definitely changed over
time, roughly along the course of straight (female) to
bisexual to dyke to queer to straight (male) to pansexual
fag to queer/gay. I was deeply repressed in terms of
sexuality from a young age, partly because of my religious
upbringing. I thought it was a terrible thing to have any
sexual feelings of any kind. I literally thought that I had
condemned myself to hell for my lustfulness each and
every time I gave in to the temptation to masturbate as a
child and teenager.

Kids called me a "dyke," "lezzie," and "lesbo" from
the age of eight. Once I figured out what the term meant, I
was worried they were right, and again I consciously
chose to suppress those feelings/fears and to try to make
myself into a normal straight girl by force of will. I finished
high school without ever having kissed anyone and was
certain I would not do anything more than kiss before I got
married.

In college, some of my friends came out as bi, which
made me reconsider my religious condemnation of
homosexuality. I soon realized that I was attracted to
women as well, came out as bi, and began dating women.
Eventually I realized that I was far, far more attracted to
women than to men, both in terms of how many women I
was attracted to and how intensely, so I dropped bi and
came out as a dyke/lesbian. When I was thinking of myself
as potentially genderqueer, I figured my sexual orientation
must be queer, and when I realized I was male I figured,
with some chagrin, that I must be straight. As I
transitioned though, particularly after I began taking
testosterone, I found that I was fantasizing about sex with
men and finding men more attractive than before—I even
started surfing for porn involving dick on the internet.

Before long, I started fooling around with
genderqueers and eventually had sex with a man (who
was also trans). It was a revelation—I loved it. I still had a
hard time really accepting that my sexual orientation had
shifted; I had developed a strong identity in terms of being
attracted to women and thought that on some level I must
just be experimenting or just trying to stay in the queer
community as a man. I'm not saying that those things
weren't going on at all, but it's around nine years after that

initial experimentation and I have been consistently far more attracted to far more men than women in that time— pretty much the exact opposite of my feelings when I had decided to come out as a dyke. So now I'm out as queer or gay (I like queer because of the radical political connotations and the lack of binary gendered implications, but I like gay because it has some degree of specificity— people can figure out that I'm especially into guys when I say it), and I've only been with men and occasionally genderqueers for the past six years or so. I don't claim to have discovered the ultimate "truth" about my sexuality. I expect it may continue to shift over time; just because I haven't been with a woman in years doesn't mean I will never be with a woman again. – Micah

Justin points out that while his preferences appear to have changed, they haven't really: "I have consistently tended to be attracted to those who are like me—does that make me really, really queer? When I identified as a woman, I was a lesbian (although I joke that I wasn't a very good one); when I was actively transitioning, I dated other transmen; and now my relationships are with men, mostly non-transgender men. It seems to me that my primary sexual orientation is towards BDSM and D/s, rather than to any particular gender. I find vanilla sex to be a fairly tedious and uncomfortable way to spend an evening, so the activities I do with a partner and the attitude that person has definitely trumps who they are in terms of their gender or other characteristics."

While social and physical transition can shake things up (or not), some nontransitioned transfolk have also reported a variety of sexual orientation changes just from exploring their gender differences. In these cases, it may be just a matter of simple exploration, but it is often complicated by the lack of a monolithic gender. After all, more gender expression means more aspects that a potential partner needs to get along with. Netdancer spoke of turning to men not out of sexual attraction but out of emotional affinity: "I identify as a dominant and homosexual. I used to be more open to bisexuality, but I had several very disastrous relationships with genetic women where I came to the conclusion that I simply could not understand them or make them happy;

based on the fact that the failing point in all those attempts seemed to be me. I also have a definite fear that I would handle a 'female' submissive or slave very harshly, more harshly then I might personally be willing to go normally. I do not have that kind of trouble with biological males or FtMs, so I confine myself to them."

On the other hand, Del went through a fairly complicated journey and continues to take lovers from all over the spectrum:

> I came out to myself as a lesbian fairly early—around 13—and started telling people at 15. Strangely enough, I still experimented with boys; I was a devout Christian and was desperately trying to convince myself that I was on the search for a boy who could make me heterosexual, so I could leave all of this sinning behind me. I gave up in college, left seminary, and dove into women's space.
>
> I thought I would love it there, but I never fit in. At 22, a girlfriend asked for a threesome with her ex-boyfriend for her birthday, and I agreed. It wasn't spectacular, but afterward he asked if he and I could start hanging out, and it was our emotional connection that fueled our sexual attraction. It actually felt good to leave the lesbian-separatist queer ghetto of a social life and fall more into a bisexual gamer-geek rhythm. Over time, I started developing long-term relationships primarily with men. Not necessarily because that's where my sexual attraction lay, but because I got along better with men and understood them better than women. I am now married to a man, but we're unabashedly poly and I have several meaningful relationships with women. – Del

What we have to keep in mind is that, whether we like it or not, orientation choices are about a lot more than just the hardwired choices of our groins. It's not that I don't believe in that hardwiring—I do; it's been proven to me over and over again that people are neurologically wired to get turned on to particular genders. The complication comes when they develop cultural markers around how that gender is expressed – which we all do, having grown up in a culture and being surrounded by one or more of them all the time. Sometimes those markers come to define "attractive member of Gender X" more than the actual bodies do.

I don't know how many transfolk have confided to me that they just didn't find themselves attracted to the aesthetics of their "new" community, such as heterosexual-after-transition FTMs who find themselves still attracted to lesbians but not so much to straight women, or gay FTMs who still lust primarily after straight men, or MTFs with the same problems in opposite directions. In these cases, it's not the physical orientation that's changed – the bodies are more or less the same in both the old hunting ground and the new one. It's the aesthetic style that's changed, and the social cues around how people flirt and interact with each other. If those cultural cues have been eroticized, the newly community-shifted tranny may feel alien and adrift in the place where they are most likely to find people who are physically attracted to them. (I know of at least two situations where this problem contributed strongly to the trans individual in question transitioning back to their old identity.) There's also the possible anchor of an existing partner who was supportive of their trans lover through transition, but has no intention of giving up their social identity and wants the trans partner to somehow fit into the old crowd. Jason reported, "I don't know how to be a straight man, even though I'm attracted to women. I don't like the role, and I don't do it well. This means that I won't date women who are primarily straight, even if they are willing to overlook my trans body."

Although most BDSM communities are pretty open about people pursuing and partnering with anyone of any combination who is interested (or at least the ones I've hung around have been), there may be assumptions about the sexual preferences of someone who is presenting as X and is or was Y, and it may take some education to get the wide range of trans orientations across. Fortunately—as I'll say more than once in this book—the BDSM demographic has absorbed a strong value on kink education, and accepting new knowledge about how things work by "experts" on the subject. If they'll listen to someone teach them how to use a single-tail, they'll listen to someone teach them about what to assume, and not assume, about the preferences of that interesting-looking trans individual over there.

(c)2008 BlackBookArt.com

Interview with Lee Harrington

I currently identify as a nice guy with a twat … but gender is a strange thing for me. Sometimes I just go as femme. Sometimes as male, or Yes. I'm a big fan of Yes as a gender identity as of late. I was always one of the boys growing up, but I was also one of the girls—tough, big, funny… but it wasn't really about gender in any direction until puberty hit.

Gender was there, but it wasn't about gender. I often wish that were still the case. Ideally, I would be able to be male about 70% of the time, female about 20% of the time, and something altogether different and/or neutral the rest of the time. But when it comes to bodies, I'm not so good at constantly living in-between, so I'm working at being "generic guy at the bagel shop" for now. I am also a drag queen, drag king, gender adventurer, and a lot of other things too. Over the years I have also been a high femme female fetish model, a butch dyke, a tough Daddy, a nervous Nellie, a shy guy, and a lot of other stuff too. It's a journey, not a destination.

Sexually I tend to prefer men, and emotionally I tend to have more regular relationships with women. But that's not always true either. I think my sexual preference is passionate. If there is passion, or creativity, or subjugation, or being taken, or high romance, or something else dramatic in the flair of the sex—I'm usually far more interested. My tastes have changed over the years about whether it's men, women, transfolk, androgynes, femme, butch etc. that I have fallen for… but the key is passion. Oh, and because my spiritual path is never far away, the occasional non-corporeal being that may or may not have gender.

BDSM has been not just my lifestyle, but my work life for a long time. There has been some damage to my interest in kink because of that. When you do bondage, for example, on screen and off, in classes and in books, constantly for over 8 years—it changes things. To be honest, I'm not sure where my BDSM activities and interest lay any more, though I'm leaning more as of late in the "Sexual Pig Bottom" realm when not in "Dominant Leather Daddy" space. And sometimes I'm both at once. I teach Kink, Spirituality and Sexuality classes as my full time living. I love it. And I love using rope bondage as a tool for artistry. I am very happy with my D/s relationships with me as the owner and/or Daddy, and love that kink is so pervasive in my life. But beyond that, it's a bit amorphous. I don't play as much as I used to any more, certainly not in public ... my interests as of late have been far more about bottoming, as they almost always have to be honest, but I am read mostly as a Top in most circles which can be tricky. I love being bound, fucked, used, held down, consumed, filled ... dirty is good, hedonistic is good. I can't take as much pain as I used to—when I actually show up in my body now instead of dissociating from it, it's hard to just float away and let the pain ride me. Not impossible—single tails and feral play I can still take a lot, but much of the rest has decreased. But since I get read as a Top a lot, I've started actively flagging, advertising and posting images of me bottoming, especially to men of all body types and birth genders, to put it back in people's faces.

I have two partners at this time, and a few long term and occasional play partners as well. My Boy/Hound Hunter and I have been together for three and a half years. He is a trans thug bear, leather Daddy, and my property. I believe fully in using what I own to its fullest, and thus when we play I bottom whenever I want to, as he is an amazingly skilled Top and why would I not use all he has? In our age play I switch back and forth between being his Mommy and Daddy, which tends to confuse other folks that I tend to ID as a Mommy a lot with him (ah, again that binary gender thing). He is beautifully romantic at times, and delightfully brutal at others.

My Service Slut/Babygirl Amy and I have been together for two years. She is a fantastically queer female femme-domme and piggy slut, but unlike Hunter, she never Tops me. She may fist me, but when it comes to bondage, pain, or D/s ... it's always with her on the bottom. We tend to also do a lot of self-improvement scenes... combining life coaching, love and kink into one big fruity smoothie. Good stuff.

I am very active internationally, but not as active locally. I still get she'd and called my old name, though I am now flat-chested and sport a beard (I was a 38DD) ... because I taught and published under my old name. People still look at images of me as a woman in my first book. It gets confusing for many of them I am told, because they got "used" to the "old me" and don't know how to "change their thoughts around me." This pissed me off for the first two years or so of my transition. I have since mellowed out, a lot. I realized I could not take it personally, because they are attached to a projection of what never really was fully true. They feel safe in their projections, their boxes, and it's not about me. Not the bad stuff ... or the good stuff. When folks praise how hot I am now, I thank them, accept the praise, but also don't let it go to my head. It's not about me—it's about their experience of me in that moment through their filters, through their life journey.

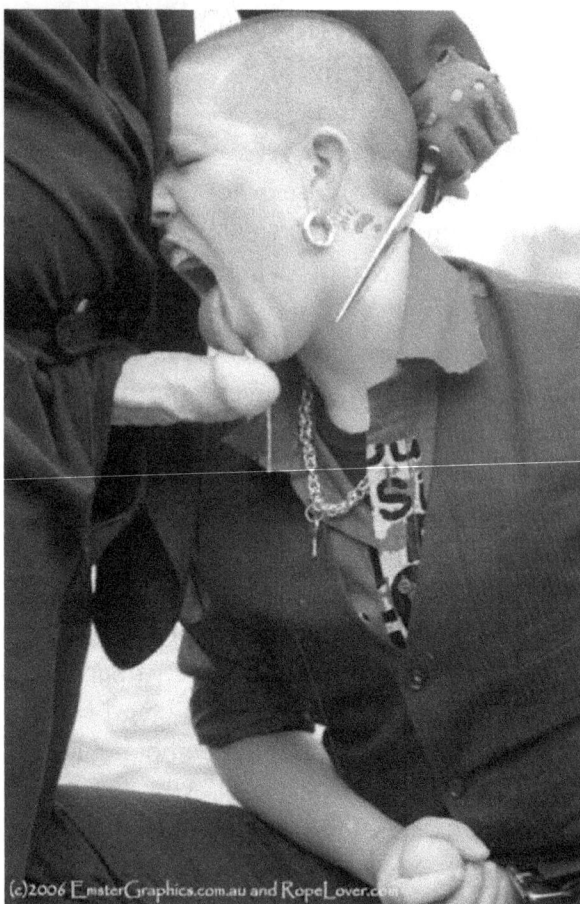

(c)2006 EmisterGraphics.com.au and RopeLover.com

Body Pain, Soul Pain:
BDSM and Coping Mechanisms

After my initial informal poll about BDSM and transgendered practitioners, I was struck by the concept of BDSM being a coping mechanism for driving a sex life through the mine field of gender dysphoria. So many of us struggle with that bizarre pain in our ordinary sex lives, and of course those of us who are into BDSM are going to struggle with it too. It's no panacea … but it does seem to help some dysphoric folk get a little more pleasure in their lives. When I did my second and more extensive survey, I asked directly as to whether my recipients were drawn to BDSM as a way to sidestep their sexual issues. More than half replied in the affirmative. Of course, this was not the only reason, and other transfolk discussed different reasons. There are all sorts of pressures, internal and external, that can drive someone to BDSM. As Vidal Rousso comments, "There is no BDSM and real life with a big border in between. Everything floats together, and for us it floats even more together, because we are more open, more vulnerable, more desperate."

Some of the transfolk that I interviewed did not use their genitals in any kind of play, and BDSM provided a context for non-genital activity. Violet-Erotica Ita says, "I've decided to do no practices including genitalia in BDSM, so there isn't any problem about that. In case of sodomization, I prefer to use a strap-on, instead of my little penis." About a third of my respondents agreed, saying that they were nearly always "stone" (didn't use their genitals) except in some cases intimately with a long-term partner. Isaiah reports that:

> My being transgender has affected many aspects of sex for me. I am not comfortable being touched or looked at. The only way that I can be touched or seen naked is if there is a lot of trust, and if I am so far gone into wanting whatever activity is promised that my brain stops freaking out over not being in the correct body. I am getting more comfortable with how my body is, thanks to my partner. She just makes me feel more manly and as if my body matches. If I see my body at all during anything sexual,

any desire shuts down and it's pointless to even try after that.

I am not okay with using my genitals when somebody is around. This wasn't always this way. It all became more difficult when I experienced how much gender mattered for other people and that I wasn't accepted as a man with the body I have. I never really got over it so I stopped using my genitals when having sex with other people. I even started feeling ashamed of the pleasures my genitals give me ... I would have serious problems with forced feminization for blatant reasons (as it needs a lot of trust for me to have sex with people, that the person conceives me as a men regardless of my "female" body), but in my fantasies, forced feminization is a huge turn-on. – Jonah

Since before I can remember I hated anyone touching my chest. This kept me from engaging in lots of sexual positions and it often kept me overly occupied during sex, focusing so much on whether my partner would touch my chest that I couldn't actually enjoy the sex. The more I come into my gender and sex identities—and the more support I receive from my partner the more I feel able to relax and enjoy sex. I am learning to see myself as a genderqueer trans man who has a chest that is only now beginning to develop positive responses to being touched.
– Mik Kinkead

Lizzie and Brianna also discuss BDSM as being a way to have non-genital sex:

My body dysphoria definitely affects my sexual and BDSM activities. It is the main reason that I avoid sex of almost any kind. It makes it very hard on my wife, I think, because she does not have issues with my body (so she claims) and yet because I find myself to be ... wrong, she is unable to enjoy it as well. BDSM really didn't become any more of a focus for my enjoyment because of my body dysphoria, as I only really enjoyed sex for a short period in my life. I think more than likely it became more important because it was a way for me to interact physically with others in a pseudo-sexual manner without there actually being sex. It's not so much a replacement for me as it is a replacement for others who wish to be with me. If that makes sense. – Lizzie

There are number of things I would like to do, but in part it is my body's appearance that prevents it. Some days I can move past it and other days the mirror haunts me like a spectre. There are certain sexual activities I cannot experience because of my nature. Regardless of being born in a male body I cannot bring myself to use that part in any way but to wash or to masturbate. The idea or the attempt to use it to thrust in any way puts my heart and body through intense pain. The physical pain is from sensitivity of the area and the emotional part is because it feels so "wrong" that it goes against every grain of my being. The feeling will not allow me to use anything to even mimic such actions with a partner. BDSM was a focus or outlet of those energies, and with some help from a few books I have read, it also began to be an outlet for my deep spirituality. – Brianna Ahava Morrigan

Siobhan Phoenix clearly explains both her issues with dysphoria and how the psychological aspects of BDSM helped as a coping mechanism:

I identify myself as a woman, yet I cannot do certain things that most women can do because of the fact that I have no vagina. I crave penetration; at one point I even said that if my surgically built vagina would not be able to be fisted, then what was the sense? I've calmed down since then (but I also know it is possible). I tend to be very "stone"—I don't want my girl touching my body sexually during play most of the time. I would probably, definitely be more sexual if I felt "whole". I'd have her serve me by fucking me, or I would even choose to experience my own submission to men. I think that's where it affects me the most. I am attracted to some men, and the men I am attracted to I want to submit to, but I also wonder why would they want a woman they could not have sex with in the same way … On the other hand, I think as I got more comfortable with who I was, the idea of things like being humiliated or used for sexual service got more hot for me. I think because I am such a staunch feminist as well, the idea of being used as a woman is so humiliating that it turns me on. One of those bottom things, I guess.

Dax also wrote about kinky humiliation being a way to get around body hatred: "There was a time when I didn't want my partner to play with my breasts or cunt, but that changed slightly when I learned to enjoy the degradation and pleasure. In any case, after chest surgery, breasts were no longer an issue. I think I'd really dig having a biological dick, but since I don't, I deal with what nature gave me." Similarly, Sejay also found a way to turn dysphoria into humiliation:

> Gender stuff sometimes makes BDSM activities more fun because it gives you a lot of material to play with. For instance, I was once ordered to perform service in a skirt and tank top, clothing which does not mesh with how I prefer to present my gender, so it was suddenly a humiliation scene (which was enjoyable).

However, this process doesn't work for everyone, or even most transfolk, as humiliation is one of those kinks that you either get into or you don't. Cordelia Wynn Shea growls, "I tried to be all right with my male body, and then with my half-female body, through humiliation. It didn't work. It just made me want to kill someone else—or, when I immediately shoved that emotion down because I was trying to be a bottom, to kill myself. At some point I just realized that I'd rather die, and I'm actively saving toward getting the rest of my surgery. If nothing else, it did point me toward that fact that I'm really a dominant."

Many of my respondents talked wistfully about activities they'd love to do, if only the junk was the right shape. The process of having sex in the headspace of the gender you want to be (a process that can ruin the sex if it doesn't work) is often fragile, and reminders of inappropriate anatomy can create a serious problem. Being as the anatomy that is most likely to be inappropriate is often the parts that are used for sex, it's a tricky job ... but many of my respondents manage it, albeit with some difficulty. Some use prostheses, some prefer cyber-interactions, some do energetic shapeshifting, and some just hang on with imagination.

> The thing that I feel the most serious lack of is the ability to penetrate my partner with a penis made off my

own flesh, and the lack of ability to ejaculate into a partner. I make do as best I can, with various dildos and a harness, and that experience can be very good but it still isn't the ideal thing I could wish for. My immersion into myself as a male does not break in Scene, so if my partner were to suddenly make some reference to me as a female it would jar me badly and possibly knock me out of Topspace. BDSM became my "thing" because I have a very deep-seated need to be in absolute control in sexual situations, and because many people around me expressed to me that they wanted to be controlled as well as nurtured. So I learned, and what I learned made me feel more able and confident about myself as well. I picked up a lot of crisis management skill too, in dealing with abreaction in my partners.

One of the things that really has been a blessing is the availability of online spaces that can be used to Scene. Chatrooms, MUSHes, and the like where it doesn't matter what the physical body looks like or acts and reacts like. I have had Scenes online that were better than anything I could have arranged offline, as there was no stress over being the "wrong" sex involved, no little jolts of disconnection where things just didn't fit together properly.

I am Pagan, and have been to many festivals and events that have clothing listed as "optional". I am not particularly uncomfortable about being naked in that contest, but that generally is not a sexualized situation.

– Netdancer

My transgender status allows me perspective I would not have had otherwise. I am better able to understand both male and female points of view and experiences, so I can relate to partners regardless of their gender identities. I try to work with what I've got when I play, and I use toys to make up for activities for which my body is not adequately equipped. Overall, testosterone makes me feel different, more energized and strong, and it does influence my decisions and emotions. I am allowing myself to be more of a manly brute when I dominate, and take what I want from the submissive or slave—it's hot to be a "manly man".

There are things I would like to do but can't because of my body's limitations. If I focus on it too much, I feel extreme frustration that I cannot experience what it feels like to fully penetrate someone with a full-grown penis, rather than the slight erectile clitoral tissue I refer to as my cock. I wish I could ejaculate. I wish I could participate in water sports without having to use a stand-to-pee device.

Gender dysphoria affects how I choose or experience sexual activities. I use strap-ons a lot. I charge them with energy, and according to partners I have fucked I am the best they've ever had. At least I know how to use the phalluses even though they are not an extension of flesh from my form. I just wish I could feel what my slave feels like inside in that very intimate way, groin to groin. But BDSM has helped with the dysphoria a lot, because it allows me to experience sex without necessarily focusing on genitals. – Lord Tom

I think my trans status does not affect my activities per se. I think it influences the *way* that I do activities. Of course if someone wanted to cross-dress me I think that would challenge me, but at the same time if I liked the clothes I would be OK with it. There are some aspects of public play I that I don't engage in with my boy because that would be too unnecessarily uncomfortable. I would never be topless in either a public or private party because I have not had chest surgery. I would never require that of my boy. I never ask my boy to be completely naked in public or private parties, because he would not be able to fully participate in the scene with that kind of vulnerability and uncomfortable feelings.

I would love to sink an attached cock deep in my boys ass when it's all warm after a spanking and I really can't do that. I would probably show off more of my body if I had surgery. I think my boy would go topless more often if he had surgery.

I am selective with both my BDSM partners and my sexual partners. I have to be sure that they see me as a man and respect my trans identity before I go to bed with them. I also need to know that if something makes me uncomfortable that the person is sophisticated enough in their communication to properly address the problem without egos getting the way. I cover my chest nearly all the time when I am having sex. I do not like having my tits bounce when I am fucking someone. I almost always cover my boy's chest when we are having sex that might make his chest bounce.

I am much more likely than other men to use my hands as a sexual tool. I like the feeling of being inside someone and actually getting some sensation. Strap-on sex does not provide that same satisfaction and level of intimacy. I do not sleep with a lot of cisguys because for the most part they are not highly skilled in the subtle and substantial differences in my body versus other female-assigned people's bodies. I have noticed that despite rigorous negotiations, some cisguys do not know how to properly stroke or suck a transman's cock.

I do think some aspects of BDSM are very attractive because normal sexual things are not possible with my body and gender. I love to feel powerful, scary, strong, and big, but given I am 5'2" and not that scary of a person, BDSM has given me a place to be all those wondrous things. I do think the fisting and needle play are about wanting and craving the ability to penetrate. Given my inability to penetrate with my genitals other forms of penetration have become more erotic. The power and control is also very attractive. Given my trans status I do not always have the type of control I would like, BDSM offers a way for me to achieve those desires for power and control. – E. Nelly

I've always enjoyed pushing my physical limits. I think some of my early experiences were driven by dissociation. I'm not sure if the dissociation was linked to gender dysphoria or to depression, and I'm not sure if my depression was linked to gender dysphoria or something even more organic. I know that as a teenager I initially enjoyed things that took me out of my head, but often went so out of my head I could no longer negotiate. I put myself in dangerous places that traumatized me because I was so far out of my body I couldn't recognize that I was being traumatized, sometimes until years later. I had a long experience with feeling stone because I couldn't let go of the trauma I held in my body. I think some of my later BDSM play, especially the more intense Daddy-boy stuff, was directly an attempt to physically work out the conflicts I'd experienced from trusting people who'd harmed me.

My SM tastes have changed some with physical transition. I've found that after going on T I stopped liking sting, especially canes, which had been a favorite before. Other things, like deep punching, became more enjoyable as I developed more muscle mass. But most things, like blood, piercing, fire, breathplay, and exhibitionism, haven't changed.

I know there're things that I can't do because of my outward gender, and most of them involve being included in the rites and rituals of traditionally minded cisgendered leatherfags. I go back and forth on whether or not I mind. I would like to find more queer leathermen who would be interested in rewriting the rites. I feel like I'm slowly attracting them towards me.

The more integrated I become into the world of radical faeries the more I see the hierarchies of body fascism among gay men. I see how many kinds of bodies are excluded from sexual rites—leather, faery or otherwise—because they do not reflect a very limited understanding of embodied masculinity, and often the existence of a flesh-grown penis is not the limiting factor. Ability, proportionality, hair growth, class and the ability to project markers of class, all of these affect the marketability of male bodies under the intense scrutiny of the normatively minded gay male gaze. Having a flesh penis wouldn't put me at the top of the stack. And even if it did, I'd only have made it to the top of a fascist stack. Honestly, I'd like to take myself out of those kinds of hierarchies.

It does drive me a little crazy sometimes to think that "If I only had a penis then x, y, z would be possible." Sometimes I worry that I will never find partners who enjoy my body as it is. My ego would love to be in possession of a body that was universally intelligible and generally marked as desirable. But then I remind myself that I would not be myself if I had always walked in this world as a man, or conventionally beautiful, or generally intelligible. My newest mantra is "you don't have to do everything or everyone to be desirable." – Blaise Garber-Paul

One thing that I love about pain is that it gets me out of my head and into my body in a way that few other things can. When I am getting beaten—or tortured, or fucked hard and fast—I am not thinking about what I look like, or my gender, or what my partner thinks of me, or transphobia, or anything else—I am just present with the extraordinary intensity of the sensation. In that way, SM really has helped me to cope with dysphoria. Broadly speaking the activities I enjoy have not changed all that much over time, but I have made some shifts in how I have engaged in them over the course of my transition.

For example, as I've physically and socially transitioned I've gotten more comfortable involving more parts of my body in play. At one point I could not handle

and always refused any play that involved my chest or my pussy. As my body changed with Testosterone and people began perceiving me as male consistently, I became a lot more comfortable with using all of my body. Now getting fucked in front and getting beaten or tortured on my chest and nipples are great pleasures for me. Also, before I had bottom surgery I had a difficult time being naked, especially if I wasn't actively getting beaten or fucked right at that moment. Now I feel quite comfortable naked.
    – Micah

For some transsexuals, body dysphoria pretty much clears up when they've made enough changes to their bodies to pass in public, even if the genitals are not yet right. Some of my respondents did report that they had more or less beaten the demon, and their only issue was the way in which they were perceived by potential partners:

Most of my body dysphoria walked away after my chest revision surgery (round 2, as round 1 was botched pretty badly). I tend to look at my lower body as being blessed with a bonus hole, as being a man with more. I get to be more piggy. The bulk of my dysphoria lay in how I was perceived at bagel shops (i.e. generic society) and my breasts. No one at bagel shops calls me she any more ... My body dysphoria going mostly away has led to me being "present" more in my play, which sometimes means less pain, or at least less pain that I do not want—but I'm told I'm still a tough cookie. – Lee Harrington

I became more able to accept my identity as a kinky pervert once I could be comfortable with the fluidity of my gender and sexual orientation. Kink became much richer, and my desire and ability to top had increased since I was able to delve into my transition ... Kink is also much more satisfying for me because now that I'm on testosterone blockers, my penis is less the focus during sexual play. It is still sensitive and is a part of my sexual play, but it's harder to maintain erection for penetration, and I experience pretty uncomfortable pain after a couple of non-ejaculatory orgasms. (Though I recently had a couple that were huge, since they've been building up the last couple of years...) Plus I'm pretty neutral on whether I use my cock or not, both because I identify as more female than male, as well as it's lessened usability, so there's less focus on it. Mostly I use it when it's someone else's desire. But I enjoy other sensations more, and since I am able to orgasm without genital stimulation, prefer more BDSM play than genital sex. – Terra Katherine McKeown

While we're used to the idea that cross-dressers—and people who don't identify as transgendered—play with gender as a sexual thing because it's hot, what happens when someone who has large emotional triggers around gender confronts those sorts of games? Is it too triggering, or does their deeper understanding of the nebulous boundaries of gender give them an advantage? Many transfolk will describe how those games gave them their first chance at exploring that painful and often repressed area; in some cases it was the door that opened to allow all the demons to come through. Sometimes, after it's all hashed through and all the changes that are going to be made have been completed, there's no more need or interest in such things. Sometimes the demons are too painful, once they're out, to play recreationally with such emotional dynamite. On the other hand, sometimes gender games continue to be a fascination for us, at any point on the continuum. Del reports:

I love, and get deeply turned on by, many forms of gender play, and I'm sure that is influenced by my own experiences with gender and sex. Strangely enough, however, I have seen a steady decline in an interest in mixing sex and SM since transitioning to a more masculine identity; I believe it's tied to experiencing more dysphoria with my female body ... The more I experience masculine identity, the more it bothers me. I have wonderful lovers who support me in the most intimate of ways—referring to my body parts in masculine ways (eg, "boycunt"), using masculine terms to refer to me as a lover, and expressing interest in relating to me sexually while packing/strapping on. These days, I don't engage in sex or sexual activities, including BDSM, with someone who absolutely needs to see me as female in order to feel comfortable. I'm open to people who are interested in having some experiences with my female body, as long as they continue to recognize my masculine identity. – Del

It affects my pervy play a lot because we're always roleplaying about bodies and gendered play. Right now I'm playing for the first time without gender roles which is also incredible, but different than boy/girl, boy/boy play. Making my body into one kind of gendered male body is a pervy practice for me, but actually one that I'm pushing away from. Like I said, I don't care that much about maleness anymore. – Simon Strikeback

It was in BDSM play spaces where I first found that I could safely explore and develop my feminine self. And after I got to the point where I was presenting to the world outside the BDSM scene, it was through an age-play Daddy/girl relationship that I was able to explore some of the needs left unaddressed growing up ... While there are parts of my body I do wish to, I was never fully at odds with my genitalia. I am, sometimes, okay with performing penetrative sex, though I do prefer extended amounts of foreplay. I guess it could be said that I enjoy some aspects of BDSM because it does relieve some concerns about performing sexually.

My interests have changed some in time with my gender and sexual identities. My initial interests focused on sexual and sensation play, energy, submission, bondage. As I started to explore aspects of transsexuality and transgenderism, I became more interested in aspects of forced feminization and chastity play ... As I went further with my transition, I started developing interests in things like erotic hypnosis and mind control. I've also since become more interested in heavier SM/sensation play as I have come into my body, taking hormones, etc. I still enjoy many of the same activities I used to, though some of the sexual play is a little more difficult since the hormones subdue some of sexual function – Sable Twilight

One of the things that I've always found wonderful about the BDSM scene is that extensive negotiation, and firmly holding boundaries, is an accepted practice. Yes, the occasional sleazy person will try to use negotiation to push those boundaries, but the community standard is and always has been that if someone says "I don't want X" during pre-activity negotiations, then X isn't going to happen. Our emphasis on safety is an asset for transfolk, who may have a long list of activities that they don't want to see happen.

Jackkinrowan points this out as an alternate reason why we stay in the BDSM scene:

> I didn't get into BDSM because "normal" things weren't working (I always had S/M fantasies), but what was especially helpful was that the BDSM community gave me a way to be able to talk about limits in a way that I didn't know how to do in my previous vanilla settings (partly probably because I was brought up to be a "good girl"). Because limits are expected and talked about and one is expected to respect them, I found a way to say "you can touch here, but not there" and that was very helpful to me. – Jackkinrowan

Naked In The Spotlight

For many people, BDSM is a hobby that they limit to the privacy of their bedrooms, or a lifestyle that they limit to the privacy of their homes. The various BDSM communities, however, tend to consider public sexplay (or nonsexual SM) at public or private dungeon parties to be part of the "ordinary" round of activities. Not everyone attends play parties, of course, but a large enough percentage attend that it is assumed to be *de rigeur* for community activities. Every large regional BDSM event makes sure to have "dungeon space" in the evenings for this reason. Creating a community where it's normal and acceptable to take your clothes off and do perverted things to each other in front of a whole crowd of people has had interesting effects on its denizens. Some non-trans perverts I've talked to have rapturously expounded on how freeing it was to be seen publicly as a sexually desirable person; it is true that people with less socially acceptable bodies can be the object of group lust if they are willingly performing activities that the watchers find sexy. In the fetish demographic, the activity can hold more sexual juice than the body type of the person doing it, and that can be an empowering experience for people who haven't experienced themselves as particularly attractive. Almost all of the post-genital-surgery transsexuals who responded to my survey waxed happily about the new freedom of being able to be naked in BDSM play space and have it be no big deal. In fact, it was practically their touchstone. As Ashley Lynch put it, "It used to be an issue for me, but now that I'm post-op, I feel I've been given a new license to exploit myself. So many outfits that I can now successfully wear without shame, and I do so with glee."

The possibility of nakedness and genital sex puts a different kind of pressure on transfolk who don't fall into that category, though. Although there are a lot of kinky activities that can be done without exposing one's body at all, the majority of "traditional" physical sensation play requires a certain amount of skin. Even with play partners who aren't going to push for such activities, trans people can feel cheated by their inability to get to any point of showing off triggering bodies. Brianna Ahava Morrigan says: "For me it is not so much my identity that makes me hesitant, but much more so my configuration. I have an intense dislike for how my body looks in ways because of how male it still appears, and for me it causes no small amount of embarrassment." Other trans people were similarly reluctant:

> I am definitely aware of how my body is or might be perceived if I take my clothes off. In a mixed public space that was not known for trans-inclusivity, I'd be aware of the potential for being the "freak on display". I might be entirely comfortable with that role, but I would not want to do a scene that was really vulnerable for me under those circumstances. In a primarily or exclusively male space, I'd be very reluctant to get naked until I really felt like people were comfortable with me being trans. I think the difference is that in a mixed space I'm already "the queer" so I am prepared to be in that outsider role. In a male space, I'm not prepared for that outsider role, and if I'm going to have to confront people about my gender or genitalia, I'd rather do it with my clothes on. – Joshua

> I have played in public space, but generally prefer not to because it interferes with my energy flow. My identity is Male Dom, I look like a Male Dom, I play as a Male Dom. By preference I generally do not strip past my jockstrap, which carries a 'flaccid' prosthetic. However several times I have had public sex by use of my erection prosthetic (strap-on), and once allowed another FTM to give me oral while using a handheld dildo on me anally as others watched from a distance. – BEAR A-M Rodgers

Being pre-top surgery, I don't feel confident to go to a play party and take off my shirts to flog my pet. I worry that my breasts would confuse others and I would get called female pronouns, or that it would change how people view or interact with me. As I get further along with hormones, it gets harder to leave the house to go do fun stuff because of all the layers I need to wear to appear flat-chested ... I never equated sex with gender; yeah, I wanted a penis and a flat chest, but sex was and still is sex for me. There are things that I don't allow now, but it took going on hormones and becoming comfortable with myself to make me uncomfortable with my body. – Cole R.

Clothing is a good example—another dom asked me to dress in a wife-beater and, well, binding shirts (which I normally wear socially) are pretty obvious underneath those; I tried an Ace bandage instead, but it fell off in a matter of minutes and was very distracting all night. Being large-breasted and wanting to present masculine also does not work so well when your favorite BDSM play involves being topless—it's hard to hit someone's back effectively and making sure breathing is solid becomes problematic when they have a shirt and binder on! Also, as someone who mostly plays with D/s, picking titles is a huge source of anxiety—Sir? Ma'am? Boy? Girl? He? She? They?—none of these really feel right, although some feel *more* right than others at different times; there have been many moments when I've had to spend uncomfortable time on up-front negotiations, stop a scene to clarify, get unintentionally thrown out of sub-/dom-space, or just play along with silent distress. – Sejay

BDSM for a long time was the only way for me to be sexual at all, especially pre-transitioning. By now I have come to be comfortable with certain trusted people to be naked and include my whole body in my sexual life. I have just come back from a week in a gay-men-only BDSM camp in Denmark. I am the first FTM that ever went there and we didn't make that public, although about half of the fifty men there knew, because they knew me beforehand. I was running around bare-chested a lot and was totally comfortable, but I didn't get naked, and since I like my BDSM sexual, that was sometimes a bummer. I'm not sure what it will take to be comfortable being naked in front of a bunch of gay guys. I assume one day it will be OK in front of a group of trusted friends, but just any gay male space? Not sure about that, as there is my own insecurity and their potential discomfort around it, although most of friends have explicitly stated that they think I have the right to be naked in gay male spaces, so there would be peer support in case of transphobic reactions.

I took my packy to Denmark, but I did not wear it a single time and at the end of the week I left it there in a good-bye ritual with my slave and my warrior, burying it on the ground there. That's how good I feel about my body as it is and how self-confident I have become in gay male spaces. So the only thing that comes to mind that I cannot do is to get a blow job at a play party or fuck my bottoms. At a queer play party I do it, though. Some of my bottoms feel I should do it at a gay men's club as well, but I do not want to risk stupid comments. It's too intimate for me. Sometimes I am sorry I don't have sperm. But then my bottoms act as if they're swallowing it, which is fun and in group sex we have acted as if someone else's sperm was mine ... so fantasy does the trick and them being inventive for me is so touching and making it all much more intimate and special that usually there are no regrets I was born this way. – TransPunk

Obviously, the "only-space" controversy (discussed at length in a later chapter of the book) affects the occurrence of nudity, especially when transfolk are passing in spaces where they might otherwise be banned. Micah writes, "I'm comfortable with just

doing just about anything else in public spaces, unless it's a space where trans men are specifically not allowed—then I am considerably more conservative in my choices." Another trans individual even begged me, when I was interviewing people for this survey, not to focus on or draw attention to the fact that some of our folk sneak into places where they know they wouldn't be welcome. Being in these spaces (and engaging in non-genital sexual activities with others in that space) was an important part of this individual's sexual and social life, and they feared that if I wrote about this sort of secret practice it would result in all manner of underwear checking. The fact that I have not honored their request is my own choice; the truth is that someone is going to bring this up sooner or later anyway, and if it is me in this book, I can at least context the practice with some background and compassion for the no-win scenario many of us face in demographically small and prejudiced local communities.

Other trans people emphasized that they do play in public space, and where it's allowed they will engage in nudity and genital sex with lovers. Some, like Lee Harrington, saw it as a form of activism. Others were simply determined not to let their personal baggage get in the way of their pleasures, an act of sheer will and courage that most nontrans people wouldn't think to see as such. Vidal Rousso sums up his struggle: "I do play in public, but my gender configuration does affect how I play. It is especially hard to have my body naked and suddenly see or remember that it is female, but I fight it. I'm happy that my body is naturally rather masculine so it is not so far from the mental image in my mind. And in my mind I do have a male body, so I don't let the transsexuality keep me from living my life the way I want to."

> I Top a lot in public, and since transition have been sexual less in big public spaces as people start messing up my gender pronouns after they see my twat getting fisted. So I play in semi-public spaces around folks who get it, or do my kink in pubic and move my sex elsewhere. And yet, I regularly walk around dungeons naked or just in boots. It's my own form of erotic activism. I do it because I've seen that if I do that night #1 of an event, by night #2, fat

people, wiry people, queer shapes and sizes all decide it's OK to be naked too. – Lee Harrington

Heh. Yes, I do play in public spaces. Some places I've been have rules about nudity and sex, but they usually don't consider anything outside of penis-vagina intercourse "sex," so no problems having fun there (since I usually only play with female assigned-at-birth folks like myself). I enjoy having sex in "public" parties and/or being naked during play, although I only do so with people who respect my gender stuff, and I dislike moving around these places naked (showing off my body to people who might not respect my gender stuff). As mentioned, it is hard to have large breasts when you play masculine, and then go to a club with a no-nipple-showing policy that forces you to put neon orange bandaids on 'em. Geez. That was awful. – Sejay

I can be naked in public, and have genital sex, if I'm in a place where I feel safe to do so—somewhere where I feel my gender identity won't be completely nullified if I take off a binder or receive vaginal sex. I rarely did these things before I began identifying as masculine, so it's not like I've seen a big change. I am one of those weirdos that mostly likes their SM and their sex separate (although not all of the time). – Del

Leather has been one of the spaces where I have felt the most free to explore my identity and my body. As a survivor of childhood sexual assault, as well as mental, physical, and emotional abuse at the hands of my parents being involved in leather has been incredibly cathartic for me. Growing up I had a profound disconnect from my body, some of that possibly being gender dysphoria but most of it really connected to my body not being something that I had ownership of. Being able to participate in leather activities, and certainly being able to give power in a 24/7 dynamic as I have for the past several years first required reclaiming my body in order to be able to give it freely. Leather has given me back my body and mind, and enabled me to present it as a gift to my Daddy. For me, being transgender has never gotten in the way of BDSM activities that I like, or want to explore. I've been lucky to exist in a very queer, very trans world where being a man who liked to get my cunt fisted wasn't a big deal. I existed within a community for whom that was a non-issue and a given that the makeup of an individual's body did not in any way dictate what sort of sex they would like, or how they might like to play.

That said, I feel extremely uncomfortable in pansexual play spaces, specifically around non-transgender men. In that respect I would say that my gender and body configuration has an impact on how I play, in that it's important to me that the individuals around me share some common experiences, and hopefully common values and perspectives about the fluidity of gender. I do not have any issue with my own nudity in relation to my gender, and in these public spaces do often have genital sex. – Sassafras Lowrey

I play in public space. I get naked. I have genital sex in public. I just had a scene playing in Faerie land where I had penetrative sex with a cisgendered man who was wearing my strap-on. I like thinking about sex as a scene. I like doing live demonstrations of how sexy transbodies are, how easy it can be to engage respectively and creatively with us. Part of the fun for me is anticipating the shock of my audience. Happily, most of my scenes are anticlimactic—I've never gotten vocal reactions from my audience beyond sounds of approval, and all the comments I hear have been positive.

I'm really into exhibitionism. I've found that I can take heavier scenes when I'm in a performance headspace. It began simply as wanting to play demo bottom for my partners (I have a long-standing attraction to teachers and educators). I felt safe with the eyes of the classroom on me. I liked the accountability. I found that I enjoyed scenes that took place in center dungeon space the best, or scenes that were specifically designed to be engaged with the audience. More recently the desire to be seen, and to see myself, has expanded into making explicit documentaries and photographs for public consumption.

I think this is directly tied into being trans: my gender has always felt a bit performed, and I've always expected my body's discordance to make an unexpected impression. By having scenes that invite spectators to watch I can feed off the energy produced by the brainfuck of finding an unexpected cunt and scars on an otherwise male body. Rather than let people 'other' me, I take the experience and set it up as a challenge—is my audience flexible enough, kinky enough to admit their arousal at viewing a body they didn't expect? – Blaise Garber-Paul

Justin recounts one situation where public play, his relationship's power dynamic, and his trans body collided in an incident that required damage control:

> We had one incident at a public space in which I really did not want to be whipped (nothing to do with gender—the energy in the space felt very voyeuristic and I wasn't feeling very well) but I obeyed my Master, of course. Some of the people watching interpreted my body language (which I guess I wasn't hiding as well as I thought) as a reluctance to get undressed and then interpreted that as my Master forcing me to reveal my trans status in public, because the people watching hadn't known I was trans until they saw me naked. A couple of days later the rumors about this were flying, and I was approached by people who were very angry that I had been "forced" to be out about being trans. We then had to go back and correct that impression, and assure people that I was okay. While on one hand it was challenging that people had witnessed an exchange between my Master and myself and had decided for themselves what it meant, I'm also glad to live in a community where, if people really felt I was in trouble, at least they came to me directly to ask if I was okay. Incidentally, the fact that I obeyed when it was challenging for me was something that strengthened the connection between my Master and me, so our experience of the situation was very different than that of the witnesses.

Right now, public BDSM play parties are being split between those that allow genital sex and/or penetration and those that don't, for reasons of legality or local group preference. If there are sexual boundaries, they vary from group to group, often based on how heterosexually-focused the group or club is. I remember walking into a play party at a club I'd never been to before that was supposedly "no sex", and the first things that I saw were a vaginal fisting scene, an anal fisting scene, and someone being fucked with a strap-on. I remember saying to my boy, "Shit, when I do that, it's sex!" On the other hand, I've been to no-sex parties where even nudity was discouraged and all the BDSM was practically devoid of specifically sexual energy.

These policies do tend to screen people in and out—as discussed in the last section, gay men tend to prefer sex-allowed clubs to the point of refusing to go to a no-sex party. On the other hand, I've heard other people talk about how they prefer no-sex clubs because they don't want to have to watch people fucking between the BDSM. Transgendered people, for the most part, tend to be prefer and be grateful for no-sex clubs because it's less pressure to do something you're not comfortable with, and your limitations aren't shoved in your face as much. I personally prefer sex-allowed parties because I love to fuck my boy at clubs, and I like to watch people fucking as part of rough, kinky sex. I would love to get blown in public as part of a scene (using my flesh junk) and don't feel comfortable about doing that, but on the other hand I realize that's my own baggage and someday perhaps I'll win that struggle and overcome it.

The most comfortable that I've ever felt at a BDSM party was at all-trans events—which, granted, are very sheltered spaces. (The events in question allowed any-gendered partners of transgendered people, and some selected allies and former partners, but the point was to create a safe space where no one present was unfamiliar with or might potentially be freaked out by trans bodies.) In the meantime, I make my way as we all do, and hope that over time we'll become so common in these communities that being courteous and supportive to us will become part of the everyday, accepted code of behavior there.

> When I was still pre-op, I was very self-conscious in the community. I remember doing a rope suspension with a friend, me being the bottom, and because of the complications of my wardrobe, it was necessary for me to strip down to my underwear to do the tie properly. As I did so, I said to the rigger with a sense of shame, "I apologize for the bulge in my panties." He just leaned in close and said, "Look, we're all in transition in one way or another." That really affected me in a positive way.
>
> I also used to become very angry at myself and life when I went to events, what with all the beautiful women

running around in various states of undress. It seemed to serve as a constant reminder that I would never look like that ... until I ended up talking to one Domme who I had elevated to the level of Goddess by how attractive she was, and I found to my surprise that she was very insecure herself and thought I was just as hot as she was. But for me, kink has never been about sex. It can include it, but it doesn't have to. If it did, I wouldn't have been able to get into the kink community comfortably until I was post-op.

– Ashley Lynch

Market Value:
Finding Partners

There's an undercurrent assumption in the transgendered demographic that being trans is a liability in the meat market of courtship and finding partners, and the hard truth is that ... it's the hard truth. The majority of people in the world are not comfortable with a trans partner. It takes a special person, in many ways, to brave our country and stick with us. It's something that our worried family members often bring up when we come out to them: "But who will love you? Who will want you now?"

At the same time, there are still a lot of people out there who willingly date transfolk, even if one only considers the numbers of us who have strong partnerships. Is it so much of a handicap that most of us are doomed to loneliness? There are many differing opinions about this.

> Being trans is absolutely a handicap. While everyone is accepting, many people just don't have interest in playing with someone like me, or being sexually involved. Of course, if I were interested in men, my kink and sex life would be a lot easier. As a lesbian, it makes it quite difficult. Oftentimes it seems the easiest solution is another trans person. – Ashley Lynch

> I don't actively look for partners, mostly because it's too much stress. I don't think being trans is a handicap any more than any sort of social oddity is. I think what is probably the heavier handicap is people who have issues with gender that do not improve when they change their lifestyle. If someone has/is in the process of transitioning but they continue to have gender issues, then they are facing a disadvantage... namely one of confusion and doubt. – Lizzie

> I have some trouble finding partners, and there are many reasons—some of which have probably more to do with my history than my trans status, although of course the two are intimately related as well. Some of the more trans related possibilities are:
> Sometimes I find that having worked hard to develop my masculinity I come off as a top when I am looking to

bottom and that can be a problem (and here is a whole other chapter about masculinity and topping, and how they are assumed in some circles to go together).

Sometimes it feels the only attraction is that they want to know all about being trans and not about me as a person.

Sometimes it feels the people I am attracted to are all 15 years younger than me and want someone who looks more genderqueer, whereas the people my age and older are looking for cis partners (or are already partnered).

Sometimes it feels I am too short (I've always been short) so I am not taken seriously as a potential partner.

Sometimes it's because I've transitioned "too much" or "too little".

When I feel good about myself and sexy in my body, I become more attractive and people have tended to respond to that and express interest/surprise about my trans status in a good way. When I don't feel so good about myself, I feel I make poorer choices and usually come off as "having a problem" and so don't attract people, people who know nothing about my trans status.

– Jackkinrowan

There are very few people—especially when it comes to bio men—who really accept me as a man. People seem to be deaf when you tell it to them, and follow their own fantasy about having a tough girl (or whatever) or agree to whatever you say just to get laid—and this is something I have to figure out and avoid. To find an understanding partner for me is extremely hard. Therefore I'm more desperate, more ready to take risks, my boundaries are more bendable and stretchable. I will admit here honestly that I will do things I won't like just in order to keep my BDSM partner happy and with me. And that happens that way directly because I'm transgendered.

– Vidal Rousso

As Vidal and Jackkinrowan both point out, self-esteem has a lot to do with it. Low self-esteem is rampant among transgendered people, caused by a wide array of torments including growing up out of place and unaccepted, being mocked or rejected by much of society, being queer-bashed on the street, being turned down for jobs and discriminated against by landlords and law enforcement, and being taken advantage of by unscrupulous people who smell that low self-esteem and use it to their own benefit. Desperation is common among our kind, and many of us are more likely to settle for anything that looks like it might give us some much-needed comfort. The importance of feeling confident about one's self was one of the main points stressed by my respondents, many of whom have learned it the hard way.

> I was having problems finding partners who would stick around. It had little to nothing to do with being trans. It was because I did not believe myself worthy of the lovers and partners I wanted in my life. The more worthy, together and centered I find myself, the more the people of my dreams manifest. – Lee Harrington

> My self-image and self-consciousness is the problem. I believe that I am damaged goods as a transperson (deep inside), and I feel that nobody would play with someone as incomplete as me, and if they did, they probably see me as a fetish object. I would like to find someone that views me as I view myself. My girl does, but I can't trust that others do. – Siobhan Phoenix

> I'm up front about who and what I am and let people know right away that if they can't treat me as the woman I am, then they have no place in my life. I also use this rule for vanilla life. As a result, I find myself surrounded by people who accept me for who I am. I've never really had a problem, but then I also live in a fairly accepting place.
> – Ashley Lynch

> Prior to my transition, I was very underconfident, I believed without a doubt that I was unattractive and not at all a suitable catch, and that I deserved the rejection I frequently received. After transition, both because I'm finally happy with who I am, and because I look really hot, I have been able to really begin deconstructing these ways of thinking. Sometimes, especially when I'm stressed or overwhelmed, I default to them, but more and more it's easy to short circuit this or recover from a bout of negativity.
> So, for those trans people with this sort of dynamic, I would say to spend time on oneself and one's worth. It's hard to feel worthy or likeable when you hate the body you

have been forced into for so long. Not all trans people feel this way, of course. But I have noticed that most of these issues are all internal. Sure, there are fewer people interested in trans people as partners, but since I'm finding partners, I have tons of friends who find partners, and because they are of all genders, sexes and orientations, I must say that it still happens. I am actually dating more now than I ever have, with the exception of when I first started investigating my gender identity and was "playing the field" a lot. The advice I would give is to learn to be as self-perceptive as possible. If you're having trouble finding partners, be a partner to yourself. Sometimes that means seeing things you don't like about yourself and either changing them, or changing one's perception to them, so that they are no longer simply negative. Doing this will allow you to be more comfortable with yourself, which is much more attractive to people. Also, having a positive attitude about how partnership works, and the like, will make it much easier to find people. We are generally the ones limiting ourselves; there is enough pressure on us from the cisgendered majority that we have to deal with, we don't have to take it on and internalize it. – Terra Katherine McKeown

First off, I think *everyone* thinks they have trouble in that department. The problem is multi-faceted and complicated. It's always difficult to be different from the mainstream, whether that's for being into BDSM alone, &/or being trans. I also think trans identity is eroticized, which makes things easier or harder depending on what you're looking for. Although my theory is that if someone's into BDSM, they're (hopefully) already interested in learning how to be safe, respectful, and open-minded about sexual things. – Sejay

Looksism can also be an extra problem for us. While everyone is subject to this burden to one extent of another, it has been pointed out repeatedly in our demographic that the standards are often set artificially high for us. It's as if being gender transgressive is such a sticking point that we have to be much closer to the top of the beauty standard in order to make up for it. TransPunk points out tellingly: "It is somewhat harder for me to find partners than if I was me with a male-born body. But it would also be harder if I was fitting the gay male beauty ideals even less than I do." Similarly, Jennifer Callanan says wryly, "I have found out that a lot of people in the BDSM community are not comfortable around trans people unless they are very cute."

Some of my respondents told about embracing the fetishization of their trans identity with confidence, which—according to them—got them plenty of partners in the BDSM scene. "Double-Edge" says flatly, "I have no problems finding partners. Mistress could hold a bidding war for me if She wished to sell me. Training and attitude are the biggest problems with most trans folk. Yes, you have to work twice as hard to fit in. But the work is worth it in the end."

> I think that being trans is not a problem specifically in BDSM "marketplace". I think instead BDSM is often considered a good pretext to satisfy curiosity about transexuality. – VioletErotica Ita

> I don't have problems finding partners. I think it's because I like having sex with other transpeople (who like

transpeople) or people who tend to fetishize my body. I understand that a lot of transfolk want partners to see them as them, and not a sex object or as "something in between", but I like the thought of it. I'm not sure if that's why I don't have any problems finding partners, or if its because I have a lot of confidence. I think confidence is the key, being proud of who you are. – Drik

> Being trans is not a handicap, but it can be a fetish for some folks, so I try not to get offended when I get fetishized. If black men, big men, furry men, twinky men are fetishized, why not trans men? Personally, I consider being trans to be a bonus—I can speak more gender languages, have more experience evaluating what I need out of life, and going after it. – Lee Harrington

In contrast, other respondents objected strongly to going along with fetishization and recounted distressing situations along that path. The objectification that is a part of fetishization didn't sit well with them emotionally, and they warned of the self-esteem problems inherent to the dark side of that path.

> Even after having many positive experiences I struggle with being confident in my transness. I don't like letting myself think that my body is a limitation. If it's limiting, then I'm asking the wrong questions of it. So I'm making promises to myself to have better experiences. I reject any partner who needs to be convinced or assured that my body is something they want to engage with. I can do that because I am certain that other opportunities will come along with people who are confident and interested in being able to engage with me. I'm not interested in being with anyone sexually who doesn't want to be my friend before, during and after.
>
> The hardest thing for me to deal with right now is finding that line between appreciation and fetishization. I want to play with men I can have sex with, and I want the men I have sex with to be attracted to the body I actually have, not a shared fantasy of remapped signifiers. I've had a play relationship that recently turned very south, with a cisgendered man. He was very interested in playing with a boy with a cunt. I, when I started it, was mostly interested in playing with his cock. It was a mutual fetishization with strong D/s overtones and some roughness. It was fun. And then it got very cold, very heartless, because we weren't seeing each other for anything beyond our genitals. It left me feeling queasy. There was something powerful about the first couple of exchanges where I experienced what it was like to be with a man who saw me fully as a man, a man who was completely into other men, and a man who saw my cunt for what it was and found that to be the most attractive, unique aspect of our exchange. I liked getting to

fetishize him back. And then I realized that the longer he fetishized my anatomy the less he saw me. – Blaise Garber-Paul

The advice I give other Trans people every day is, "Do not advertise yourself as a Tranny, and do not lie by saying you are not. Let people get to know *you* first instead of your birth defect." I present *me*, all the good and bad, first and foremost. If people pay attention, the clues are all there that I am not the standard-issue cisgender male, yet I never get identified as a Tranny either. Blatantly disclose only to those who are affected by it, your chosen physical partners. Trans people handicap themselves in BDSM community and in general sexual marketplace, due to encouraging fetishization or discrimination by flagging their Trans status before their real personae. – BEAR A-M Rodgers

Finding the right partner was always difficult for me, partly because of my need for a dominant kinky person, and then the issue of him understanding my identity and being attracted to me. With a feminine/female identity I didn't have much of a problem finding men who were attracted to me, but finding one who would accept me as I am, *and* have similar fantasies, was no easy task. Living with a male identity made me receive drastically less attention from men. My advice: The internet is great. Be safe and make sure you meet in a public space, and that a friend knows who you're meeting. Being trans is definitely a fetish for some, the "trannychasers". Some people are just plain curious, but both of these categories of people don't equal a trustworthy, respectful partner. – Dax

One solution mentioned in passing above—dating other transpeople—is a viable option mentioned by about a third of my respondents. Ten years ago, that was a lot less common. Mental health gatekeepers stressed the importance of getting a partner who was a "real" man or women in order to validate one's gender identity. For many of us, that was the "holy grail" of having succeeded at transsexuality. However, some of us (like myself and my two partners) loudly challenged that model, wondering why of all minorities, we alone were discouraged from marrying our own kind. A decade later, the tide has turned and transfolk are just as likely to date each other as to date nontrans men or women. This solution met with enthusiasm in many of my surveys.

> I've never had an issue finding partners for sex, play, or relationships because of my gender identity or expression. Some of that I know is sheer luck, but a big part of it I believe is that gender aside I'm incredibly queer. In my community gender transgression is seen by many to be attractive. I also for the most part only play with other trans or genderqueer people. This is a pretty important boundary for me because it at least to some level insures that things I need to feel comfortable in my body will be recognized, understood, and honored making it possible for me to fully surrender. – Sassafras Lowrey

> I get laid because freak trannies who are artists and queers and have a relative amount of privilege to run around and meet up with each other and write zines and travel and party stick together. We're also poly, which helps! Sex positivity is really rare in trans communities, and that's why a lot of trans folks don't get laid enough. Shame, especially around sex, is something I'm personally working on eradicating from the world. – Simon Strikeback

> I date other transfolk, both MTF and FTM. It's easier. We understand each other, we respect each other's psychological boundaries around sex, we are never ashamed to be seen with each other in public. I've dated biomen and biowomen too, but I always come back to my own kind. – Jonathan

On the other hand, that isn't always the answer for everyone. Some people are just more attracted to single-gendered lovers, and always will be. Others find that two (or more) people with the same triggers will continually remind each other of their mutual pain. Being without the anchor of one partner's inflexible identity can make some transgendered people feel adrift. Blaise Garber-Paul writes about facing the back side of trans-trans relationships:

> I had an encounter getting cruised by a man who I'd read as cisgendered. At the end of the exchange, while asking for my number, he said that he preferred transmen. I was surprised, felt fetishized, and made that clear. He

asserted that he was trans as well, that it was a camaraderie thing. I didn't believe him ... and then he showed me his top surgery scars. It was a complicated moment for me: at that particular moment I wasn't looking to be involved with another transman. I was trying to take some space from an intense relationship with another transman, and hooking up with a transman was too emotionally loaded for me. That experience changed how I react to gay men who hesitate with me—I feel like having been on the other side, it's given me a little more distance from taking a rejection like that personally, a little more sympathy to the internal complexities that go into selecting a lover or play partner.

There are challenges to being with nontrans partners as well. They may have trouble grasping some of the more esoteric but still horrifyingly crucial issues of our complicated existences, and they may not get just how much they don't get it. Micah articulately talks about the difficulties of getting them to understand:

Some people don't want to have sex or play with trans people; some people love to fuck us but have a very fetishizing/exoticizing kind of attitude toward us. I think there are some similarities to navigating any sort of nonconsensual/societal-based power difference in relationships. If I'm white and my partner is a person of color, or if I'm Muslim and my partner is Christian, or if I'm able-bodied and my partner is disabled, or if I'm trans and my partner is non-trans, there's going to be some sort of power dynamic there that we're going to have to deal with in a responsible way in order to have a positive consensual fun relationship with one another. To me, it's worth the challenge. I don't want to have to go around seeking out partners who are demographically identical to me and I often feel like my partners and I learn a lot from each other based on our different experiences in the world.

I used to be pretty wary about playing with non-trans people, because I was worried that they would say or do things in our relationship or scene that would be hurtful to me in terms of my gender or that I would experience as transphobic. Eventually I realized that everyone—including trans people—is transphobic to some degree. I have internalized transphobia too. Even in relationships or scenes with other trans people I have often gotten hurt or triggered in terms of my gender at some point. Non-trans people are human and diverse and some of them can be pretty damn great trans allies, although naturally none of them is completely free from transphobia. I believe that everyone, including me, deserves to have a partner or partners who are kind, respectful, and supportive and accept us as who we are. I also believe the only way not to risk getting hurt by another person is to stay completely alone, which is certainly not what I want. Also, as my transition progressed I began to feel a lot more confident and less easily hurt or triggered, which made it easier for me to feel good about taking more risks.

I now mostly date non-trans men, which has sometimes worked out wonderfully and sometimes poorly. I try to give everyone the benefit of the doubt and I have some patience and compassion as guys I'm with learn about trans issues and make mistakes along the way. I try not to dwell on the little inevitable hurts, whether I'm with a trans person or a non-trans person. At the same time, I also speak up when partners say or do things that don't work for me. I don't stick around if I think someone is being disrespectful, overly defensive, or mean or if I'm just not happy with what's happening between us. Most people are pretty great in my experience, though, and I'm really happy with how many of my relationships/scenes with non-trans people have gone. Admittedly, my passing privilege makes it easier for me than for some other trans guys.

Being with non-trans people can be difficult, of course. Their bodies are not on the line the way that ours are when it comes to trans issues; real solidarity can be hard to find. I remember once years ago I was hanging out with three people with whom I had variously close and kinky relationships. Two of them were friends of mine, a trans man and non-trans woman, both Tops whom I played with pretty regularly. They were old friends with one another and co-Topped me from time to time. The third was a non-trans woman and my primary partner, who was also friends with the other two and often had vanilla sex with the trans man. The phone rang and I picked up. The news was terrible: another trans man, whom none of us knew well but all of us were friendly with, had just been arrested for using the men's room. He was being held at the police precinct as we spoke. The person who called urged me to call the police precinct, explain that the guy had been in the right bathroom, ask for his release, and try to get as many others as possible to do the same.

I told the others and made the phone call to the police precinct right away. The other trans guy picked up the phone right after me and made the same call. The two non-trans people in the room, though, exchanged a glance and said they didn't want to call—they felt awkward about talking to the police. The other trans guy said, in frustration, "How would you feel if you got arrested for using the bathroom!" They changed the subject. The truth is that they could not imagine getting arrested for using the bathroom. The other trans guy and I could—we lived with the fear (and at times the reality) of that and other horrible things happening to us every time we used a public restroom. There was no question in our minds that we would take 30 seconds to do what we could for a member of our community sitting in jail because of transphobia, even if the police might be a bit brusque or refer to us as female. The two non-trans women liked trans guys well enough: they slept with us and played with us and hung out with us. Still, the thought of a brief awkwardness on the phone was enough to deter them from trying to get one of us out of jail when it counted. Of course there were a lot of non-trans people who did call that night, but for me it was a searing example of how our lovers are not always our allies.

(I still remember that moment clearly, even though it was years ago. I realized once that I was doing the exact same thing that they did when I decided not to call a district attorney to advocate for someone who was in trouble just for being a young Latina lesbian. Embarrassed at my own hypocrisy, I belatedly made the call. It's important to remember all the different ways we can be allies for one another.) – Micah

Nontrans partners may be attracted to transgendered partners for many reasons besides mere fetishization ... and besides a uniquely personal attraction to that special person who happens to be transgendered but that hardly even makes a difference. Often their desires for us are complicated, and they may be confused about them, or unwilling to share their motivations for fear of insulting us. Blaise Garber-Paul speaks of his experiences with nontrans male partners:

I've come across an increasing number of gay men who have started seeking out experiences with transmen. They recognize themselves as gay men, but are beginning to detach their attraction to a person's energy from their expectation of particular anatomy. These men range from men who had positive hetero experiences before deciding that they were gay (they miss cunt, but weren't attracted to women), men who fetishize men with small cocks, or with extra pliable holes, and men who simply don't find their primary attraction to a person to be genital-focused.I find that this is especially true in BDSM circles. What I've got between my legs says nothing about how well I throw a punch or take a needle.

When it comes to advice to each other in finding partners, transfolk also stressed the importance of simply being who you are and having faith that it will come, rather than trying to become something artificial that would attract the wrong people. Many had solid and sensible advice coming from a place of blunt practicality, but it was practicality rooted, again, in being centered in one's self. With our changing and flexible identities and our often meandering journeys, being centered in one's self and existence is something that may take a lot of time and struggle for most of us. It's not a new message: once you are fully yourself, you will attract the people who want you as you are. It's a message that many will have trouble believing, but it still rings true even in the face of all fatalism and doubt.

The only trouble I have in finding partners is when people cannot get past the genitals. Advice for other transfolk: Be yourself, this cannot be stressed enough. If you are yourself, the right people will be able to see you and will be attracted to you for who you are, and this wide world is so diverse you will find someone. – Lord Tom

First you need to be honest with yourself, and learn to open up about what it is that you want to accomplish. For me, getting sex isn't the problem. Finding a person you can live with is the problem. I have been lucky in both instances. – Mistress Cayenne

Spend time alone and really reflect on your wants, needs, and desires. Being an accomplished well-put-together person is attractive to most people. Desperate, confused, and needy is not sexy to most people. – E. Nelly

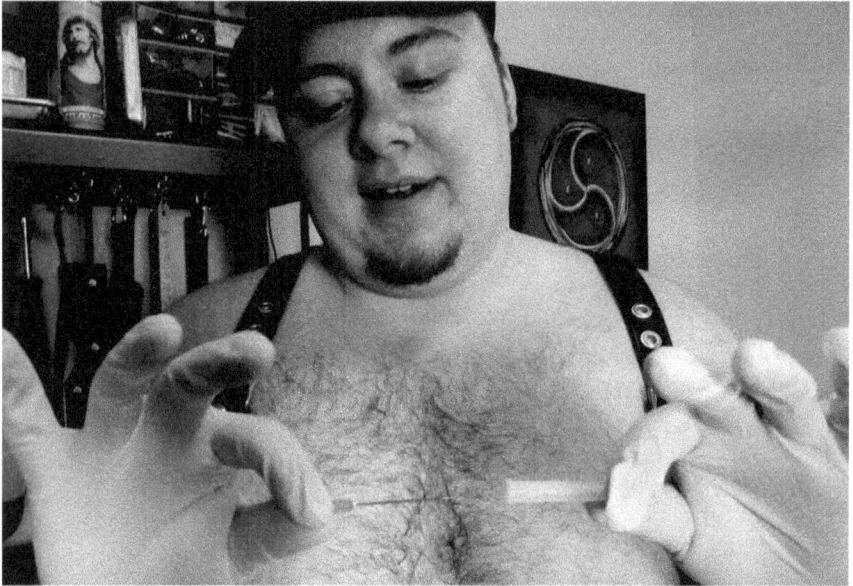

I don't have trouble finding partners, but I believe in fate. Not sure I can give that kinda of advice to others. I think I don't have trouble finding partners because I don't let me being trans affect my relationship. – boy bailey

I advise trans people the same way I advise anyone else on finding partners—be yourself, be honest about what you want, be gentle but not invisible, and have no attachment to the outcome, and you'll do fine. People are attracted to confidence, honesty, and consideration as much as they're attracted to physicality. The hardest part is that non-attachment; you have to keep your emotional investment in people low until you know whether or not they're interested in you. It does no one any good for you to pine secretly for someone for a long time, to the point of feeling devastated if they turn you down. Remember this is supposed to be fun and lighthearted in the beginning.
– Del

I don't always get the partners I want. No one does. Sometimes I have amazing experiences with people I might not have thought of sexually before they approached me. I think that people attract partners as they are able to. I think that it's a combination of having a good sense of yourself, a solid grounding in yourself, and having an ability to reach out to others. Being trans is a challenge in the sexual marketplaces, but so are a million other variations in body and mind. I don't like the line of thinking that goes "if I only had a 'normal' body then I would find lovers *so* easily...." because it's simply not true. Most folks I know have a lot of trouble finding satisfying sexual and play connections. Finding partners is a human problem.

In terms of finding partners in a BDSM context ... I would tell transfolk having trouble finding partners that they should look to everything else first. Look to your sense of self satisfaction, self confidence, self ease. Look to your ability to please yourself—sexually, creatively, intellectually, etc. Engaging people are engaging, regardless of what their anatomy looks like. And the trans part, I think the most important part is simply to rock it. Make it fabulous. Acknowledge it. Aim for comfort over fantasy. Learn how to make your body happy so you can show other people. Make human connections well before worrying about having sex or play connections. – Blaise Garber-Paul

Love Is A Many~Gendered Thing: Being Partnered

As discussed in the last chapter, partnering for transfolk—and especially for kinky transfolk—can be like hunting for a needle in a haystack. Finding someone who is content with your gender identity, and who also shares your kinks, can be a tall order ... and yet people manage it. My interviews were fairly evenly divided between the partnered and the unpartnered. Some discussed former partners, including the ones who left them over issues of gender, and the ones who left them over issues of kink. At least half, however, were ensconced in loving, supportive, kinky relationships that suited them well. TransPunk says of one of his partner relationships: "I am the Master to my warrior, who is also a switch and more on the top side and not my property. He is also my soulbrother. With him I explored the shamanic side of BDSM and we are on a similar spiritual path. He was the first one, after my surgery and after a long period of my not being comfortable with my cunt, to fuck me in the cunt, which was due to mutual trust and our deep bonding and the need to have intense intimacy. To both of us it was a very intimate gesture, much more than other sex. He invented the term "dickhole" for my cunt and compared it to fucking a fisted asshole, which was such a fag thing to say that I felt very much viewed as a man despite the vaginal sex. Since I met him, I

have slowly become more confident about being naked in front of other gay men and sexual partners."

One Or Many

Some of my respondents were in monogamous relationships, but a surprising number were actively polyamorous (as opposed to simply single and looking in a variety of places). Since this is a book about transgendered people involved in BDSM, and the BDSM demographic tends to be rife with people who embrace all sorts of alternative love arrangements, this was not unexpected.

> I've had a pretty significant number of other partners over time. At various times I've tried BDSM with strangers, with friends, with partners of partners, and with lovers. Some have been quite experienced Tops, but I've also hooked up with a fair number of other bottoms. I usually win the "who gets to be the bottom?" fight. One partner of mine who was exclusively a bottom when we met ended up becoming quite the Top in our relationship and now, years after we broke up, is a switch. When I was playing with another friend of mine who was a bottom, we switched pretty evenly. It was fun, actually—pinching, hot wax, and similar activities are ones that I've found I can enjoy as a top, even though I would prefer being on the bottom.
>
> I've also been with a fair number of people who, at least at the start of our relationship, were vanilla. Some I've corrupted—or rather, introduced to the beautiful world of BDSM. They found they loved it and I helped them learn to be sadists/Doms/Daddies/Tops from my position as a masochist/sub/boy/bottom. With others I've just contented myself with vanilla sex, but I have often found something about what we did that I was able to experience and enjoy as a sub/masochist even though it did not carry the same meaning for my partner. Being polyamorous makes it easier to be with some vanilla partners; I know that I am always free to seek out BDSM elsewhere. – Micah

> I'm in a committed, polyamorous, BDSM relationship with my husband, Ninja. We've been together for six years, and legally married for two. We are in a power exchange relationship that has changed over time; right now we're identifying as "Daddy/boy", although I refer to him as "my Sir". I have a girlfriend whom I see rarely, with whom I

engage in SM with. I have two women who are in service to me, formally—that is to say, we have some form of long term agreement/contract that makes arrangements for a balanced D/s dynamic. One of them wears a "trial collar", which may will become permanent over time; the other is currently collared to someone else, but her owner knows and supports our relationship.

I have several other people who serve me casually, usually attending SM or pagan events with me. They get in for free in exchange for acts of service, including packing/unpacking, driving, scheduling, gofering, and the like. I have about six casual lovers, only some of whom are kinky in some way. I also have several people with whom I have engaged in SM, and I plan to continue doing so in the future—I call them "play partners". – Del

Our Own Kind

As has been mentioned throughout the book, any given transgendered individual may be attracted to or choose to have a relationship with men, women, or other transfolk of any stripe. Yet as we've also discussed before, many are now turning specifically to that third category, deliberately choosing to partner with each other in numbers that were formerly unheard of. It may be that the "taboo" was easier to break through for people who were already breaking through a number of other sexual taboos, and didn't care much any more. Many of my respondents were in trans/trans relationships, and described their partners eloquently:

> My one parent died before I was able to tell him that he never had a son, just a daughter who was trying so hard to be one, and my mother abandoned me after hearing of it and refusing to acknowledge it in the slightest ... It was not until my current partner, my present Mistress, that I had someone who was healthy and understood what I was going through as I transitioned. I had a couple of partners in the years before I met her; one raped me physically and the other did so emotionally. The reason my Mistress understands so well is that she is also a transitioning MtF. At the beginning of July 2009, we had our one year anniversary ... Besides her being my Mistress, she is also my wife and in ways my big sister and the mother I never had. – Brianna Ahava Morrigan

My current partner has been with me for close to three years now. He has been my fulltime slut for about a year and a half now, and is a domestic and personal service slut. He is my special little guy/boy in the ageplay sense and in the Daddy/boy sense. I am not a real domly-dom type and I take a more loving approach with our power exchange. He was relatively new to the SM world when we got together and we have both grown quite a bit in our understanding of ourselves through kink.

My boy is also an FTM guy so we connect a lot around gender issues as well as sharing lots of the similar fetishes. We have so much in common in terms of our BDSM desires. We enjoy lots of hot breath play, impact play, and edge play of all stripes. We are both big time blood fetishists and rough body play fans. When we play there is this energy connection and transfer that is truly unique.

He's a bratty type bottom—he can be demanding at times and often requires a reminder of his place. He is playful and charming with a distinctly nasty side when he wants to be. He loves to exchange power with me and loves to be scared by me. I love our relationship because despite the fact that we have known each other for four years I can still scare him with just one look. – E. Nelly

I tend to date androgynous/genderqueer people who either identifies as androgynous/genderqueer or who may appear to others as being androgynous or genderqueer. I realize those are two different terms but I want to be specific as to the kind of body type that I generally find attractive. I have dated men and women and folks who identify as both men and women and people who identify as neither men nor women. Currently I am with someone who identifies as both genderqueer and female.

I have not noticed any change in my own BDSM practice based on the gender, sex, race, or age of the person I am dating. As I mentioned earlier I began using BDSM as a way to both explore my gender identity and to practice safer sex. My first serious partners were all female identified non-trans women, most of who identified as bisexual. In these relationships I was generally asked to be more dominant and I definitely practiced a more aggressive attitude including topping and using bondage as a way to dominate. With my current partner—who is also a bisexual and female but also identifies as genderqueer—I have felt freer to investigate bottoming and switching. My partner refers to me as a "bossy bottom" or a bottom that tops.

I think due to my partner's transgender identity I feel more comfortable explaining my own gender identity and asking to be dominated. I know that she will not see my sexual desires as undermining my sex identity; a fear I had with all my previous partners. She is also assisting me in exploring all the possibilities of my gender identity in terms of BDSM. My partner is teaching me that although I was denied my identity for a long time that doesn't give me the right to deny anyone else theirs, so I am learning how to switch and dominate from a comfortable position.

– Mik Kinkead

I like to call myself "stone-sexual", meaning that I nearly exclusively partner with individuals whose sexuality manifests itself as "stone". Most frequently, I have dated/played with/had relationships with stone butches who also identify as transgender and/or genderqueer. My partner/Daddy and I have been together for over 5 years, during which time our genders have shifted considerably. The joke around our house is, that "we were fags when we got together, but not in a factory-direct sort way." At that time, I had just stopped taking testosterone (for the first time) and ze was just beginning to consider starting. There has been a very natural (to us) ebb and flow to our genders over the course of our relationship so far. We both believe and understand gender to be something constantly shifting and changing and so there has never been the crisis of "oh goodness my partner is presenting or identifying differently!" that I've seen other people's relationships struggle with.

– Sassafras Lowrey

Bridging The Gap

Being the nontrans partner of a transgendered lover isn't an easy job. There's pressure from inside the relationship from all the challenges of their triggers pushing on your triggers, and even if you clear all that up, there's still all the pressure from outside. You constantly deal with all the people who don't understand and who make you want to, as nontrans partner Ruth puts it in another chapter, hit them over the head with a chair. Add to this the social stigma of both of you being perverts, and that can mean an awful lot of closets, or else an awful lot of education and grinding discrimination.

However, the nontrans partners who responded to my survey were very clear not only about their love for their partners, but how much of a great bargain they'd got with this person. There was no question about them loving "in spite of" the trans nature. TransPunk mentions another of his partners: "He was the first one actually turned on by the fact that I have a different plumbing. But he was really careful and self-critical in order not to fetishize me as trans. When he saw my scar on the chest the first time, he said it turned him on, because he saw it as the sign of a warrior and felt I had fought harder for my masculinity than bioguys." Similarly, Mingdestiny wrote about her FTM partner:

> Lee is the most fascinating creature on the planet: super intelligent, very grounded and impeccable morals, totally goofy, deeply affectionate, unbelievably sexy, and lives a strict adherence to his erotic authenticity. I think that after meeting him (he was one year on T) I fell in love with the person in the middle, between male and female. We used to talk like girlfriends for hours and hours. As he has been on T I am noticing that he has switched to the "guy" category—being less chatty per se, but our conversations are deeper and more to the point. He also takes more of a "fix it" attitude. His being trans does not seem to play that much of a part in our relationship but occasionally he'll be more volatile, or moody directly after a shot of T. It only changed the dynamic in the sense that he got more Daddyish, more protective of me, spent more time with me. But I don't think that is because of the transition, I think it the evolution that we are on. Lee is always a guy with me, but he has a "Mistress Meany-Pants" character I have played with.

Ian MacAlister went into depth about both his own questioned assumptions and his relationship with his trans girl, and how her trans experiences have added to their compatibility:

> My girl Zennie is a transwoman. I'm her Daddy and her master and I tell her what to do. We are also in love and it is a very romantic relationship. I'm bisexual and I tried both sex and intimacy with women and men. What I

came up with, for myself anyhow, is that sex is sex and it's the person, not the anatomy that makes it special. Relationships, that's different. I like being dominant over feminine people, I like the "heterosexual" romance of dominant male and submissive femme. I don't apply it to the rest of the world, it's just one of my fetishes, and I wish people who share that fetish would admit that's all it is. I put "heterosexual" in quotes because real heterosexuality is about unipolar body preference, not relationship dynamic, so what I do is neither. I come to it as a queer man, I know it's a role. (Although the D/s is not a role for us, it's real.) Anyway, I also found that I like men as companions because we think similarly and have mutual interests. I am uncomfortable with where that road leads— the idea that women are for marrying and men are for friends and fucking. That seems stereotypical in a way I don't like.

Zennie makes that whole thing irrelevant. She is my girl when I want romance and because she was raised male she can be my friend and companion from that perspective. She can do "guy things" with me—I felt weird about asking her to come to the shooting range with me when we were dating, then I brought her and found out that she'd owned guns before and was a better shot than me! I do see both masculine and feminine in her, and I love both of them. She used to be uncomfortable about that, but after a couple of years seeing how my liking her masculine parts didn't make me see her as just a man, I could relate easily to her as a woman and that was just as important, she became comfortable with it. To me she's just beautiful. It took a long time before she believed that, though.

Ruth, on the other hand, didn't see anything special about the trans nature of her lovers; they are just who they are, and were special because of their own personal characteristics. She wrote: "The idea of someone's trans status changing how I react to them at first seems as foreign as asking if I treat blondes differently than redheads ... but then I remember that in one small way, it can. I generally do not ask cisgendered submissives what body parts are off limits in the same fashion that I do transgendered submissives. Then again, were I to top someone with another obvious physical issue, I would be equally concerned with qualifying those particular limits. I do not see specific qualities or skills being solely the domain of trans people any more than I see them only in cisgendered people. Each person is a unique and wonderful banquet of strengths and weaknesses."

The Earthquake Of Transition

Transitioning in a relationship is never easy, and some nontrans partners had that ambivalent privilege. The difficulties of transition do seem to break up more than half of relationships that go through it, due to a variety of reasons—the trans partner or the relationship is no longer the other partner's sexual preference, the trans partner needs to focus entirely on themselves during that time, or the general instability of the situation triggers other issues which crack the foundation. However, some manage to hang in there and stick together in spite of all that. Lord Tom recounts:

> I have had a few partners in my BDSM journey, and each one of them had a unique perspective on the lifestyle and community. They have been understanding of my mistakes and I am humbled by their patience and by their willingness to try again when things did not go exactly as planned. My current primary partner and I have been married over three years, and she has a beautiful slave heart. When I decided to physically transition from female to male a little over a year ago, she encouraged me and supported my decision to be my true self. I love her deeply, and I want to give her the guidance she deserves as her Master.

On the other side, the issue of physical attraction is a large and frightening problem during transition in existing relationships. Even when a partner is supportive of their lover, and wants to do their best to go along with the switch of public sexual orientation that may occur (or may be assumed to occur by outsiders), the vagaries of the crotch can interfere. Some of the transfolk that I interviewed made reference to the point after the initial period of hormones when their bodily scents changed, and suddenly something went off in their partner's attraction for them. (Scent means a lot more to unconscious attraction than we often think.)

Others referred to the moment when they looked in the mirror and began to really see someone of the sex they wanted to be perceived as ... and at about the same time, their partner stopped looking at them with desire. Lee Harrington dryly comments about his transition relationship: "My former husband and I got together with me being out about being two-spirited and identifying male part-time, and he told me he was bi-sexual. Slowly, as I became more masculine, this shifted to bi-sensual. And when I decided after 7 years together that I needed to transition, this became straight."

Sometimes a transitioning partner can expose and challenge all the hidden gender assumptions of both parties. We all grow up and live in societies with set gender roles, and it's almost impossible not to absorb some of those assumptions. When one partner becomes a different gender in an existing relationship, the programming and ideals about how both should act toward each other—alone and in private—and how they should keep to or deliberately transgress roles can be an enormous problem. While sex is also a proving ground to be figured into this equation, the daily interactions over breakfast can be just as crucial in determining the fate of a couple. Even if the nontrans partner is supportive of the change, the forcible surfacing of ingrained gender patterns can become too much to bear. For example, Joshua's relationship of the time did not survive transition, even though his partner was reasonably open to his gender explorations.

> My boyfriend during transition, J, was a five-year tumultuous "egalitarian" relationship. He loved me very much and was an amazing lover, but we fought constantly and treated each other terribly. Sex was the one area where our relationship really seemed to work, and we quickly got involved in BDSM and swinging. The swing clubs were very conservative about gender roles and very heterosexual, but the local BDSM scene was more open-minded.
>
> J and I lived together, but it was an entirely open relationship and I had a great deal of casual sex with both men and women. I started getting involved with the local GLBT community, and felt increasingly comfortable with a somewhat butch "dyke" identity. However, while I certainly enjoyed occasional sex with women, I strongly

preferred men as both friends and lovers. I had a harder time relating to women.

J was very open to me exploring different gender roles and just about anything else in our sex. He had been reluctant to explore his attraction to men, but once I began to transition I was surprised by his sexual enthusiasm for my new body and his eagerness to be socially perceived as a gay man. Unfortunately, the experience of socially transitioning from female to male prompted me to examine my social and interpersonal relationships, and highlighted for me the ways in which J and I brought out the worst in each other. He had anger management problems, and I would needle him in order to get him to lose control so I could feel superior. One day I drove him to the point where he slammed me up against the wall and was just about to punch me in the face. Ironically, I realized that meant that he definitely saw me as male, as he would never have hit a woman. After that, I knew that we just weren't good for each other, and I ended the relationship soon after transition.

Nanette's journey also brought up issues for her wife, which eventually ended their marriage: "My wife was supportive at first of my cross-dressing, but eventually as I got more into kink, my outfits got more extreme and my fantasies less vanilla, and she began to object. I started to transition, and it went badly. We divorced, and I thought it was because she wasn't attracted to me as a woman—but she then got another lover who is also a cross-dresser. In fact, she met the new 'girl' at a support meeting she came to with me. When the dust had settled and we could talk to each other calmly, we discussed it and she told me that it was the image of womanhood I'd chosen—sexy and provocative—that she was turned off by. Her upbringing made her think badly of that style of femininity, and she didn't want to think about that because it triggered her own issues around attractiveness. She said that she could be with a woman, but not a whore—that's what she'd say I looked like when I wore miniskirts or spike heels or any sexy clothing. Her new lover wears women's business suits and they have vanilla lesbian sex. My new lover is kinky and we wear black leather corsets together. So for us,

I guess it was as much the BDSM as the trans stuff that broke us up."

It isn't all difficulty, though. Some nontrans partners that I interviewed were reasonably sanguine about the ups and downs of their partners' changes, even when difficulties arose. Ruth writes about the transition of three of her partners:

> I have had a number of transgendered partners over the years. They have ranged from out and proud to seriously closeted. My partners have also ranged from FTM to MTF, from gender-fluid to gender-rejecting, and in varying states of surgical reformation. My wife came into my life as male, transitioned to living full-time as female, and is now rejecting gender identification as a whole. Since she is a foot and a half taller than I am, sometimes clean shaven, sometimes sporting a full beard, and almost always skirt-wearing, this can make life rather interesting for us as far as public perception is concerned.
>
> My wife did transition while we were together. During the time she was transitioning, she lost interest in most of the sexual activities we shared, including being a submissive. Having seen a number of my friends go through similar changes in their sexual desires during estrogen use, I admit that while disappointed I was not surprised. I think that knowing people who had experienced similar changes during transition made it somewhat easier to not take things personally, though I do admit that it times I was too insecure to be certain it was because she did not love me. As she has become more confident in herself and who she is, she seems to have shed most of the desire to submit in obvious ways, and turned instead to the things she feels are what I need. My sexual response to her has changed both very little, and a great deal in the past decade. I still find her incredibly arousing—that has not changed at all—but I am now more reluctant to turn to her for my sexual needs. While she reassures me that she is perfectly comfortable saying "no" when she isn't interested, I have too much past history with other lovers feeling they had to "humor" my libido, and being unhappy with that situation. We have cast aside the Domme/sub side of our relationship; I keep the collar she wore for me as a reminder, but she will never wear it again. Sadism and masochism are still active in our lives, it's just more about switching for each of us at this point.

I am also involved with an intersexed FTM dominant who identified publicly as female when I met him. While I was out of state during the time period in which he transitioned, he was never far from my thoughts. He is a powerful man, well respected in the BDSM community as well as other groups to which he belongs. He also transitioned during the time I knew him, but I was not around to be a support to him at the time. He did not express a desire to have me wear a collar with his name on it until after transition. While we did not have a stereotypically accepted sexual relationship before this, I had bottomed to him, and from that I see no change in the experience. I have always found him exciting, and will continue to do so regardless of gender or anything else. The only changes I can see in our relationship are the ones that come with time and becoming more comfortable with each other.

One of my girlfriends is an MTF, and is successfully accepted in society as female. She can be a very femme girl, though occasionally will surprise me with a burst of unabashed stereotypical masculine behaviour. My girlfriend came to me identifying as a drag queen, and had to have this idea redefined for her. We were introduced by some mutual friends who were in her company in the military. They felt I would "understand" her, while they found her to be a fine joke. While her identity was largely in her when I met her, she stayed a boy in the military until she was finally asked to leave. Once she left the military, the path to finding who she was and could be seemed very difficult for her both in bed and out. Our sexual interactions have changed mostly in her desires to have certain parts of her body touched or not. My sexual response to her has increased over the years, but that is not due to her gender identity but the fact that she has grown out her hair.

Any change in the way that others see those I am involved with has not changed anything for me at this point. – Ruth

For some nontrans partners, being with a trans partner can definitely widen their horizons, if they let it. Justin writes about how his late master was affected by their relationship:

When my Master first collared me, he identified as straight; near the end of his life, he identified as pansexual.

I would say that my gender identity, since I had transitioned years before I met him, impacted his sense of his sexuality more than it impacted mine. We did have an intimate relationship and my identity as male (as opposed to my trans status) was challenging at the very beginning. But we both agreed that the right match of Master and slave, and the right dynamics of how that played itself out in the dungeon and the bedroom, were much more central to each of our senses of our sexuality than our gender or the labels of our sexual orientations. I really don't feel like my gender identity _per se_ played much of a role. Gender was a bigger dynamic between us. My gender required him to challenge himself to expand sexually and he also taught me an enormous amount about what it means to be a man. His combination of fierce protectiveness and responsibility with a compassionate and gentle side was a very powerful role model for me of the kind of man I want to be.

Crstlbella, a nontrans slave partner, poignantly describes the process of her Master's transition and her reactions to it:

My Master is actually the only transgendered or transsexual partner I have had. In fact, until I met him I was barely aware of the existence of transsexual, transgendered and intersexed individuals, despite being an active member of the bisexual, lesbian and gay community. For years I identified as a heterosexual-leaning bisexual female. I have since come to the conclusion that I am not bisexual—but rather, I am submissive. I am attracted to dominant men, women, intersexed individuals and transfolk, but not so much to other submissive people.

When I met my Master, he had neither transitioned nor had he seriously considered transitioning. Frankly, I do not believe he knew it was _possible_ to transition successfully enough to pass and therefore seemed determined to make a go of it as a woman. We initially met though an online role-playing game where we were both playing male characters. Though we eventually both played several characters (both male and female) and all sorts of sexual orientations, the majority of our online interactions were as part of a D/s dynamic bordering on an M/s dynamic where he played the dominant role. However, we did have some interactions where we reversed that and I was in the dominant role.

When we met in person a few months later, I believed at that time that he was a woman. Transgender was still not truly a part of our shared vocabulary at that point. I had long considered myself to be bisexual though I had had only very limited sexual relations with other women, and nothing that I could actually call a true relationship. Complicating matters was the fact that we are actually 15 years apart in age—and I was the more experienced of the pair of us. I believe it was this combination of factors, along with the manner in which we met, that led us to utilize role-play on a fairly regular basis for much of our love-making, usually incorporating other aspects of BDSM as well. During that time we swapped roles and genders quite frequently. However, I felt that we tended to have a great deal of tension between us whenever I was the dominant of the pairing and whenever he was female of the pairing. It was also during this time that we moved to Massachusetts so that we could marry— and I would say that we were generally perceived as an "out" lesbian couple both inside and outside the BDSM community, at least when we were perceived as a couple at all.

But when my spouse finally confided in me that he really was *male* and that part wasn't so much a role, I have to say that I was not terribly surprised—and I tried my best to be supportive. As we began his transition and for almost a full year of him receiving testosterone injections, we pretty much continued as we had—swapping roles and genders, though I felt that some of this began to cause more and more tensions between us. Eventually, and after much soul-searching on both of our parts, we finally confessed to each other that this was not what either of us wanted. Role-playing was all well and good—and BDSM was fun, but we were both seeking something deeper. Something closer to who we each were spiritually—and we jointly made a decision to turn more strongly to the M/s dynamic we had already begun to develop. We still do role-playing and occasionally swap gender roles for the sake of a short scene but not as often as we did. We've also pretty much stopped swapping roles as far as the power dynamic is concerned—he remains firmly in the dominant role and I am quite happily in the submissive role now.

This gender fluidity was through role-play during sex as well as in every day interactions. Sometimes it *did* make me uncomfortable, and sometimes I couldn't do without it. I think part of it really depended on the headspace I happened to be in at the time and how comfortable I was at that moment with my *own* gender fluidity. And yes, we have both interacted with all of each others' genders in a sexual capacity. As for how things are different ... that's a tough one. Not because it's difficult to distinguish his different sexual genders—but because we have done so much with role-playing, and each role has been so wonderfully distinct from the next, that I scarcely know where to start. Each *role* has been different, even ones that have the same sexual gender, though, so I think it's more that my Master just likes variety—and happens to be creative enough and insightful enough as an individual that he is able to take on *any* role, regardless of gender, and do it justice. Overall, I think it's a bonus, though—as it's really hard to get bored when you and your partner are forever changing things up.

As for how I feel about these changes, well, they've actually been rather affirming for me. It was through our playing with gender that I came to realize that I wasn't really heterosexual, lesbian, or bisexual … and I'm still not entirely clear on what pansexual is. I just don't have that kind of sexual orientation. I'm the submissive, the bottom, the slave. *That* is my sexual orientation. The rest is up to him.

I also believe that the lingering stereotypes in our culture about the gender roles that men and women "traditionally" occupy have actually made it easier on us as other people's perception of my Master's sexual orientation and gender have changed. It was difficult for people to see him as dominant when he looked like a pretty blonde girl, fifteen years my junior—and difficult for them to see him as my partner at all even as an equal or my spouse. Since his transition, people no longer question so much that we are a couple. Instead of thinking we are sisters, they recognize us as married. When the check is brought to our table at restaurants, it is generally placed near him as the man and therefore presumed dominant person, rather than by me as the older woman and therefore the presumed dominant person. These may seem like little annoyances, small complaints … and they are, but added together I felt they used to quietly undermine our dynamic. Now, I find our dynamic to be somewhat reinforced by the stereotypical assumptions people tend to make about our gender roles. Not that I'm big on stereotypes… it's just that for once they've been helping.

Imagination and Gender Play

It's been said repeatedly that the most important quality that a nontrans partner can have is imagination, because it's useful when confronted with anatomy, roles, or past history that doesn't match. Fortunately, the BDSM demographic is one where erotic imagination is praised and valued, and being with someone sexually in a way that may be different from the ordinary public life that you both live isn't so big a stretch for many people. Being able to stretch one's sexual flexibility to include new activities, or to make unusual sexual activities your mainstay, is also a skill that we are more likely to find in this lifestyle. To have a partner who can say, "Sure, this isn't any stranger than most of the things I do anyway, and if I can get into them, I can get into that," is strongly affirming.

TransPunk in Germany tells a beautiful story of acceptance and mutual imagination: "As a transguy, of course I don't have sperm of my own. So one time when I was topping my slave and my warrior, we ended up in a situation where one of my bottoms was on his knees sucking my (biological) cock and the other's cock. At some point the other bottom came over my cock and the kneeling one licked it off (note that we have carefully negotiated fluid bonds). We later exchanged our perception of that moment and it turned out that in all our minds we felt that my bio-male bottoms' sperm belonged to me as their Master, and that my bottom's sperm was mine. They sacrificed it to me and it was magically transformed to be mine. It was one of those situations that felt really healing, and since then I haven't really felt any lack for not having sperm produced by my own body."

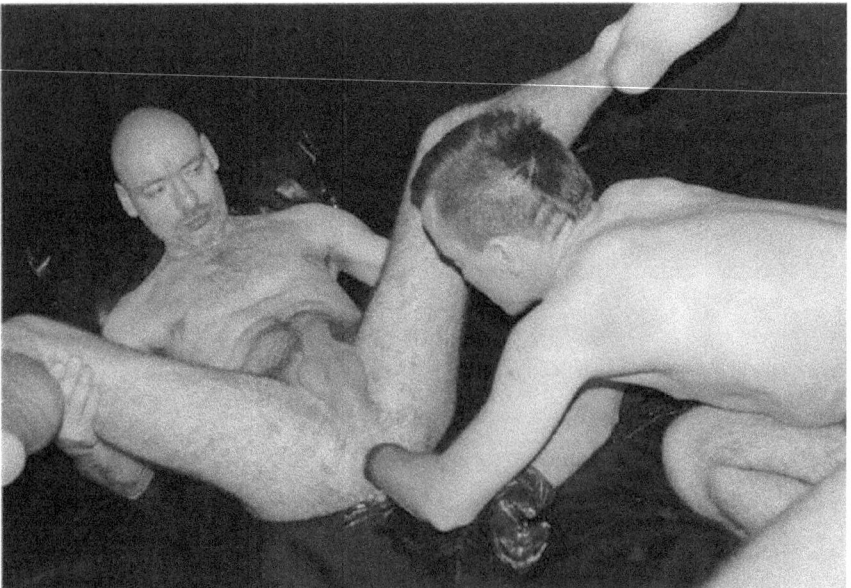

The need for imagination and flexibility is especially true for transfolk who play with gender—and especially for those who play with it back toward the direction they once came from. Of course, this doesn't always work out, as MTF respondent "Double-Edge" says dryly: "I was asked to cross dress as a man one time. Mistress says that will never happen again. She could not stand me as a man."

Still, some partners end up playing with the smorgasbord of gender that some trans individuals can be. Ruth says: "The only lover I have had who openly identified as gender-fluid to me was not one of my three transsexual lovers. They would occasionally shift the energy they were experiencing during sex and BDSM "play". It was part of who they were, and as such I embraced it as part of the experience of being with them. It did not make me uncomfortable, and at times was a major part of our interactions. The experience of having physically subdued and bound a fairly submissive male, only to have an incredibly powerful female start fighting the chains and verbally abusing me was certainly different from any other relationship I have been in. In some ways I would think that it is not unlike dealing with someone who exhibits DID. While I can't tell you if I interacted with *all* their sexual identities, there were certainly differences between the pieces I was shown. They had a very strong-willed and powerful female identity, and at the same time a very submissive male identity who desired nothing more than to know their place and be put there."

Similarly, Karen, a nontrans partner, wrote: "My husband is FTM and used to be my wife. We met and committed to each other shortly before his transition—I was aware that he was FTM from the start. First I got someone who was basically a stone butch switch—s/he could top me, or I could top but the pants (or cock) always stayed on. Then for seven years I had a male partner who slowly became able to allow me to touch his genitals during BDSM, and then during sex, and then he got to really like it. And then, seven years later, he came to me and told me that he wanted to engage his 'female side' in a scene. I got to take 'her' virginity. It was one of the most moving things I've ever done, and it did not change

the fact that he was a man and my husband twenty minutes later. Once in a while I get to have sex with 'her', maybe twice a year. I feel like I'm having a secret affair, but it's not infidelity! The rest of the time he is unabashedly a man. I consider myself to be very lucky."

Some years ago, my FTM partner and I attended a group of transgendered people who were exploring the sacred aspects of sexuality, and how that worked uniquely with us. Sometimes there would be "exercises", which people would take home and do with their partners, or do a variant with themselves if they didn't have partners. One of the exercises—designed for trans/trans couples—was to have sex four separate times, each time roleplaying a different gender combination and trying to understand the energetic component of each one. Over the course of a week, we played with male/male (our standard format), female/female (which was not without its issues, as it was where we came from), male/female, and female/male. The two things that didn't change were our D/s dynamic and our 14-year age difference, and we discovered as we switched the genders around that those two polar axes became more prominent.

The male/male sex was pretty ordinary—it was what's for breakfast. When my boy got to be the girl, it went fairly easily—he has done drag and played with female sexuality before, so no dysphoria was triggered. He wanted to be a young girl being seduced by an older man, not exactly virgin but inexperienced and easily scandalized, and we did find that my "normal" male persona isn't much good at the heterosexual romance, even the dark predatory version. I tended to move too fast and be too rough for his "girl", but in the end she surrendered anyway. (Of course.)

When it came time for me to take the female role, I had to think about it for a while. Unlike my partner, I still had a lot of problems taking a female role sexually, and not just due to gender dysphoria. For me, the first 15 years of my sexual experience, my "drag queen" era, as I put it, consisted of female-role sex with both men and women where I was always deeply dissociated. I put on a polished performance that I never actually showed up for in any real way. I had to figure out how to harness the female energy in myself (which I knew existed, it just wasn't in the majority, and it was not strongly linked to my sexuality) in a way that didn't encourage dissociation, and trust my lover to pick up the cues.

The person that emerged, surprisingly enough, was that of a woman much older than myself—in her sixties, perhaps, sort of a homesteading Tasha Tudor type, but more sexually dominant. With a male partner, it was as if she had decided with the turn of the seasons to get herself a nice stud, who would then be shooed out the door to do the haying and not bother her for another few months. With a female partner, we reverted to a sort of schoolmistress/ schoolgirl scene. My boy confided that it seemed to be the most unseemly of all, in a hot way, for two FTMs. It was also "unseemly" in a different way, which was actually exciting to him—the young schoolgirl doing it with a much older woman. We did notice that even when the gender scenario changed, our power dynamic was still firmly in place … and, oddly enough, so was our age difference. In fact, as we shifted, the age difference became more prominent, especially in the F/f scene, where my persona's age was supposedly even further away from his than my natural one.

The interactions taught me a lot about myself, my genders, and my sexual responses. I cleaned out a lot of old psychological debris, and put some old demons to rest. I could not have done this without a partner who was willing to go there with me, and be patient as I worked out my issues, even as I was patient for his. I also couldn't have done it with a partner who was not just as much of a polymorphous pervert as I was. Our multiple axes of difference have deepened and enlightened not only our sex life, but the entirety of our lives together.

Interview with Terra Katherine McKeown

When I was younger, between all the worrying my parents did about my ambiguous genitalia and the strangeness of my upbringing, I thought everyone wanted to be both a girl and a boy. It was just a given to me that if given the opportunity to switch back and forth whenever I wanted, I would take that up in a heartbeat. But, as I said, there was a lot of pressure on me growing up. Not only was I a hyper-sensitive queer boy, I was also an artist, I was Pagan, and I was obese. Raised in a small, rural Western Washington town, I was one of my cohorts' favorite targets for abuse and ridicule. In addition to that, my father had molested me as a very young child, and I was wrestling with my fear of him in light of past and ongoing abuse. The combination of consistent abuse, the confusion I felt about my gender, and sexual feelings towards other boys caused me to implode. Aside from suicide attempts, I found solace in scratching and biting myself until I bled. My identity was very fluid, even then, so I didn't identify with anything. I became androgynous and asexual in dress, cutting off all attraction to other people. My hair grew out and I draped myself in black clothing; I would sometimes be seen as female. It would have brought me joy had I even given myself the chance to even think about gender identity.

After college, still androgynous and confused, I met my first girlfriend. I was amazed someone was actually attracted to me, and it began the transformation that culminated in my exploration of gender identity … *many* gender identities. She told me, "I am so happy to finally be with a *straight man*." Did you know that you can actually check books out of the library that teach you how to be a straight man so that you can "flirt with women" better? I'd watch other men and how they'd take up space and talk and walk, and I tried very hard to learn how to be one. Of course, now that I was a *straight man*, I began to get hit on by gay men. Still untied to my gender and sexual identity, I experimented and finally started falling in love with men. One of my lovers told me, "Honey, admit it, you're a gay man," but I didn't really feel satisfied with that. I had been hearing about "pansexual" as a term, and decided that I was that; after all, I could conceive of being with more than just women *and* men. It didn't quite fit, but it was a better choice than *bi*-sexual, if by nothing more than semantics.

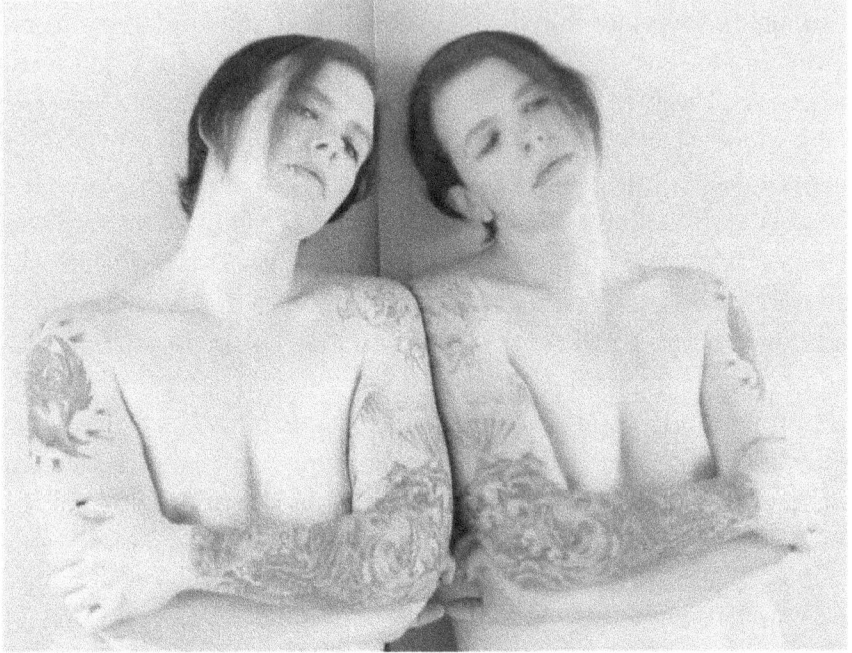

Soon after I went to grad school in an art therapy/depth focused Psychology program. While there I took a cross-cultural mythology and symbolism course, the first semester split into the Feminine and the Masculine. The instructor for the Feminine section told the men in the class—including me—that we couldn't understand any of this information, so just shut up and listen! She was very much an essentialist. Having some social psychology and psychology of gender under my belt, I argued with her ferociously about her essentialist view of gender, and especially the *archetypes* of gender. (I wish I'd had access to the book *Hermaphrodeities* at the time!) My final paper studied the Gallae, berdache, and many other cross-cultural examples of those who transgressed gender norms.

The Masculine section was just as bad; the instructor solicited the men in the class—including me—to give examples and insight from our own life to illustrate what we were talking about. I hated it, and passed each time I was asked. Finally, he nailed me down and told me he wanted to know about my experience *as a man*. Letting the anger out, I pounded the table and said I had nothing to add. I scared my cohort and I scared myself, but he stopped asking. I told my cohort as I railed, outside of class, about this seminar, "Why don't they have a section for the Psychology of the Androgyne?" They all told me I should write the book. I was still clueless, at the time, as to why this ate me up so badly, and *transgender* wasn't even in my mental dictionary.)

After graduate school I returned to Seattle broke and jobless. While I tried to find employment with my new degree, I found my new family. They called themselves queer and introduced me to queer politics, something in my white "male" life that I'd had the privilege to ignore. In addition to this, they called themselves *genderqueer*. This turned me on! Following their advice, I read everything I could get my hands on and considered myself *genderqueer* ... It was during this time that I met many of my best friends, and I had the support and the knowledge to really investigate *my own* identity—not one given to me by girlfriends or boyfriends, by doctors or parents, or by anyone else in society. It had never occurred to me that I could choose my identity.

I have been on hormone replacement therapy for nearly two years, transitioning to a more feminized body. I still identify as gender variant or genderqueer, rather than as a woman, but I am a very fluid person. Sometimes I identify as a woman, especially when I go stealth. I tell people I'm a genderqueer person on the transfeminine spectrum. Sometimes I use transfeminist, or transfemme, or my favorite, a "gender nomad". My gender expression is very fluid, though usually more feminine than not. I often get confused with a trans man when I'm not completely femmed out, as I often dress as a dyke and then tell people I'm trans. Most often I try to express myself in a genderfuck way, with ties and skirts, or combat boots with dresses, but once in a while I'll bind my new breasts, put my hair under a hat, and try to actually be read as male. It usually doesn't work, which doesn't bother me all that much, but I still try.

I have always had more interest, socially as well as sexually, in women. My father abused me, most of those who beat me up or teased me were boys, and there were a couple of boyfriends who didn't listen to "no" when I didn't want to have sex with them. In general I found men to be a turn-off, people to be feared, and for the most part I didn't trust them. Since my mother was a feminist, and she taught me some of the first things I knew about social justice, I was pretty anti-man from the start. However, even as a child, I had attractions to men. From celebrities on TV to schoolmates, there were those men who turned my head and made me wonder if there was any way could be with them.

Currently, I identify as queer and as a dyke, as I have a greater emotional connection with women. In addition, the few trans people that I knew about, and especially those people who were androgynous by nature or by choice, were a huge turn on for me. "Pansexual" may be a better choice than "bisexual" (which reminded me of a binary that, even uneducated at the time about gender, I was turned off to). But "pansexual", while perhaps an etymologically accurate word for my sexual orientation, does not have the political aspects that *queer* and *dyke* have to them.

For me, sex has to be rough. I especially like bondage, impact play, wrestling and struggling, sensation play and sensory deprivation, roleplaying and rape play. I also like ritual and sacred BDSM—not that most sex, for me, isn't sacred, but ... it's the overall intention with everyone involved, right? I am entering into the world of doing more play piercing and cutting, and being the open minded adventurous girl I am, I enjoy trying almost anything once. I am a switch—it really depends, mostly, on the energy I have with someone. As a switchy, intelligent, somewhat sadistic trickster, I enjoy making people work for it and really have strong intention and focus. That can either be topping from the bottom, being a bratty bottom, or having my top buttons pressed and topping someone. I have less experience, however, as a top, and am currently intentionally focusing on improving my comfort with and skills as a Domme.

As a spiritual person, and one who has felt a calling to do spiritual work, my personal approach to being trans and genderqueer *and* my approach to BDSM is also a sacred one. For many cultures, as many of us know, trans people were the holy ones that could be in the liminal places, the between places, and usher people back and forth between one state to another. They were the psychopomps and the shamans, the priestesses and the muses. Not always, of course, but it makes a sort of archetypal-symbolic sense. I feel that much of my liminality (gender, sexuality, kink, just to name a few) is a part of my vocation, and that I use that to look beyond binaries, to find healing and direction for people, to really be able to put faith in the ineffable. In scene, the altered states and the healing, growth and magic that can be done in that space is one that I believe can be reached by transgressing the norms. Kink does that. Gender variance does that as well. Not that trans people will specifically be shamans, always, but they teach, they are "out there" in ways that some people will never experience, and that allows them the role of shepherding others into those spaces.

I consider myself a servant of Aphrodite. My life is dedicated to sex positivism, sexual healing, and sensual living. As a priestess, as well as a liminal holy person (and I try to say that as humbly as possible), I bring all of these aspects of myself to the people I work and play with, dedicated to bringing healing and growth. I can't live on this, of course, but it permeates all I do: sex work, social work, spiritual work, even simply being in community. This is how I, as a trans person, have evolved, and my gender journey has informed a great part of it by allowing me to pass through a different gate. Maybe not a better or higher one, but a different one, and a different perspective is sometimes all that is needed, too.

Trans Master, Trans Slave: Queering Up Power Dynamics

To the world outside the BDSM demographic, power dynamics—dominant and submissive, master/mistress and slave, owner and property—seem par for the course. Of course every one of these kinksters is groveling at someone's feet or barking daily orders. The truth is that people who live daily power dynamics are a minority among BDSM'ers, and people with intense power dynamics of the owner/property type are even rarer, a minority among minorities. Many of the more egalitarian kinksters look askance at power dynamic relationships, and many of the people in limited power exchange look askance at the full-time highly controlled slaves with few limits and little recourse. It's a hierarchy of disapproval all the way down in many places, and some M/s or O/p couples (or triples) feel like outsiders in the more freewheeling BDSM communities because of this. Crstlbella sums up the experience by saying flatly, "We haven't really had much to do with the BDSM community, primarily because we've had trouble finding a place where we feel like we fit in. But it's not because of gender— more just trying to place our M/s lifestyle in the BDSM world."

When gender issues are added to power dynamics, however, the "traditional" roles often fall apart and participants have to create new archetypes of power and surrender. Some seize on and rework D/s subculture customs, such as Karolyn Amara Quinterlin, who says wryly, "We are in a D/s relationship that is based mostly on Gor, but with a lot of the inherent prejudices removed to try and make it more equitable for all in the household, due to the fact that I am MTF and my slave is also MTF; as such we would not be welcomed in most Gorean homes."

Still others use parental terms. Siobhan Phoenix says "I identify as my girl's 'Mommy' and have a loving, caring, but firm role established over her. I probably would have been a 'Daddy' if I wasn't so opposed to using male gender markers for myself." Netdancer describes his D/s relationship as "...a nurturing dominant, a 'Daddy', for the most part. A lot of what I do is mental and emotional, and I am very interested in seeing anyone I partner with become stronger, more self assured and more able to move towards their own goals. I am in a 24/7 Master/Slave relationship, with a strong Daddy/boy slant to it. C runs the household and takes care of me, and we rather lean on each other for support. There is no Master without a slave, and no slave without a master. The whole thing is a symbiosis, where I provide mental and emotional comfort and I receive contact and assurances that I am what is desired. I can see my objectives being achieved too, as C becomes stronger and more self-assured over time."

Power Exchange as Transitional Initiation

Parental roles are often used in the BDSM community at large as an initiatory period, helping adults to fully come into their adulthood, as it were. ("Daddy/boy" relationships in the gay male leather communities are the most indicative of this custom, but it appears in other gender combinations as well.) It's not uncommon among transgendered kinksters to use parental-style power exchange during the transitional part of their journey, as a way to "make them a man" or "make a woman out of them". Sometimes the parental role is filled by non-transgendered men or women, who hold up their expertise for the would-be "new man" or "new woman" to follow. Blaise Garber-Paul tells his story: "Since beginning my transition I've had several very significant BDSM/sex partners who fell into mentor roles. These people were all cisgendered men, some straight-identified, some queer. They were individuals who were at least 10 years older than me, some more than 20 years. They weren't romantic—we didn't go on dates, talk about "being in love", or setting up domestic spheres together. We were consistently emotionally involved, though, with most of our play revolving around a D/s structure that enforced my masculine socialization and rites of passage. It fit into my feeling that I needed someone to "teach me to be a man"—a concept that I've mostly let go of, partly because I pass as a man, and partly because I've realized just how many different ways there are to be a man."

In other pairings, the parental figure is also transgendered, in the same direction as the "youthful" partner. In these cases, the initiation is into the experience of actually being a transgendered adult in the world, with knowledge and experience drawn from their survival as trans rather than as the "target" gender. Jonathan says, "All my boys are FTMs like me. I mentor them and teach them to survive, to feel sexually confident, to be socially confident as men on the street. Most of them leave at some point; they 'grow up' as it were, and move on. Some stay in that liminal phase for a long time, if they've got a lot of damage. Some go on to become tops, some stay bottoms but in a more adult-male way. It's part of my job as Daddy to see that they are brought up right."

Some transfolk I've spoken with have used power exchange relationships to work through transition in a different way. Coming to a decision-making point about one's gender can mean working through all the difficult assumptions and fears one has about that gender. It's not unusual for transition to bring up a wealth of suppressed trauma from the psyche, and it's best to clear that out before one can cleanly make such a huge change in one's life. A power exchange relationship, whether for a single scene or for a longer period of time, can be a safe place to work that through. It has boundaries and is negotiated; you know what you can expect and that it won't disintegrate into abuse (assuming that you've chosen the right people to help you go there). Several FTMs and a few MTFs in our sample mentioned how it had been useful for them to have submissive relationships with dominant biomales that they respected, in order to get over their issues with biomales in positions of power and to see positive male role models in action. Sometimes this was in response to earlier abuse, as Siobhan Phoenix relates: "I have found the need to submit towards men in my life more strongly. I think this is about processing the trauma of my younger life of being locked up and abused by a group of men. I have started to let go of the knuckle-whitening control issues I have, but I have only explored this sparingly so far."

Healing can also come from the dominant side of the equation. When I transitioned, I was immediately confronted with the spectre of my abusive father. I found a great deal of healing in "being the monster" in scenes with a former boy who liked ageplay but was more interested in the intensity of a scene with a mean Daddy than the comfort of a cuddly one. I found my experience echoed in reverse by transwoman Cordelia Shea Wynn: "I have a lot of mother issues. I spent years both wanting to be female and avoiding it because I thought I'd turn into my mother, and who wanted that? I prefer men sexually, so I avoided women and tried hard to be gay. I finally got over myself enough to have relationships with women friends (and one lover) who convinced me that there were many ways to be female, and not just the crazy abusive model I'd grown up hiding from. But something in my subconscious needed to deal with the fear of becoming my mom, even though I'm so not her. So I created an evil Mommy character, far worse than my Mom ever was, and played with a lot of subs who were into that and found it fun. It showed me that I could stop whenever I wanted, I was never out of control, I wasn't like my crazy mother. I only needed to do that for about a year during my transition, and then I was over the problem. But it really helped—much better than therapy!"

Transition and Master/slave Relationships

Other couples (or households) prefer a more formal master/slave situation. Crstlbella writes: "My trans partner is Master and I am his slave in our M/s relationship. We frequently use a God/priestess archetype as a short-hand for describing the relationship. We view this as a lifetime commitment and more. Our relationship is full-time, 24/7, and, at the moment it is a live-in arrangement. I do not believe my Master's trans status has changed how I react to him; however, his confidence and level of comfort in his body have grown as he has transitioned and I have found that *these* changes have helped me to see him as more my Master than before. I believe that his experience living in the world of women has made him much more insightful as a Master, particularly as a Master of someone who is in a female body. He also seems to have a better understanding of the cultural differences between men and women as a result."

Her partner, Lord Tom, describes how their relationship changed to a more formal and distant M/s dynamic: "We both realized, after a few years of marriage, that we needed to break out of the more vanilla 'in love' stage, the 'Hi honey, I'm home!' routine that was a little too familiar for our liking. While that sort of relationship is perfectly fine for some, we knew we could no longer be close in an informal way as partners in equal roles. Now that we have more distance in the power dynamic, we are closer in other ways. It is more satisfying than any relationship I have ever been in. The choices we made are not without sacrifice, but those sacrifices are worth it and we would not have it any other way."

Cordelia Shea Wynn relates: "I know that some people are going to say that something's wrong with me, or that my behavior isn't very 'feminine', but I am not terribly interested in the kind of one-on-one relationship where two people are intimate and in each other's heads and business all the time. I had that with a wonderful man once, he died, I'm in a different place in my life now. I am an artist and musician and performer, and my art and music is the great love of my life right now. So I enjoy having submissives who serve me and give me sex and BDSM—I have three right now—but I am not sentimentally romantic with them. I'm the mistress, and they serve, and there is a formal distance that we both enjoy. It reinforces respect. I am not contemptuous of my male slaves like so many biofemale mistresses—I think that having lived as a man, and especially as a gay man, prevented that. I care about them, I am affectionate with them, I am protective of them. I like them as people or I wouldn't have them around. I'm not in love with them, and I don't believe that they are in love with me. When I need intimacy, I have two transwoman friends I talk to."

Ruth, the nontrans partner of three different transgendered partners, tells about her D/s relationship: "While not fully submissive by nature, I get as close as I will with my relationship with my Top. We have both, at different times, described our relationship in dog terms. I described it as being like a Lord's hunting dog; I spend much time ranging the woods, but always feel I am welcome to come to the manor and lay at his feet, adoring him.

While I am a half-wild beast, I am *his* dog, not yours. Once he gave me a similar description of how he viewed our interaction that delighted me—he saw me as a vicious dog who would obey him and lick his hand, but would rip *your* throat open if he allowed it. I suppose this would be why his term for me is fitting in so many different ways; I am his bitch, and will be as long as he will open the door when I show up and scratch at it. While our situation is not currently live-in, that may theoretically change in a few years. The distance is not long, but our interactions are not as frequent as either of us would like. I am always his bitch, whether near him or not, but I would say our relationship would be viewed by anyone outside my head as part-time."

Transitioning Paradigms

One of the most interesting questions answered in our surveys was the issue of whether transition changed people's orientation between dominant and submissive. About a third of my respondents (including most of the switches) reported that their gender presentation may have changed, but their preferred roles and activities didn't. BEAR A-M Rodgers says: "I am the same D/s orientation post-transition as I was pre-transition, no role changes. My partners relate to me the same, it is how they relate to themselves that may have changed. There is no 'new social gender role', no one assigned a role to me pre-transition."

His point about partners having to learn to relate to themselves as people in a relationship whose orientation is now seen as being different (and likely not what they expected) is a parallel issue. Many relationships have not survived the partner's transition because it meant they were now perceived as straight, or lesbian, or gay, or something that they felt didn't really describe their identity. Slave Anneke describes her mistress's struggle with the issue, paralleling her own:

> My lover and mistress was there for me all the way through my transition. She's basically a straight woman, although she makes exceptions—sort of a Kinsey 1—and it was hard for her to deal with my needing to become a woman. I think it might have been tempting for her to use

her authority over me to stop my transitioning, except that she saw how unhappy I was and she honestly wanted me to be better, and that's why I can trust her to have control over me. But it meant that we were seen as lesbians, and she had problems with that. Then she met straight mistresses who had girl-slaves too, and gay men with dyke-boys, and that helped.

It did mean that she brought in another slave who is male, and she had to do a lot of work with me to make sure I didn't think that I was being replaced. I was terrified for a while, but I like Bobby and it all settled out, and she's not getting rid of me—I'm alpha slave and see that Bobby is prepared for things. So now she is not a lesbian, but has a girl-slave and a boy-slave. It was just really important for her to be seen as a particular preference. But then, it's important to me to be seen as a woman! So if she can be good about my need, I can be good about hers, and we can compromise ... I think that the key was the fact that I was still her slave. Being her slave meant more than being her boyfriend or girlfriend. She's said, "You're my possession. It doesn't matter how you're redecorated, so long as you're still all mine." So the D/s was the anchor for our relationship when everything else went upside-down.

On the other hand, two-thirds of the respondents did find themselves flipping their orientation after transition. Some found that the amount of soul-searching they had to do in order to cleanly transition also extended itself to soul-searching activities, especially about the way that gender "ought" to be done with regard to power and surrender. Mik Kinkead says: "I have felt trapped by the paradigm that all masculine people should be dominant. I was always expected to be dominant even though I was much more aroused by being submissive or by playing roles where I got to equally dominate and be dominated."

Others found that hormones played a part, or that their resistance to roles that were closer to their hearts were affected by having the wrong bodies or having low self-esteem. The reasons were as colorful and varied as the demographic itself, and I give a selection of them in the following pages:

Before I transitioned, I identified entirely as a sub. But now that I've transitioned, I've discovered I'm much

more of a Domme. It has a lot more to do with me embracing myself as the powerful woman that I am. Before transition, that was impossible because I didn't like myself.
– Ashley Lynch

I was raised to be a successful and independent woman, and I strongly rejected the "housewife" role. Before transition, I refused to do more than "my share" of housework with my bio-male partner, and when I was financially supporting him, I expected him to keep house for me. It was like I couldn't be relax into being the submissive I wanted to be as long as I was female; it would be "letting the side down" in some way. (I wasn't even a feminist, but this feeling dogged me.) I'd tried to be submissive to a much older man when I was 15 (my master today tells me that this was sleazy, but at the time I was just flattered) but it didn't work out and I rejected the whole concept. So I was a loud-mouthed, dykey, aggressive woman who came off looking very dominant, and just did pervy sensation play in clubs. Me, do what people told me? Forget it.

After transitioning to male, I suddenly came down with the strong urge to submit and be of service. My male gender manifested sexually as a submissive gay boy, and I found myself poring over books of formal etiquette and dreaming of serving a master. Becoming male gave me the freedom to express my innate submissive nature; with a masculine-presenting body I was ironically much more comfortable settling in to a submissive "housewife" role. I was being my authentic self, both in gender and in role, and it was still transgressive! What more could I ask for?

Also, the process of socially transitioning made me so much more aware of the gender-based inequalities in my life. I had thought my relationship with my partner of that time was free of that, but it was amazing how transition highlighted all these assumptions and patterns that I couldn't see.

I still remained primarily attracted to men, and wanted very much to be part of the gay leather scene. I wanted to immerse myself in a fully masculine role, and I wanted very much to be accepted sexually as a man by other men. However, before I had much opportunity to explore that, I entered into the service of an FTM master. I moved away from the city and have very limited involvement with the gay or leather scene. I think that having an FTM master is very good for me, because it helped me to accept my body as it is, and allowed me to settle into a more comfortable gender identity. I worry that if I had gotten involved with a biomale dominant, I would have had a lot more trouble accepting that my body will never be 100% male. – Joshua

Yeah, when I was first contemplating transition, I had an idea that I wanted to be someone's slave and live in chains at their feet. That was partly reading too much porn—I'm amazed at how much I absorbed from bad crossdressing and kink porn and had to deprogram myself of later—and partly because I was scared. I looked at the outside world and my chances in it as a non-passing (and I knew from my body and face that I was unlikely to pass) transsexual and they terrified me. I saw people in my support group tell their horror stories of lost jobs, lost housing, unemployment, ridicule, violence on the street ... of course some vague idea of sex slavery sounded better than that! Prince Charming in black leather, come to rescue me from social oppression. And yeah, I sort of tried it, awkwardly ... and I found out that it wasn't what I wanted. I'm not submissive enough, and anyway once I'd transitioned and had a decent job and apartment (luckier than many!) and I was over the terrifying part, it stopped turning me on so much.

Now I'm a Mistress, and it's much more my style. I was afraid that being dominant would be seen as being unfeminine, that part of the masculine habits I had to unlearn was getting rid of assertiveness and (especially) aggressiveness. Like no one would take me seriously as female if I wasn't a shrinking violet; I'd have to choose between expressing my femininity or expressing my dominance. I feared that any attempt to act dominant (especially as I don't pass completely and never will, I'm too big and masculine-featured) would just make people think, "Oh, that's really a man pretending to me a woman—and not doing a very good job of it!" And, to tell the truth, that wasn't unfounded, it happened a lot. I had to get past the point of caring. I had to be secure in who I was and not need that outward validation. Getting a slave (or three) who saw me as I am really helped. – Cordelia Shea Wynn

I started BDSM very young, in my teens. At the time I was attempting to buy friendship and connection, and I played out the submissive role as the 'coin' I had available to purchase those things. It wasn't something I especially wanted to do, but I felt that I had to, or no one would like me or find me desirable. Over time I became more switchy, as I grew a bit and realized that you can't purchase what I was looking for. I settled firmly into a dominant role in my 20s and I've remained there since then. – Netdancer

My D/s orientation changed from a part-time switch to a full-time Master and Dominant. Part of this change with my transition happened because I am more comfortable with myself, and the other part is hormone-related. When I began to feel the full effects of testosterone, it was a profound awakening. Testosterone helps me think more clearly, contributes to my ability to make quick decisions, gives me more energy ... there's an edge to me now that I didn't have before. Overall, testosterone has contributed to my dominance. I'm not saying this is how it affects everyone, but it certainly pushed me in one direction over the other. My slave treats me differently now and respects me more because I am more sure of myself and I have direction in life.

When it comes to what my "new" social gender assigns, I must say it is interesting how people see me as the dominant now, and they didn't when I appeared female. Sometimes this is a good thing, other times people mistake me for a chauvinist when we are out in public and I speak for my wife. The social roles are still new to me but I am aware I have to be conscious of how I present myself in public. Today people tend to frown upon blatantly dominant heterosexual men.–Lord Tom

My D/s orientation shifted completely after transition. I have not served anyone. There are probably two reasons; first, my nearly four years of service to my previous partner ended in very damaging ways, and secondly, during my transition I found myself identifying more in the role of a top. What has evolved over time is my understanding of myself as a Top. I have learned new ways to get him to do the things that I want without having to constantly keep after him to do those things. – E. Nelly

Personally, the more I play with masculinity, the more I have explored my dominant side, and have less and less interest in being submissive. However, I also think this is tied to me getting older and more disabled. I feel in some way I've earned the privilege of being served, of having people who want to do for me what I've done for others over time. But I'd be dishonest if I didn't admit that being seen as a dominant in my community is linked to how I feel about my masculinity as well. – Del

My first attempt at being a master was with a transwoman who told me that she wanted to be a slave. It was great at first—I dominated, she swooned, I ordered, she did it. I was on top of the world—look, I had a slave! It filled something in me I didn't know was there, some hollow I hadn't noticed yet. She had a lot of self-esteem issues, and of course as a good master and lover I did my damnedest to help her with that, to build her up. It worked. It worked so well that one day she told me that she was no longer interested in submitting. It had made her feel safe when she had no confidence, it had made her feel like she belonged when she had no family, it was a position she felt she couldn't do better than, and of course it was hot. When I'd fixed the first three, she didn't need it any more. After surgery her libido crashed and our sex life—by that time egalitarian—fell apart. We parted amicably, and I went looking for someone who wanted the position for real, soul-deep reasons. Still, I meet a lot of transwomen who romanticize being a slave, and I wonder if their reasons are like hers. I want to say to them, "Get your life together, do something meaningful, get therapy, get your self-esteem up, and then see if you still want this." It has to be done for the right reasons or not at all. – Ian MacAlister, nontrans partner

Justin muses thoughtfully about his experience of being a slave who has changed gender: "My D/s roles and desires don't feel to me like they were impacted at all by my transition. However, I am significantly more comfortable as a male slave than as a female slave. I think that it feels freer to chart my own path about what slavery looks like, rather than worrying that I am simply falling into or becoming a sexist stereotype. I feel like I have a better sense of being grounded in the strength of my submission this way, probably in large part because I am so much more comfortable in my own skin. It would be naïve, though, to not recognize the ways in which society demeans men who are not in charge. It is significantly more comfortable for me to be around gay Masters and slaves, where male dominance and submission are equally seen, as it is in the straight community, where it often feels skewed towards dominant men and submissive women."

It's not lost on me, reading these and the other descriptions of transgendered people and their D/s orientations, that we as a community completely scramble the hoary theories of male dominance and female submissiveness as biologically hardwired. First of all, if such theories were true, how would we fall into them, ideally? Who would count as "male" and thus be "hardwired" to be dominant—the MTF who was born and raised physically male, or the FTM with the masculinized brain who ends up there? The same thing could be argued in reverse for "females" who would supposedly end up submissive. The truth is that we are all over the spectrum. There seem to be more submissives than dominants—in both genders—but anyone who's been in a mixed BDSM community will admit that this is true for both men and women. There is a surprising amount of switching back and forth over the line during transition, for a variety of reasons. Our existence and the truth of our behavior answers the theories by saying, "It's not nearly that simple." Of course, it is also not lost on me that many of the individuals who hold these theories most closely would strongly prefer that we not exist at all.

Dysphoria and Sexual Control

Some participants described their power dynamic relationships in highly sexual terms, but others talked about contexts that were nonsexual, or where sex was relegated to a back seat. Jonathan wrote: "I've had a few FTM boys (and one MTF girl) in service to me and we didn't have sex. In some cases we did nonsexual S/M, and certainly I would have welcomed sex with any of them if they had wanted it, but the point of the relationship was to give them a place to serve that was entirely safe. For them, their sex life was in such confusion from the dysphoria that there wasn't any such thing as safe sex, emotionally speaking. Not pressuring them for it was the best thing I could do for them. We were affectionate, but pants stayed on. I've been there, I've had those days, so I understood."

E. Nelly describes his boy's routine and emphasizes its practicality rather than romanticism:

> I have a mostly 24/7 D/s relationship with my current boy. We have negotiated a contract which has not yet been signed because the boy is not willing to give up his paycheck or smoking entirely. The boy works outside of the home but has been tasked with numerous duties including both personal and domestic services. We began using a system of rewards and punishments which included a chore chart to clarify expectations as well as a way to provide meaning to his work. Over time we have phased the heavy rewards system out. I wanted to initially provide those rewards so that he felt valued and appreciate which was a major issue from his previous relationship. He is now in charge of creating his own chore chart based on the season and executing those chores in a timely fashion. We do share some of the house duties, but there are specific tasks which are exclusively his.
>
> My boy certainly feels owned by me and knows that serving someone else is on a "permission only basis." It was important to me in the beginning that he became fully engulfed in service. His work outside of the home is based on service to adults with developmental disabilities. His time at home is dedicated to domestic and personal service. My boy is not a sexual servant. I am not particularly interested in that type of service. He is responsible for my sexual satisfaction but his primary service role is not sexual.

Some participants who lived as slaves or submissives described the practice of chastity or sexual limitations in glowing terms. For them, having a controlling partner place limits on their sexual expression helped them to avoid the social pressure of sexual contact and the risk of having an attack of dysphoria in the bed of some unwitting date. When one is facing down body dysphoria, partial or even complete chastity can look like a good thing. Finn in Germany extols the contract between himself and his mistress as a saving grace:

> She is my Mistress, and I am her special, devoted boy; this fortuitous situation affords us both not only sexual arousal but also profound happiness and harmony ... Another new, but central aspect of our relationship is that of chastity in relation to orgasm, which may seem incongruous to a polyamorous relationship but which has allowed me a great freedom. I frequently become despondent about the difficulty I experience in reaching orgasm, or the depression into which I sometimes fall after having done so. Therefore, we have agreed that my orgasms will subsequently be under her control, a fact symbolized by my wearing of a bracelet which represents a conceptual chastity belt. Each time I glance at this bracelet on my wrist, I experience a wonderful jolt of excitement; this keeps me in a permanent state of arousal, and encourages greater productivity. Since orgasming for me is now a reward, and often an infrequent one, I am keen to serve my Mistress to the best of my ability and constantly think of new ways to impress her. I have abandoned my former sexual selfishness and devoted my energies to pleasuring her; from which I in turn receive great satisfaction. The relationship has already caused my confidence and understanding of myself to develop with a shocking and profound rapidity, which in turn has generated a positivity about my body and its sexual capacity which I previously thought impossible.

Similarly, Joshua finds the external limitations set on his sexual behavior to be a comfort:

Early in my transition, I felt pretty good about my masculinizing body, but worried about how people would relate to my still-female genitals. I was reliably passing as male socially, but nude was a different story. I had previously enjoyed a lot of casual sex and SM play in situations where there was extremely minimal conversation or negotiation beforehand. I played primarily with men, and they tended to assume that I wanted vaginal penetration unless I made it really clear. While I did enjoy vaginal penetration, I felt like I was in an uncomfortably female role when it was the assumed default activity, rather than one option among many. I wondered, how can I clearly communicate this to a casual partner in a way that feels natural and comfortable to me? I was heavily into the body modification scene, so I decided to get three pairs of deep labial piercings. I could wear one ring through each pair, as a sort of self-imposed chastity device. It would be a way to non-verbally communicate that vaginal penetration was "off limits" without discouraging other genital stimulation. I had grown quite a nice phallus with testosterone. I didn't want partners to feel like they had to be "careful" to avoid certain types of play (people are hesitant enough with unfamiliar genitalia!) and I didn't want to have to worry about whether I could trust them to not to misread my enthusiasm for another activity as consent for penetration. They could do whatever the obvious physical limitation would allow, and if I really wanted vaginal penetration I could remove the rings. As someone who has never considered phalloplasty to be an option, this was also a way of making my genitals into something different than the ordinary female equipment. I thought it was a great idea.

But before I had a chance to implement this clever plan, I got involved with my master. I moved from the city to a rural area, and opportunities for easy casual sex plummeted. Even when a chance presented itself, my master made it clear that my former rampant promiscuity was no longer a real option for me. I could play with other people, but no penetration or even any genital contact of any sort (that was reserved for him), and they had to talk to him first. He didn't want rings getting in the way of rough fucking, and neither did I. And interestingly, once I stopped having so much casual sex with strangers, I no longer thought of my genitals as part of my "public" gender presentation. During the same time period, physically I went from being someone who was *almost* always read as male, so long as I was careful about my presentation, to someone who couldn't pass as female even if I tried. In light of all that, my master vetoed the genital piercings as being unnecessary and redundant. The "invisible chastity harness" was enough. (Plus we do have a real one, just for fun, that he has locked me into before sending me off to have casual sex.)

On the rare occasions that I do have casual sex, my off-limits genitals aren't even an issue, which is a big relief. My master has done a huge amount of work to help me to open up and be less emotionally guarded, and as a side effect, certain types of sex can put me in a fairly vulnerable place emotionally. Going there with my master is a wonderful thing, but I wouldn't want to do that with just anybody. Since I got involved with my master, I have not had a single casual sex encounter that triggered uncomfortable feelings about my body or gender. Sexual limits can be very freeing when your sexuality is an emotional minefield. – Joshua

Service and Control

One of the interesting divisions we've found while interviewing and counseling D/s and M/s people over the years is that there seems to be two main motivations for submissives— serving, or being controlled. Similarly, the matching motivations for dominants are controlling or being served. Some are all about one or the other (although submissives may be forced to do their less favorite one), and some enjoy both. In the general BDSM community, the primarily control-oriented submissives seem to greatly outnumber the primarily service-oriented submissives. In our dealings with the transgender demographic, we did find some purely control-oriented people on the bottom side; Sassafras Lowrey tells us that: "Honestly, my primary interest is in being controlled. It offers me a sense of safety, and happiness, and also, is incredibly grounding for me. That said, service is something that I work to find pleasure and interest in. Boot blacking is one example of service that has really spoken to me, and that I have under my Daddy's guidance explored. I work hard to excel and prioritize service, because I believe it's important though it is not my primary motivation."

The great majority of the submissives in our sample, however, were surprisingly service-oriented regardless of whether they were FTM or MTF. Joshua spoke for many of the submissives in the sample when he says, "I enjoy being controlled, but service is what is really fulfilling to me. I need to feel useful." This puts our small sample in an interesting juxtaposition to the majority of D/s practitioners. The reasons for this anomaly are anyone's guess.

Similarly, a few dominants preferred control. Ashley Lynch says, "I like the control aspect the best. When someone gives that trust to you, it's exhilarating!" Lord Tom says poetically about his desire for control: "The idea of controlling someone else who submitted to me turned me on when nothing else would. I am a writer and a lover of stories, and I drew from artistic and literary instances of power exchange. To me, such stories in which one person vows to protect the other, where fealty is sworn, when the person is taken by force and ends up loving it, these are all romantic. Now that I practice BDSM daily, I also realize it is a consensual and relatively safe outlet for my darker proclivities … Being served is an integral part of my M/s relationship, but what really turns me on is controlling my partner. I love being able to tell her what to do, and she will do anything I say. With that ability to control comes enormous responsibility, but I use that power wisely, in as many kinky ways as possible. We find this an exciting aspect of our dynamic. It leaves her breathless, and it makes me feel deliciously twisted. The power is a rush."

However, they were also in the minority; most seemed to be more inclined to service. Those who were or had been switches came up the same.

> It's all about being served. Very little of our relationship is about control. Much of my disabled status has led to the service interest for me. – Siobhan Phoenix

> As a submissive I think I prefer the idea of service. While I do sometimes fantasize about being controlled, and having some elements of control are important in my submission, I recognize that what I am really looking for is structure in ways I can serve and be of service. As a dominant, I think I look primarily for service there as well. Though control is important, but not in so much rules or protocol. I like to use my dominance as a means to help build up and improve the submissive I am working with. And to that extent, I exert control of things like how they talk about themselves or how they confront situations.
> – Sable Twilight

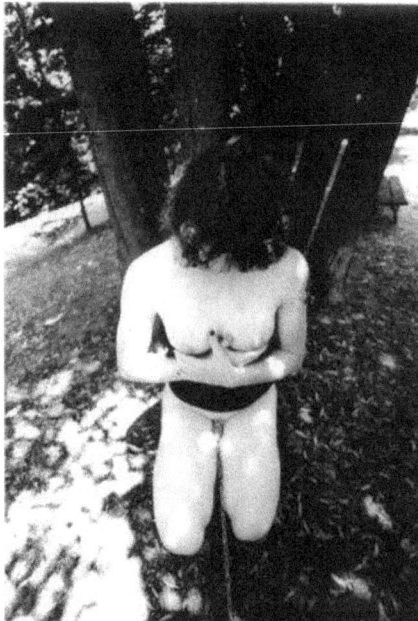

> I'm interested in service and being served. I don't like control, even more if it's taking control over the

partner's sexual life, or to be controlled in my own sexual life. – VioletErotica Ita

I find service infinitely fulfilling and it is a stronger motivation for me. However, being controlled can be a powerful and beautiful thing. It does seem to me that the socialization that I received as a female child and young person prepared me to be a different kind of male slave. I was taught to be attentive to the needs of men, that women should engage in what we'd call domestic service, that deference to a man's wishes is desirable. (My mother was very traditional in her understanding of gender roles; my father is not.) I think that there are some gay male Masters who find this kind of attention to detail and attention to them very pleasing from another man and that it is different from what they may encounter in men who are socialized as men. – Justin

I love, absolutely love, being served. Even something as small as a cup of coffee being made for me gives me a warm feeling, the knowledge that I am loved. I don't need to apply as much sheer "control" pressure to C as I once did; as his self-destructive tendencies have waned as he has become happier and more self-assured about himself and his place in the world. I still find it erotic to give orders and see them obeyed, to be able to drop him with just my voice alone. I don't think that will ever change.
– Netdancer

Some, like E. Nelly and Slave Anneke, are clear about finding both fairly equally important:

The appeal as a bottom was definitely about the attention and the service—I was a detail oriented service slut. I loved the guidance and direction my life had with the care of a loving dominant. As a top now, the appeal is not all that different; I have a service boy and that service is an expression of his love, devotion, and loyalty to me. I love the type of love that we share which is distinctly different than vanilla love, or vanilla love as I understand it. There is a bit of a parental love that exists between us, there is love as a Dominant and submissive, and there is a love as partners. There is a closeness that we share that could not be shared unless we have the type of relationship that we do. I love sharing different types of love, which can only come about when a relationship takes on a certain form.

But when I think about the root of my BDSM, I come to the idea of control. I love control and when I am in service, I love to give up control—total control. There is so much socialization about what control is appropriate to relinquish and what is not. As a submissive, overcoming that socialization is far more challenging than whatever task I have been assigned. I am also intrigued by what the long term affects control and behavior modification have on others. I am also intrigued by pain and punishment. Managing pain, addressing punishment, and vulnerability are all issues I am currently exploring through BDSM. As a top though—I am also fascinated with control. I want to get as close to full control as possible. – E. Nelly

At first it was all about control for me, because the gender dysphoria made me feel so out of control of my life. I tried to use slavery as a way to ignore those feelings, and then when I couldn't do it anymore, as a way to have someone else say how it should be done. Once I transitioned, though—big sigh of relief for my soul!— service came to be just as important. I now have a new appreciation for service. It makes me feel useful and good about myself. Before, I couldn't feel good about myself no matter what I did, so the delight of a job well done and pleasing my Mistress in a way that no one else could, that was kind of lost on me. I had to be forced into everything because my soul was miserable and balked at doing anything, and I needed the cattle prod to feel alive and move at all. Now I am myself, and I have myself to give, and I can now give freely and serve. – Slave Anneke

Public Assumptions

When these power-dynamic relationships are enacted in public BDSM communities, they face whatever biases and assumptions are endemic to that particular corner of the world. Non-trans masters/mistresses and slaves have complained about assumptions made by community members on the basis of gender, size, and presentation for years. The most common complaints are dominant women being assumed to be other than dominant if they are not arrayed in stereotypical fetish gear, and large, burly male submissives being assumed to be dominant. It's par for the course for people to try to guess if someone is dominant or submissive, and not only for the purpose of attempting to hit on them. In some demographics (and in the internal worlds of some D/s couples) there are appropriate and inappropriate ways to approach or speak to someone who might be an owned slave, for example. Most people simply don't want to offend, so they watch and make assumptions based on whatever information they can glean and whatever personal biases they may have. When the participants have mixed gender cues, it can create confusion, especially among people not used to transgender as a working concept. Brianna Ahava Morrigan points out that: "I haven't experienced problems with being taken seriously in *my* preferred role per se, but I have on occasion had to correct or clarify to people when they see my Mistress and myself. At times, from an initial look, they assume she is the submissive and I am the dominant before that can be corrected, because of our body types. Mistress has a lithe and willowy build and I on the other hand have a very voluptuous and broader look."

Similarly, TransPunk has been misinterpreted, but gets the best of the situation: "I have experienced a few problems, as I am read as young and cute a lot and not taken seriously as a Master. (By now I have started to refer to myself jokingly as 'the cute Master'.) People still assume due to my being much smaller than my bottoms (my slave is two heads taller than me and my warrior also taller and much bulkier than me), that I have to be the bottom. When we start playing and these two big tall guys kneel in front of me mouths drop open all around us, which makes us snicker. But this refers only to strangers and idiots, not to my inner circle and my play partners. Sometimes out of ignorance men don't get how I could be Master without a bio-dick, but again, this does not apply to the bottoms I end up with, who I screen beforehand."

Confusion runs rampant when someone changes roles, whether that is a long-term change after a different long-term identity, or simply switching from day to day. People may fall back on gender stereotypes, typified by Sejay's remarking, "As a sub, I often get referred to as 'she' against my wishes, even after reminders.

But as a dom, I am always called Sir." Some spectators who are stuck in male-dominant/female submissive worldviews may also see all transgendered people as some sort of female—MTFs, in their view, "gave up" being male and are thus no better than female, while FTMs are really still women. This may mean that they file all transfolk mentally as submissives, and have a hard time taking them seriously as dominants. Joshua echoes: "I don't think FTMs have trouble being taken seriously as submissives. I can see how it might be a problem with some straight female dominants who do the female-superiority thing, though, because we rejected the female role."

Sassafras Lowrey tells of the difficulties with a frequently changing identity in the public eye:

> Over the course of my relationship with my Daddy my gender has shifted, the most major instance being my quitting T for the final time. It was then that I admitting to myself and to him that I wanted to begin playing with gender by being transgressively feminine instead of in masculine ways, but that I was still a boy. I'm incredibly blessed to have a Daddy/life partner who loves and values my gender exploration and who has been my support every step of that. My transition to femme happened right before our relationship transitioned to 24/7 and I found the D/s to be very comforting during this complicated time, though my D/s orientation did not change nor did my role. My gender is "femme" and I transitioned here from genderqueer FTM so for me there isn't really a "traditional D/s role" assigned to my current gender in the most traditional of senses. That said, there is a larger queer community assumption that all femmes are submissive, whereas when I was read as transmasculine it was not assumed that based my gender identity had any bearing on my D/s orientation. This is an issue that a lot of femmes I know grapple with, especially those who are tops and who struggle to be respected as such. It's extra complicated for me because I am 100% submissive, and so I have to grapple with my orientation being part of the stereotype of what my gender is "supposed" to do.

On the other hand, some transgendered dominants have no trouble with community perceptions. BEAR A-M Rodgers says,

"Even when my Trans status is disclosed there is no question or ridicule of my Dominant role. I may be discriminated against for being Trans but they still understand and accept I am a male Dom." In some demographics, transitioning can even bring a solidifying of and new respect for one's identity, depending on the direction of proclivity and the ideals of that community. Lord Tom says, "Most people take me more seriously now than they did pre-transition. They see my transition as a courageous act by a person who truly knows what he wants. They see what kind of man I am, and the key is in my quiet confidence and inner strength. I am unashamed to be myself, and people have told me they admire that."

It would be naïve to say that a transgendered lover isn't something of a social stigma for a nontrans partner, even if that's an unfair situation that shouldn't exist. When a nontrans individual makes a commitment to a transgendered lover, they're not unaware of the social risks that they take, and the way that their choice will be seen. For some, it's too much; for others, loyalty in the face of all disapproval becomes a stubborn, immovable shield against the opinions of others. That includes people in the BDSM communities who might make assumptions about power dynamics from the outside. Ian MacAlister points out: "Look, I'm a pervert. No matter what kind of relationship I have, someone's going to disapprove. So I might as well do what I want, and what my partner wants. Doing BDSM, being a master, being queer, being into my transgendered lover … I can't purge myself of all of those anyway without going mad, so why should I hold back on any one of them? BDSM taught me that there's no going back. You are who you are, just go with it and fuck 'em all."

TransPunk speaks of his biomale partners in a similar vein:

> Sometimes my transsexuality connects in a secondary way with my being a Master—e.g. after my chest surgery, my slave took care of me (and my parents). We both found that to be a suitable D/s dynamic. My slave and warrior both know they are supposed to switch to guard dogs in the event someone lashes out with transphobia at me. They would defend their Master; sometimes they even see me as superior due to my third gender status. And it fits well with my status as Master

that I can have multiple orgasms while they are only allowed to come off and on at my command (when in protocol). It enhances the sexual service situation and makes me look more potent. In general, my bottoms use the D/s to reaffirm my masculine status, e.g. through worshipping my beautiful chest or my clit-dick or praising my everlasting hard-on (while strapping on).

In the end, however, it is the responsibility of the observed to communicate their identities to the audience, if they value that audience's opinions and reactions. Calm confidence in one's role is the best solution, better than strident overcompensation that may come off as insecure and add to the problem. As Ashley Lynch points out, "I've experienced more internal problems in my intense need to be taken seriously than I've ever experienced problems due to other people. Often we're our own worst enemies."

Dirty Secrets:
Seeing Each Other

The most controversial part of my survey was where I asked people to make comments—general or specific, snarky or nonjudgmental, it didn't matter—about how they saw people in the scene who inhabited D/s roles in different gender combinations, and how they believed that other people in the scene saw those combinations. I realized, when I put that in, that some people would not be comfortable with making those judgments—at least, not where people could see it. Saying, "How do you think people in the BDSM scene tend to see this sort of person?" or even "How do you, personally, see this sort of person?" is not something that most feel is useful conversation ... unless, of course, we're gossiping over a few beers at the bar.

The truth is that we all have assumptions about these BDSM subgroups, and assumptions about other people's assumptions. We all talk about them when we think that no one's listening, and bitch about them on Internet lists, and make great sweeping generalizations about them. Of course it's a problem, of course it's not fair ... but like all such problems, if we don't drag it out onto the table and look at it, it's not going to go away. These sorts of assumptions never die when ignored and kept in darkness. They thrive on that. It's the light of day that starts to wither them.

It was also very interesting to see the comments about transfolk who fall into these categories ... and how many other transfolk sadly said, "I've never met one of these. I'm the only transgendered person in my local group, or for miles around as far as I know." (All right, so who's going to hold the first Double Edge conference, and how many local BDSM groups will sponsor out their one lone transgendered member as a representative?) My heart went out to them. While there are more and more of us all the time, while our numbers keep rising (especially among young people), there are still not enough of us to be there for the rural tranny in the middle of nowhere in the underpopulated state, and too often it's the BDSM group where they turn instead of a nonexistent local trans community. We don't all live in San Francisco, after all.

So how do we see each other—or think we see each other? About half of my respondents declined to answer these questions, not liking the idea of generalizing. A few others assumed that I was asking how sexually attractive they thought these different groups were, and answered accordingly. The remainder answered usefully, and I got some very interesting information.

The first category, and the most controversial all-round, was that of nontrans male dominants. Troublingly enough, most of the commentary was extremely negative. It seemed that nontrans dominant men were the most feared and reviled of all the categories, regardless of the gender (beginning or ending) or sexual preferences of the transfolk involved. Some of the comments included "…the roughest of all dominants, little aftercare compared to others," "…think their penis gives them the right to be Doms," "…more genitally focused than females," "Tough Guy, must be very self assured, tend to be loud and wanting to assume control of everything from a club meeting to who uses what bathroom."

E. Nelly was honest about his ambivalence with this population: "I think of the straight ones as pigs with big egos for the most part. I can't help but think they top women because they are misogynists. It's not always true, but I have met enough 'domly-doms' to know it is true some of the time. I think of them as the flashy flogging and whipping show, know-it-all types. I think of them as totally unaware of queer people, history and culture." Similarly, Sejay comments on how those traits can be seen as positive or negative by different people: "They are very confident in doing and/or asking for what they want, sometimes not even asking permission before doing it. And why not? They have all the privilege. It is difficult for some gender-role-savvy female assigned-at-birth individuals I know to trust these folks, at least initially, for the cultural assumption that allowing them to dominate reinforces the societal patriarchy; then again, some women find that really, really sexy."

TransPunk in Germany, like other FTMs, made a distinction between straight and gay nontrans topmen: "A majority of the straight ones seems to think they are on top beyond the consensual role and entitled to anything, but I'm not sure if that's just typically biomale, regardless of being a BDSM top … I usually stay away from them, though luckily there's great exceptions to the rule! The gay male ones I hang out with tend to be very caring and not so hung up about their masculinity. But I see plenty of guys around who mistake being assholes for being good tops."

While FTMs tended to cut gay men more slack, MTFs tended to paint both straight and gay with the same brush. Terra Katherine McKeown summed up both the stereotype and her own issues with it by saying, "I don't really like them, in general. Both because of my own trauma, but also because I think most cis-men don't look at their privilege at all. (Why would they want to, with all that power?) I think that they are bullies, annoyingly cocky, wield their privilege like a penis, are mostly insensitive, and (especially if they're gay men) openly hostile to just about everyone. They usually are way too harsh in their play, reluctant to scale it down if you complain or safeword. However, I have a handful of cis-men in my life who are absolutely not like this, examine their privilege regularly, and they are really fucking hot because of it. So I recognize my own damage around cis-men, and I try to own that … but I get reminded of male privilege every day, especially from the gay men in my life, and it's difficult to speak about my own issues through the gritted teeth."

Sable Twilight also spoke of her disappointment with nontrans dominant men as a MTF: "Most heterosexual cissexual male dominants are uninterested in transsexual women. I think they don't see transsexual women as potential mates. Homosexual cissexual male dominants are pretty much uninterested in transsexual women because of the whole femaleness thing. So over all, cissexual male dominants either don't see trans women as women, and so are not interested, or they do see them as women, and so are not interested. However, there are a handful of heterosexual cissexual male dominants who seem to like trans women. Overall, these men are pure gold for the trans women community. I wish there were more of them."

On the other hand, some respondents had good experiences with nontrans male dominants, and were willing to stand up for them. Del pointed out compassionately: "I think these guys get the worst rap of all people in the scene, period. People have all these stereotypes of 'Sir Lord High Domly-Dom' who expects everyone to kowtow to them, or that they're potential predators looking for some young thing to take advantage of. I can't think of one nice thing that's ever said about cisgendered male dominants, even in queer community." Ms. Jen commented that "Many have been quite nice to me, and are usually very respectful," and boy bailey suggested that he had "met several who are soft and caring despite hard exterior."

Blaise Garber-Paul had an easier time with straight biomale dominants: "Straight men are easier for me to negotiate with than gay men. I like watching the confusion in straight men, though generally they hit their stride pretty easily, as long as really they're queer underneath it all. I'm too furry for many of them to get confused about what they're dealing with. Bears are wonderful, older men seem to be more receptive, but I worry sometimes that that's because they think they couldn't catch a young guy unless there was a catch, which makes me feel a little demeaned, but it's probably just in my head."

Vidal Rousso proclaimed "Well, I like biomale dominants. Most of my experience comes from the leather gay world, though. Biomale dominants are the hardest to find, since they are also the hardest to accept that an FTM isn't a girl, but these are the people you can get the most rough, most adventurous, most primal sex from. Unfortunately I also think that this is the most conservative group."

It seems like in any public scene there are more nontrans men billing themselves as submissive than anyone else. This may be due to the fact that women are less willing to go to public events in general, and that there do seem to be more submissives than dominants in the scene. (Online, the numbers are somewhat reversed, as female submissives are more likely to be stay-at-homes with plenty of computer time and fewer inhibitions on discussing highly personal things, and tend to make up the majority of most online groups.) Of course, not all these men are subs per se; some are simply fetishists. But they all agree on one thing: they vastly outnumber the dominant women (and even the dominant gay and bisexual men) that they lust after, and most end up unpartnered and unable to find what they want. Comments about this population by the gender-savvy transfolk tended to concentrate on the difficulty of being raised male and having to break through that programming in order to embrace their submissive natures.

> It's hard to find true male submissives. Most can only handle it part time for short periods of time. The ones who are very submissive often don't want to admit it for fear of being seen as weak and taken advantage of.
> – Double-Edge

> They either think subbing to women is the ultimate kink, or subbing to men automatically means they are gay or lesser men. – BEAR A-M Rodgers

> For some reason it seems easier for people to consider them odd, weird, weak, sick, or perverted than male doms. – Sejay

> Gay ones tend to either struggle with their role or are very strong personalities. In my community, most gay guys switch. – TransPunk

> There are so many unattached male submissives that they often feel they have to be very assertive just to be noticed. This gets them seen as not submissive. Men aren't taught how to be gracefully submissive. Male upbringing gets in the way, too. Many of them need to feel strong control in order to keep their early programming in check. At least in the beginning. They challenge their dominants a lot until they have settled down. – Slave Anneke

> For the most part, I think that they are either hellions in their non-kink life (professional go-getters, for instance)

and are submissive because they have huge control issues (and also have the same hang-ups and annoyances that I spoke of in the previous section), or they are quiet, sensitive and *appear* to not really know what they want. Many of them do, however, but they are just quiet. – Terra Katherine McKeown

Most of them can be rather feminine in their expressions and body language, possibly trying to justify the submission with being feminine for the time being. I personally think that justification is unnecessary, for it is perfectly normal for a man to want to be submissive. Of course there are also just men who are submissive and feminine by nature, that's another business. It can also happen that the dominant has to *really* do all the work with these men. Simultaneously, for a dominant, some of them are the most beautiful things ever. – Vidal Rousso

Some transfolk had had negative experiences with them. VioletErotica Ita characterized them as "often boring and insistent"; Netdancer refers to them as "…extremely needy, many trying to top from the bottom", and boy bailey notes that they are "…often not able to put words to their interests." Sable Twilight is similarly ambivalent:

I'm going to talk primarily about those cissexual male submissive who are interested in playing with transsexual women. Most identify as straight, but seem to fetishize transsexual women for their genitals. Most seem hyper focused on the fantasy of being on the receiving end of penetrative sex. Another common fantasy I have seen is a desired to be feminized as well.

Others were more positive toward them than toward their dominant brothers. Ms. Jen says that "…Most I've known have been straight, and aren't really experienced. The few that have experience have been a joy to work with." E. Nelly says, "I think of them as usually being sweet and gentle boys, both straight and gay. I always assume straight guy subs are into domestic service and CBT. I also assume many straight male subs are into forced feminization or crossdressing." Blaise-Garber-Paul laughs, "I don't know what to do with them yet, but I'm figuring it out. Mostly I turn them into puppies."

Del sarcastically points out: "They exist? I mean, of course I know they exist, but outside of the gay community, people act as though they don't. In general, I find it interesting that we almost never see cisgendered male submissives as kink educators."

Nontrans female dominants are the rarest people in the BDSM scene, statistically anyway. Ironically, their very rarity puts them in high demand, and creates the atmosphere that allows many of them to charge money for domination as a service, or demand large sums of money from submissives. Not that all are professionals or require financial slavery by any means, but if they were more common in BDSM communities, the desperation that funds those activities might be lessened. Their reviews were somewhat more positive than their male brothers, but still somewhat ambivalent. VioletErotica Ita wrote dryly, "Here in Italy, most of them are overweight." Netdancer had "run into the man-hater stereotype a lot." BEAR A-M Rodgers growled that "the hetero ones usually have a chip on their shoulders, and the bisexual ones are usually latent hetero but find other girls kinky."

The comment about chips on shoulders can probably be put down to the fact that, as Cordelia Shea Wynn says, "Dominant women often have to walk a gamut of sexist male dominants who don't respect their dominance, entitled submissive men who want them to conform to their fantasies, and het couples pushing the tired old dogma of 'all men are dominant, all women just want to be slaves.' It's no wonder that they get sharp about it, although it can be wearing if they're overly defensive and that leaks into their play. The more high femme they are, the more defensive they may feel the need to be, and sometimes that ends up being meaner as well." As a positive correlation, TransPunk compliments them with "High femmes tend to be real hardcore players."

There was a strong division between butch and femme dommes in most comments, with one compassionate comment that "there doesn't seem to be any other images of female dominance for them to model themselves after." E. Nelly explored his mental images with: "I usually think of straight females as very sadistic, into corsets, and untouchable or distant. Gay female dominants are usually butch or extremely high femme in my mind and into leather, like the leatherdyke archetype."

Del wrote me about this population: "I think they get stereotyped as either for-pay dominatrixes or power-hungry cuckolders. Some go a little power crazy with titles like 'Goddess'. Think about it—if a cisgendered male dom wanted his subs to call him 'God', there'd be no end of eye rolling and accusations of chauvinistic behavior! There's a real overlooking of cisgendered female dominants who aren't lifestylers, and those who are the more 'mommy' type of dominant, rather than a harsh mistress."

Some FTMs liked nontrans female dommes, but felt that they would be turned down due to not wanting "stereotypical" activities with them. Boy bailey complained that they were "often very interested in CBT, which doesn't work as easily for transmen." Blaise related, "I have very limited play relationships with them. They seem to expect a lot of service, and I'm generally not inclined to serve women. Butch dom women generally trigger my gender issues."

Positive commentary on nontrans female dominants was fairly common, and included:

> "Most of them really have the air of domina, they are self-assured, queen-like, strong and blossoming women. They can have immense mental domination power while biomale dominants are working on more physical level. They are much less conservative and more open-minded than their male counterparts." – Vidal Rousso

> The Goddess's gift to humanity and submissives. Women who know what they want and like to be in charge. Many need a lot of training from other dominas in order to believe that it's really OK to be who they want to be. There are not enough of them. I see women all the time in the vanilla world who would be wonderful dominants, but they wouldn't want to be associated with "perverts". So they keep trying to find egalitarian partners and then fight

with them. I wish that more dominant women could find themselves. – Slave Anneke

> Most of the ones that I have met have all been down to earth, motherly types. I think they like being "bitches" (for fun) and of course get off on being sadistic (that's the point, right?) but that they generally fall into the stereotypically nurturing role. My first Mistress, however, was a lot like a cocky man (but more controlled and kinder in general) instead of this type, so I'm well aware it's a stereotype. I think there are a lot of control and trust issues that Dommes have, though, scarring perhaps from gender stereotyping in general. That's just my own conjecture, though. – Terra Katherine McKeown

Nontrans female submissives take a lot of heat outside most BDSM communities, either from predatory males who are looking for easy meat, or angry women who feel that they are "letting the side down" and making female independence look bad. While gay male subs may have a role (in some erotic and leather imagery) that allows them to be tough but submissive, female submission has nothing of the kind, except perhaps for butch dyke subs whose style is often lifted from gay male imagery. Del speaks of this problem: "The general perspective on cisgendered female submissives is that they're in abusive relationships, and can't stand up for their own rights, even when they protest that they chose this, and want it."

Comments about this population concentrated on how much they tried to identify with the stereotype of the helpless female, including "...needy and clingy, seeming to exaggerate the stereotypical 50's woman," "weak, silly, cute, sexy, small," "looking for a daddy type," and "heavily, negatively, influenced by dick waving Doms." MTF Double-Edge said sardonically, "Life has trained woman to be submissive throughout history and the trend is still relevant."

Ms. Jen says poignantly, "Many seem very unsure of themselves, almost lost. I get the feeling that some were looking for something completely different from BDSM, but this was the closest they could get. Just my take." Similarly, Ian MacAlister, a nontrans partner, comments, "I think that there are a lot of submissive women on the edges of the scene who are not all that kinky but are looking for an old-fashioned relationship, a man who will take care of them, but someone who is conscious about being dominant rather than just doing it unconsciously. You can only really find that in the BDSM scene, ironically, or else in some fringe religious groups. So they will put up with being kinky in order to get the relationship they want."

Others explored their perceptions in more depth:

> The straight female submissives I have met are usually very sweet, sometimes flaky, but usually toys or doll-type submissives. I think of them as femme. For queer female submissives, I almost always think of them as butch. – E. Nelly

> Many of the ones I know are giggly and fun-loving, almost to the point of being too "airheaded" to take care of themselves "because their top will do that for them." They all have shown that they have the capability of going beyond that, but they choose not to, perhaps because that's what's expected of them. Thankfully, that's only about half of them; the other half seem pretty grounded and down to earth, and are great self-advocates. If they are new to the scene, they generally have control and trust issues, but want to find a way of releasing them. If they aren't new, they really take BDSM as a way of liberating themselves and learning more about themselves. – Terra Katherine McKeown

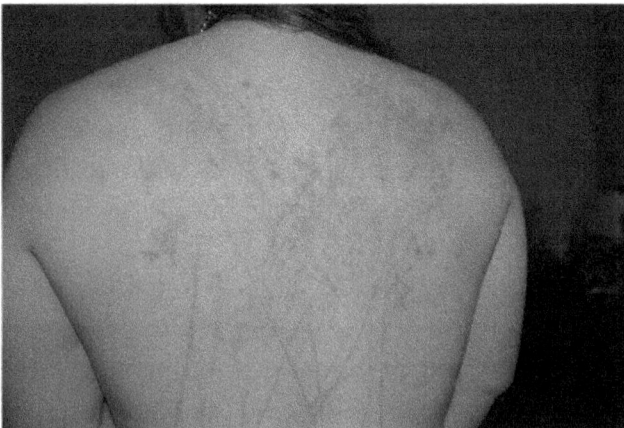

FTMs, in general, were less likely to desire nontrans female subs but more likely to find them easy to find partners among. Blaise exults, "Submissive dykes and queer women are fabulous, flexible, fun. They bring out the butch in me like nothing else." In contrast, most of the MTFs who responded were primarily interested in biowomen (and no, I don't know how I managed to get all the lesbian-identified MTFs and so few of the straight-identified ones) but less able to find ones, especially in the submissive population, who would accept them. Sable Twilight points out that: "Most cissexual female submissives are interested in either cissexual men or cissexual women. Again, being transsexual eliminates one as a potential candidate for scening. The handful of bisexual cissexual female submissives who enjoy playing with trans women are real gems."

There was sketchier information on how we tend to see each other, due to the fact that many of us hadn't ever met people in one or more of the four transgendered/power exchange categories that I listed. There were a significant number of MTFs who had never met an FTM; high concentrations of FTMs in kink groups tended to be an urban phenomenon as far as I could tell from my limited survey. Since women are less likely than men to take part in the public scene, this may be an area where female upbringing affects that statistic, at least in non-urban areas where an FTM may be solitary. There is also the possibility that more MTFs get involved with the scene as initial cross-dressers, and FTMs who cross-dress tend to be reluctant to identify with that in public. It may also be that FTMs tend to stick to lesbian leather groups, regardless of actual sexual preferences, rather than pansexual groups during their pre-trans-identification periods (and even afterwards in some cases). It may take them longer to transition into pansexual space, if they ever do (some attempt to go straight to gay male space). However, as with all things, this is conjecture and not to be taken as an across-the-board situation.

Transman dominants were the first trans category. Del wrote of them, "There's a perception that FTM dominants are overcome by their newly found male privilege and take it to the bedroom in the guise of SM," and this stereotype was borne out by the comments of others: "Sometimes overcompensate and act like the worst of bio-male dominants." "Often feel like they have something to prove when out in public." "Exercising their projected manhood; very often can only dominate biofemales and other FTMs." "I only know one, and he is the poster child for the classic 'Napoleon Complex'." Terra Katherine McKeown comments:

> Hot. Oh, sorry, that's not helpful, is it? Early in transition, I have noted that there's a desire and impulse to be as stereotypically male as possible, so there's a lot of cockiness and carelessness that seems to crop up. I have noted that many, however, seem to find more balance after a few years and tend to be some of the strongest-yet-sensitive tops I've ever played with. Sometimes, though, there are insecurities about being sensitive and it being equated with femininity, and I have often not commented at all, because I don't *believe* that, but also because it's something they have to figure out for themselves. Most of the FTM Doms that I've met are very insightful and strive to be as balanced as possible.

Several people referred to them positively as male-identified, male-looking people who had the fortunate trait of not having been conditioned into repressing their emotions. Double-Edge enthused, "Some of my favorite people. Men with feelings!" Others made reference to their supposed proclivities; Sable Twilight mentions, "Sadly, I've not had much direct with trans men dominants. Most I've seen in scene space seem primarily interested in cissexual woman, other trans men or, on occasion, gay cissexual men." As an FTM himself, Blaise muses, "I've played with many, but with most I find we bring the switch out in each other. I find it fascinating to watch all the assumptions we make about each other, assuming that since we're both FTM we've experienced the same things in the world, or even had the same experience of gender."

Sejay wryly sums up the three general perceptions he's noticed about FTM dominants: "(A) 'Cute'; not taken seriously as male or as a dom or both. (B) 'hot'; eroticized and a rare commodity in the

BDSM scene. Or (C) invisible, and appear to have a lot on their mind; guarded and aloof."

I once had a conversation about submissive transmen with a noted nontrans gay dominant and presenter, and he said that in his experience they were some of the most service-oriented people he'd ever met ... and really, really into bootblacking. While I've certainly met some FTM subs who were neither, it was an observation that I've heard again since, repeatedly. Ian MacAlister, a nontrans partner, commented, "I think that transboys really want to be seen as useful, possibly because they were told that being ornamental was so important when they were girls, possibly because they know that they are at a disadvantage in the meat market and they want something extra to offer."

At any rate, my respondents concentrated on the dilemma they had seen FTM subs struggle with over the dichotomy of being seen as male and simultaneously being seen as submissive. The hallmarks of submissive behavior are, in some cultures and some people's minds, something that is associated with femininity. For biomale subs (especially heterosexual ones, as gay male subs have more of an accepted role as submissive but still masculine) this often ends up with them exploring limited femininity in order to figure out the boundaries of that dichotomy. For many FTMs, who have had all the forced feminization they can stand, thank you (although there are a few who engage in forced-femme as a post-transition fetish just because it's forbidden), that's not a direction that they are willing to go in. Some struggle with the problem, some find solace in more "manly" gay male submissive roles, and some simply don't mind being seen as effeminate. Vidal Rousso points out that: "My perception is that they can be more lively, open and active than biomale submissives; also they tend to be more masculine. Unfortunately many of them have a problem with acceptance of their body which makes things more complicated and emotionally harder for both them and their partners."

Many of the comments about them played on this theme: "They try too hard to be manly, when their natural demeanor is quite enough." "Oddly, I have seen many 'sissy' boys here." "Seen as 'cute'; male identity is taken as playful more than serious." "They're seen as incomplete, because real men aren't submissive." "They tend to be playful and faerie-like." Ironically, one FTM dominant commented that: "They are probably more free to express their needs than FTM Doms."

TransPunk comments that "Most of the transfags seem to be submissive and more on the 'boy' side." It is true that a "boy" identity can be a real asset to an FTM who is early in their transition and still learning about masculinity, in the way that a biomale teenager might. Since FTMs also look younger, the title can seem more plausible than a more authoritarian one. It is also an asset to the FTMs I've talked to who are pushed by their brain wiring to live as male, but who are so ambivalent about men and manhood, largely due to bad experiences with nontrans men in their childhoods, that they prefer to identify as a boy rather than as an adult man. Of these, most remain submissive or switch with other boy-types or girl-types; it's very hard to be taken seriously as a dominant when you are identifying as a youth, except by someone else who also identifies that way. Older FTM submissives who still identify as "boy" have mentioned that they think of the label not as an ageplay marker but as a servant-marker, as in the "houseboy" or "stableboy" who might be any age but are referred to in that way as a class diminutive.

There were several comments regarding the self-assumed FTM labels of "boy" and "boi", the latter of which was coined by some transmasculine-spectrum individuals to specify boy-identified people who were not biomen. It's a label that some FTM transsexuals reject—one snarked that it "I keep thinking it should be pronounced 'bwah'." Another remarked: "On one coast, the word refers to genderqueer girls who play like boys but aren't trans, and on the other coast some young transmen who have transitioned are now using the word. It's created some misunderstandings."

Of all my categories, the general perception of MTF dominants got the largest number of comments related to fetish outfits and activities. Many wrote about "...often into high heels and boot worship," "high femme, into fishnets and high heeled shoes," "really into corsets, heels, and humiliating biomen." Many compared them to nontrans female dominants, some as being more sadistic and some as less so. Coreyboi pointed out: "I have found that dominant MTFs and biofemales both are not as genitally focused. They tend to play with more of the body than biomales, which is a good thing for us."

As described earlier in the book, MTF dominants face some of the same cultural difficulties as FTM submissives, in reverse. Dominance and aggressiveness can be seen as masculine, especially when paired with a body which may have lingering male cues that can't be erased. On top of this, since female (or, rather, *femme*) dominants are in short supply and command market value, some MTF dominants who find it hard to get loving partners may follow in the footsteps of their biofemale sisters and become professionals. This puts them in a position where their biggest "selling point" may be traits that they dislike in themselves and that give them trauma, but the temptation of cash (especially considering the financial disability that being a transwoman can create) and ready partners of some sort can be very seductive. Some of my respondents referred to this dichotomy and the struggle that ensues:

People assume that they are either extending their indoctrinated dick privilege, or are enjoying the fetishizing of Trannies. – BEAR A-M Rodgers

They're seen as she-male dominatrixes who commercialize their gendered identity as a fetish. – Del

There are too many pros out there charging for 'services'. I realize that everyone needs to make a living, but it means that there is almost a permanent meme that these are all 'She-male dominants' with pay services.
– Netdancer

There are very few of them. I suspect most of them are expected to engage in penetrative sex, and perhaps get rejected when they don't. – Sable Twilight

I was scared to play with them at first. I thought that they would be more like men, which was silly because I belong to a biofemale Mistress and I am a transwoman. But my mistress lent me to a couple, and it wasn't all that different from playing with a biofemale mistress, except that afterwards we talked about having the same hobbies. For one of them, I was the first trans slave she'd ever met. She later confided to me that she had really wanted to involve her genitals in the scene, but felt that she couldn't because she was worried that I might not think that she was "really" trans if she had. The funny thing is, I was thinking the same thing when she started in on me. – Slave Anneke

I have met several, and in general these are women who know what they want and go after it. I think they're often very intense; they protect their identity as trans *women* very strongly, and sometimes come off as "masculine" to many people. Being on the MTF spectrum, I personally take offense at that, though I understand the roots. Some trans Dommes I have met embrace that as a part of their gender exploration, however, and that's a trip to think about! I think there is a perception that many MTF Dommes do not have the "nurturing streak" that cis-female Dommes have. – Terra Katherine McKeown

I speak as one of them: We're damned if we do, and damned if we don't. If we want to use our male organs during sex, we're not really women. If we don't, we're not pandering to the fetishes of most men—and we don't get any orgasms. If we are aggressive, we're seen as male. If we're not, we're not dominant enough and male subs will be rude and disrespectful, because they want that boot on their asses. If we wear the fetish gear, we're being stereotypical and simply copying male ideas of femininity. If we don't, men don't find us sexy because we're "out of uniform". It's hard for me to find male slaves who can see me just hanging around the house in sweats, hat, and no makeup while they clean, and won't then stop thinking of me as an actual woman, and feel vaguely cheated. Men are visual creatures, and they have a hard time with replacing what's in front of their eyes with what I am asking them to see in their imaginations. And let's not even bring up that movie *Silence Of The Lambs* where Jodie Foster says that all transsexuals are passive! Don't even get me started, I'll rant at length.

Ironically, while I've seen plenty of transwoman submissives who are really only submissive because they fear the workplace or think that female equals sub, I've also seen quite a few transwoman dominants who aren't really very dominant and are only in it for the money or the attention. When you live in a sick society and they want you to be a whore, being a pro-domme can look like a good deal. – Cordelia Shea Wynn

Of the few MTF dommes who replied to my survey, many seemed suspicious of each other. Unlike nontrans women, there was not as much bonding between them, perhaps because of leftover male upbringing. Ms. Jen explored her ambivalent feelings: "They are mostly fakes, in my experience. There aren't many really, considering most MTFs seem to be submissive. The ones I've met were actually dangerous to themselves and to others. I know some from online chats that seem to know the deal, and are cool folks. I'd love to get together with them over a drink or coffee."

When it comes to numbers, submissives are in the lead with both FTMs and MTFs ... but then, from what the rest of the BDSM demographic looks like, that's normal for all genders. There always seem to be more subs than dom/mes to partner with them. (One could make a case that not all the so-called subs are really subs— that they are just fetishists who aren't really submissive when push comes to shove—but then one could make such a case for dominants as well.) However, among transwomen, the ratio is extremely exaggerated, or at least it seems that way anecdotally from what I and my extensive network of transgender friends have seen. Nearly all transwomen identify as submissives, including those on the part-time end of the spectrum. Speculative reasons for this ranged from cultural assumptions about femaleness equaling submission, to fear of the world and wanting to be taken care of, to having been beaten down emotionally as children as a side effect of being an effeminate boy. Del speculates, "It's part of the traditional feminine experience to be submissive, and I think quite a few MTFs feel that in order to truly be feminine, they have to submit."

Terra Katherine McKeown shared her own observations as someone in this position:

> The bulk of the trans women I have met who are into the scene are primarily subs. I hate to say that I think this has a lot to do with the *idea* that women are subservient, and it's a way of getting into "female" mode for many people: becoming passive, becoming subservient, being quiet. Many I have met and spoke with really crave attention and to be seen as a woman. Many take themselves *far* too seriously, in my opinion. I am mostly an

"MTF submissive", myself, and I can see myself having had to deconstruct these things, too. Some were easier to deconstruct than others.

Commenting on the general perception of submissive transwomen, images again revolved around clothing and fetish activities, although not so much as for dominant transwomen. Some remarks included: "I think of the sissy maid role. I also think of MTF subs as being into spankings." "Excessive feminization almost to the point of caricature." "Usually into costumes and leather, often shy and get treated like doormats." "Most people think of them as tall, awkward, obvious—not able to pass very easily, wearing a lot of perverted outfits." "I see a lot of them who want to be slaves so that someone will buy them their surgery—I wonder what happens when they have it?" Ms. Jen complained, "Lots of walking trainwrecks and people with no idea as to what BDSM is all about. Especially amongst the CD crowd."

On the other hand, Double-Edge felt that they were "...great submissives. They try very hard to fit in; unfortunately too many start too late in life to really change their habits. I find the younger they make the change the fewer problems they have." Cordelia Shea Wynn's experiences are similar:

> The way that transwomen are taught to be female is not honest. We are taught to act stereotypically female in the hopes that it can offset our discordant physical gender cues—our voices, our large-boned bodies, our wide jaws and receding hairlines. It's fakery that the average biowoman would rebel against in a heartbeat. It doesn't teach us how to be women, how to cope with partners as a woman, faced with their expectations of us. It doesn't teach us how to winnow out partners and find the right ones. All the skills we learned about that when we lived as men don't hold up here.
>
> Not only that, but growing up male, femmy, and something other than a cast-iron bitch can really wreck someone. It's the submissive personalities, the ones who really want to please and don't want to be confrontational, who take the most damage from a traditional "male" upbringing, not to mention one where they try to beat the femininity out of you and you live in fear all the time. I'm

one of those cast-iron bitches and it nearly broke me. I see submissive transwomen all the time who have terrible social and emotional skills, and it's because they had such a bad time as children that they just shut down. They are still about 12 inside, a 12-year-old girl who never learned to be an adult in the world in more than a shallow way. They crave guidance, but don't trust it.

So between the fakery and the damage, I see submissive trannies getting the message that they should sit passively and go along with the first dominant asshole who walks up and deigns to tell them what to do, and it's really a shame. Transwoman subs can bring something great to the table, if they're self-aware and have good self-esteem. They can give service without being tied to gender roles. I see male subs who think it's humiliating to do the dishes, and female subs who wouldn't change the oil in a car if ordered. A good transwoman sub can bring all the skills that she learned in her male life, plus all the ones she is ready to learn in her female life. They just need training, mentoring, and reassurance that they are fine just as they are.

Some respondents referred to MTF submissives as being the most likely of all the trans subgroups to allow abusive relationships out of desperation; many voiced their concern for them over this. One dominant wrote, "These sadly seem to be the ones confused about gender stereotyping to the point of allowing dominants to truly abuse them." Another mentioned, "Desperation is rampant among this group, and they will put up with anyone, no matter how crass and uncaring, so long as they validate their female gender identity at least some of the time."

Ian MacAlister, the partner of a submissive transwoman, wrote a heartfelt and poignant piece to me that, I think, deserves to end this chapter. Let it be something to take with you into your futures.

When my girl Zennie came to me, she was covered with scars emotionally. She was honestly submissive, and had been since she was a young boy—which was when the relationship scars started. Being a submissive effeminate young boy is so not safe in this society. Neither is being a submissive transwoman. People assume that they can be taken advantage of, and they do it again and again.

Yes, there is an assumption that they are desperate, and there's some truth to that statement. But doesn't almost everyone want to be loved? Perhaps they choose poor companionship over isolating loneliness, but that's a brave choice, even when it's a dangerous one. Sometimes it's a fatal one; I'm well aware of the statistics, of how many transwomen (and some transmen) get murdered because they were desperate for contact. But that doesn't mean that they shouldn't continue to seek out contact. It's a human need, and nontrans people also sometimes make poor decisions out of desperation and get hurt. Yes, some of them isolate and become obsessed with their fetishes, and that's a stereotype in the community too. But doesn't everyone need something to hold onto when love isn't forthcoming? The cure for that is more human contact, something that the finger-pointers should remember.

Those of us who love transgendered people, their partners, their friends, the people who care about them— we are the ones with the most important voice in the scene. We have the opportunity to change things. It's not fair that we are listened to more than our transgendered partners and friends, but we can use our voices to get them heard. We are the ones who have the most power to speak out against stereotypes, so we have an obligation to do it. Since we are trusted the most by transgendered people in general—we're on their side, and even when we criticize it's done out of love—we can help them to get past *being* those stereotypes. People often are what you treat them like, especially if they are still exploring their fluid identities, which is even more likely with a combination of transgender and submissiveness. That fluidity can be a wonderful asset in a relationship. It should be guided and appreciated, not scorned. It's the lovers, friends, allies—and owners—of transgendered people who have a chance to communicate that information to the rest of the scene. So let's start doing it.

Interview with Vidal Rousso

I was born female, grew up unaware of the anatomical differences between the sexes, believed that I could choose whom I can be, and that I was a boy even if for some reason I had to dress as a girl. As long as I remember I was living in two worlds, the outside world and the world in my head, in which my closest people also were allowed in. The separate worlds are still here, and I prefer to stay in the inner world, from which I also get the strength to meet the outside world. I'm trying to make both worlds meet, but it is hard work with myself.

I have some very strong weed roots in my thinking, probably from when I was growing up and the society around was traditional and mainstream. Those roots keep coming up sometimes as a very negative self-image, you know, as if I had a devil sitting on the ear and whispering "But you have a female body, that means you are a female … a crazy female, BOOO!" So I have had and still have a lot of fighting to do with finding myself as a third sex male. The next step is probably to be able to convince people that a contradiction in terms is possible, and that I can enjoy vaginal sex and be proud of the beauty of my body while still being a guy.

I figured I was transsexual about the age of 20. Before I had tried to "be a girl" but it has always ended with bad taste in my mouth. Most of the time I was dressing in male clothes anyway, even if it got me bullied at school. When I was 25, my only goal was SRS; it was not possible at the time, and later I understood that the main reason I wanted SRS was to be accepted and seen as male by society instead of trying to live with my female body. Seeing SRS as a make-up for society's approval, I dropped the idea. It is a hard choice, and one must be strong to face society, to face being called female; still, what I want is to live as if I was born in the right body.

Right now I see myself as a man. I am non-op, but insist that I'm a transsexual FTM. I see myself as falling in some third-sex niche (well, I can't escape it even if I do SRS), and I try to live as people did before SRS was possible. I try to find myself and my body there, to learn how it could work more harmonically.

My mother once told me that I'd never be what I was, and if I was born male I would've been a transvestite. Then, on the spot, I protested, but now I see the truth in it. If I was born male I would've been cross-dressing at periods, and that is also what I'm doing now. I'm well aware that an FTM ain't allowed to be more feminine than a Texas cowboy, but since I just follow who I am, I don't let fear stand in the way of exploring the more feminine sides of myself as well.

I used to be into classic BDSM; now I am into something I call post-BDSM, to give it a name. I have had many years of very good, active BDSM. I tried all I wanted to try, it was a great period and I had fantastic sex, but now it is over and doesn't arouse me any more. I need to go further than that, to a place where BDSM becomes more real and lifelike, where most of the rules and restrictions disappear, and everything is about the genuine feeling (as much as possible). I know several other people previously into BDSM and now wanting the same thing I want. For me, too many regulations and prescriptions makes classic BDSM too mechanical, too systematic; I don't want to follow any lists or guidebooks of how a good master or slave should be either. Thinking too much spoils the fun. I want it all to be a real play in that sense that anything can float and change in the process, one person doesn't know what the other one is about to do, the only thing the partners stay true to is their characters (and a few pre-agreed notions, such as "no vaginal sex" or "I want to come out of the play the way I went in, apart from some bruises and welts"). Feelings can come pretty close to real; I'm sometimes looking for real fear. Neither part has to think about "Was it okay to use handcuffs or did she prefer rope?" or "Is this the correct position?"

A classic scene like this: "You are going to get 20 lashes. Are you ready to receive them?" "Yes." "Yes what?" "Yes, Mistress,"— belongs to classic BDSM but not post-BDSM. What I'm interested in is rather a life simulation, a scene from an improvised movie, where everything happens the way it would happen in real life. An example: late in the evening a guy crossing a meadow meets a girl who lures him to her home (well, at this point the guy lets himself be lured, since he recognizes his girlfriend and knows that something is about to come). Once there, she attacks him and cuffs him. She might torture him, if she likes. She might make him do things under real threat, or have him as her sexual toy; he can either resist or give up, or maybe come to like the situation, but he doesn't decide anything here unless he breaks free. It's also up to the girl when she will let him go. It's like a real-life situation, and the communication between both is not boyfriend and girlfriend playing, having a classic BDSM scene, but between a captor and a captive. I play without safewords, without having the faintest idea what will come next, and in as real environment as possible. That is what brings me pleasure.

(P.S. I must add a note that this type of BDSM is only to be done with psychologically stable, trustworthy partners. Although I wouldn't do classic BDSM with somebody unstable or untrustworthy either.)

I'm very much into dominance and submission (especially forceful), and real life-like roleplays. My patterns vary depending on the partner. I know I will sound as if I can't get past traditional, primal instincts when I describe how I relate to my partners. But I'm not a traditional man from the bushes, far from that, and I'm working hard to be free and open in my mind and I'm daring to tell it loud. If I'm with a male-dominant partner, he has to be able to make me submit physically. It is weird, but it feels like I'm not able to get past my instincts, as I seem to be born with a male hierarchy already in my brain. If a man is stronger and can fight me down, I will give it all up to him and feel it is right. The closer match the guy is for me, the more important is the physical strength, and the more alike we are to each other, the stronger is my need to overpower, submit and take him instead. It might be something about my own submissive identity and that I see men of my type as especially attractive when they have submitted. It might be the projection of my wishes and needs onto the guy, trying to make him feel what I want to feel and enjoy it through him.

The situation is closely connected with my identity. I'm myself quite tall and quite strong; many guys are a fair match for me in a fight, but certainly not all. Since instead of SRS-ing myself and butching myself up I try to live in my body the way I would've if I was born male, I fall pretty low into the male hierarchy physically. But I don't need to be the samurai, I'm happy being the samurai's homosexual lover. With women, strength plays no role. It feels like women stand outside such bullshit as male hierarchy and physical strength, and don't need to overpower me in order to make me submit. Can it be I respect women more because I fear them less? Still working on it.

When it comes to me being dominant, it's mostly turned against the men in my league, men who resemble me. Then I want their pain, mental, physical and sexual submission. When I am dominant with women, the dominance shows up as rough sex and use of force. I'm not the right person to whip bloody somebody who identifies herself as female; the same brutality against women as against men won't arouse or interest me. Why? Can it be the age-old instinct of not hurting a body which is softer and more beautiful that I can't get over? I don't think that it is only my sexual preference, I believe that everything has deeper reasons.

Belonging:
The Gates of Community

So, after half a book's worth of talking about how many transgendered individuals find solace and pleasure in the practice of BDSM, and how it can be a supportive place to work out the kinks (as it were) of gender identity, attention does need to be paid to the aspects of BDSM community that are troubling to many transfolk. It's not all happy whips and chains and everyone accepting everyone else. Many transgendered people have found themselves at odds with well-meaning but uneducated community policies, and when they speak out, they may become a focal point of general disagreement and disharmony. This makes people a lot less willing to speak out, and pretty much guarantees that the ones who speak the loudest are often likely to be the ones with the worst social skills who just don't care any more or don't know how else to address the problem. In the last five years, the "transgender issue" (which is actually a whole bunch of different issues attached to our existence and varying needs) has spread to the point where some community leaders wince or flinch when I bring it up.

Some transfolk will quietly check out the welcoming temperature of a community, and if it doesn't feel right, they simply move on. We tend to get tired of constantly forcing a place for ourselves, and sometimes we just have to conserve our energy. As Coreyboi says, "I guess it is a matter of choosing my battles ... if I am not accepted as myself I would not want to be in that space. There are plenty of other places."

A few had even given up on belonging to local groups, after years of bad experiences. Ruth struggled with issues of being able to go to supportive places with both her MTF and FTM lovers, and finally writes: "Having been rejected by the BDSM community long ago, I don't really feel I have a place in it any more. I can only say that were I to want to be a part of it, I am aware that there are places that would reject not only each of my partners for various reasons (including the cisgendered ones I have not mentioned here) but would reject me as well."

The Ism Game

People aren't perfect, especially in a group linked only by enjoying certain sexual-fetish activities. Sexism is everywhere, including among BDSM practitioners, and so is transphobia and stereotypes. While it may be less of a problem in such demographics, picking up a whip doesn't guarantee any political sensitivity. As I mentioned in the introduction, the fact that "transgender" is listed in so many BDSM books right alongside sexual kinks can make a lot of nontrans people assume that it's just another sexual fetish, and that means trans people are in BDSM space "doing" gender transgression in order to get their gender-fetish needs met, supposedly with someone who can also fetishize it from the other side. MTFs tend to take the brunt of that, because of the proliferation of "she-male" porn. Ms. Jen complains, "I suppose the one thing that has changed since my transition is my intense dislike of men in the scene who expect transwomen to be nothing more than free hookers. This seems quite common, unfortunately, and it's indicative of a lack of understanding regarding TG people. Many, many men do not understand the idea that we are people, just like them. We aren't simply objects for their amusement."

It's hard to explain to sexually interested people that some transfolk are fine with you fetishizing their bodies and natures, and some aren't, and there's no way to tell by looking. Del carefully suggests, "Something that is neither fully negative, nor fully positive, is the fetishization of third gendered people. Many lesbian-identified women, and hetero-identified men, love to play and have sex with people who are third gendered. It means I get attention from those people, and some of them can see that the fetishized body has a person and a soul behind it. Some, not all."

Trans people may also find that while they are treated as their chosen gender face to face, when the rumor mill gets started on their name, what's whispered behind the back may be quite different. Since BDSM practitioners have a long history of being proud of "grapevine warnings" as a way to prevent abusive couplings, gossip is rampant and unvoiced assumptions can bounce back in people's faces later. Siobhan Phoenix writes sadly, "There have been times, especially in reference to my divorce, where abuse that I had suffered had been written off because I was the genetically male partner in the relationship. It's the sexist nature of those who believe that only men can be perpetrators of sexual assault/abuse."

While few people of color responded to my survey, a few commented that they had a double burden of inclusivity—trying to get both race and transgender included. Sejay commented on this dilemma: "As an Asian person, I have noticed a great lack of ethnic diversity everywhere in the BDSM scene as well. Even the 'POC' events that I've attended were mostly geared toward African American individuals, which is great, but not what I was hoping for in terms of a diverse community."

A few passing, transitioned transsexuals complained about other transfolk in their community who, they felt, made their trans status too big of a deal, and would come across better if they paid more attention to their presentation. "Double-Edge" complains: "I feel a transsexual person should pass as whatever sex they are trying to be. This would solve the problems with fitting in. Boobs and makeup does not make you a woman. I have a couple of friends whom have done total transformations and their dress, mannerisms, and voice still give them away."

On the other hand, those who identified as genderqueer or third-gender objected to this policy, and felt that their more gender-conservative brothers and sisters were supporting barriers that they ought to be tearing down. E. Nelly tells of his experience with local politics: "The president of the local group is transsexual identified, and while he does not really hide his trans status, he is very passable and virtually stealth in most aspects of his life. He is treated differently than me and my non-passing partner. I do not think the group leader makes much room for genderqueer people because he is the type of trans guy who loves and embraces the binary. We don't go over preferred pronouns at the beginning of the group and we do not discuss trans issues openly." Genderqueers with particularly unusual presentations may even lose the support of the rest of the trans element in their community, as Sassafras Lowrey explains:

Right after leaving home as a teen, I became heavily involved in my local LGBTQ youth center. Here like in my first relationship which would come a few months later, BDSM and leather were the norm rather than the exception. Adult volunteers who were active in the leather community would come and give BDSM 101 workshops. The logic being that pretty much all the kids were playing, so it was best to make sure we were doing things as safely as possible, and that we learned skills about how to negotiate what we wanted, and find ways to play that affirmed our identities.

That said, even for some transgender people my shifting of gender identities has been too much. When I quit testosterone and transitioned into a queerly feminine presentation, I lost many of my closest transgender friends. For them, my expression of self was simply too much, and they felt as though I was giving all trans people a bad name. Because my leather community was so closely interconnected to my trans community I did experience some fallout in terms of loss of friendship and community but the issue was less about leather and more about gender.

Even passing and closeted transfolk are not entirely safe from discrimination, because closets are notorious for vanishing as soon as word gets out, which it does all too often. While it is usually easier for someone who has lived and worked in a community for years, it's hard to guess whether the result will be "It's just Janey, it doesn't matter to us what she used to be," or "Why didn't she tell us, all this time? It's kind of dishonest." There can be a lot of reasons for ostracizing someone, not all of them rational. BEAR A-M Rodgers writes grimly, "I have been a director of local BDSM educational groups, and educator for regional BDSM communities for many years. However, in October 2008 I was 'outed' as a Transsexual and so was subsequently ostracized by those same groups and community. Even the FTM Leather community ostracizes me for being mainstreamed instead of in-your-face, I guess because my history started as an accepted male instead of being a once-female fighting to get in."

Pillars of the Community

Some transgendered people are active in their local and BDSM communities, and a few even run for national offices or for leather titles ... and get them. Some are mainstays of their community structures, and some simply settle in and find them to be supportive friends and allies. Ashley Lynch wrote about her group's support for her: "Everyone in the community is great, many of my best friends are there and they accept me wonderfully. When I returned from Montreal for my surgery, I came back to find my apartment decorated with balloons and a big cake congratulating me. The next event I went to, everyone lined up to have a chance to hug and congratulate me and they all insisted on singing happy birthday for me. The only negative thing I can think of is that the kink community has a tendency to attract a lot of crossdressers, and while there's absolutely nothing wrong with that, it made it difficult for me in the beginning because people kept assuming I was a crossdresser too and just marvelled at how good I looked. It took some work to educate everyone that I was a woman, but I got there."

I am involved with my local group. As far as I know, those in the group that knew me pre-transition are highly curious about me. I'm kind of the info center for them on trans stuff; at least it feels that way sometimes. I feel that they're constantly looking for physical changes—how well my beard is coming in, how much my face has changed and so forth. And granted, that could just be my dysphoria kicking in. – Cole R.

People don't think of me as trans; I think it is because of my Old Guard training. All they see is a good slave and sex does not come into it. I have seen other transfolk whom had problems at different functions, but it all came back to how they acted or reacted to the situation. – Double-Edge

I've had more acceptance from the BDSM community than just about any other I'm a part of. I can be honest about my gender identity and very few, if any, ask those very basic questions that most transgendered people get tired of hearing about six seconds after they declare their intent to transition. – Del

I am part of my local genderqueer BDSM community as much as this exists—i.e., it's not a formal organization, but there are regular play parties and such. They've been very accepting of my trans status. I have started to expand and attend more straight-focused events. Mostly, they are accepting of my trans status although I think now it's easy because I look very normatively male—what I mean, most people have no problems with my pronouns for example. I have seen the same people who accept me and my being trans have a lot of trouble with people whose gender presentation is more ambiguous for whatever reason. So in general (and this is a generalization) I would say that the community is accepting and well-meaning in theory but in practice has not done a lot of work or informed itself greatly about the trans community. But I think there has been progress—a local organization that did not accept trans people (of either spectrum—or only if the transwomen had had genital surgery) now accepts a wide variety of trans people and there are a few more queer spaces where people can gather. In these spaces there also seems to be the possibility of being genderqueer,
There's also the issue of reputation. while when I transitioned there was a definite pressure to identify with the M or the F and get all the surgeries etc. I see more people comfortable and open about their varying genital configurations for example. – Jackkinrowan

Transgendered people can be the blade that peels back a BDSM group's mouthed platitudes about wanting diversity and makes them face whether they really want it, and want the influx of searching people who might show up if they got a diversity-friendly reputation. Sejay points out that: "If transfolk or trans allies speak well of a BDSM party/space/person, than that party/space/person is automatically assumed to be open-minded, considerate, and politically savvy. These attributes are very desirable in a place you choose to patronize or space you choose to spend your time or person you might want to play with, especially because BDSM play desires, if not demands, safety (because you're playing with things that could permanently damage you) and open-mindedness (because not everyone is accepting of 'leather' folks)."

Pricing options can be a challenge. Some clubs have different prices for men and women; some add a third price for cross-dressers, but generally prices are assigned by what the person at the door decides you are. Micah notes the problems with this policy: "That particular party is a bit frustrating to me from a policy level too, though. They have one price for men and a much lower price for women/trans. To me that means in order to get in the door I have to choose between being male or trans—which I can't—and that to the extent I am a man I am less welcome in the space. Also, the pricing policy is obviously a disincentive for non-trans men to go. Since I really like playing with and having sex with non-trans men, the policy seems quite unappealing to me on that level as well."

He also comments sharply about the difficulties of making pansexual space trans-friendly:

> I've been to some pansexual/straight spaces too, but I have never disclosed or found anyone to play with there. Some of the language they use about gender and bodies in workshops in those spaces has not worked so well for me. Once I was at a workshop where a non-trans man and a non-trans woman were presenting on water sports. The discussion of differences between men and women when it came to pissing was pretty triggering to me, given the way my trans male body works. Then an audience member asked a question about positions or aiming or something for when women piss. The female presenter kept trying to respond, but the male presenter kept cutting her off. He explained he was a tranny-chaser and lurked on some FTM lists. Then he started to describe some of the strategies FTMs use to pee standing up. Listening to trans men being described as women and as totally fetishized sexual objects was fairly horrifying to me.

The Iron Gates of Gender Segregation

Women-only or men-only spaces are, of course, the biggest demons when it comes to the problem of trans inclusivity, and have been for the past decade. The situation has become more and more intense as transfolk become more out in the community, and as visible and well-respected members of the community have transitioned and then asked, "So where am I welcome now?"Groups have reacted in a number of different ways, and there has been a lot of angry debate on all sides which continues to go on.

When I asked my respondents the million-dollar question about gender-segregated clubs, groups, and parties (or "only spaces", as I referred to them), I was prepared for the deluge of impassioned writing that came in from all sides. In fact, this section is the largest in the entire book, which didn't surprise me. Dozens of people practically wrote essays about it. In fact, I decided that I didn't have to express my own opinions on the subject, because so many people had said it so much better than I ever could.

What I didn't expect was that the opinions were all over the place, which proves that we as the Tribe of Trans are not in any sort of agreement over this most prickly of topics. We have a whole array of strong opinions, and most of us don't know that. In fact, there was a lot of assumption that "of course this is the way that my trans brothers and sisters all feel", when that wasn't true at all. We need to be honest about that, especially to BDSM group organizers who are probably flustered enough as it is. This means that one thing this section *isn't* going to be is one long preaching about what any given group or club or party-givers ought to be doing. Instead, it's going to be a number of different and eloquent perspectives that will help them to make the individual decision that is right for them.

Many of my respondents were completely against the whole concept of only spaces, and wanted them completely abolished. Simon Strikeback says in disgust: "I worked on Camp Trans for 7 years and frankly I'm pretty over only spaces. I host queer-focused events all over the place, but not only queer people go there, and it's got lots of trans folks because we're the ones that put on the best events! The idea of trying to figure out how to be the kind of trans person I am in an 'only' space doesn't really make any sense to me. I think trannies should be able to do whatever the fuck they want, and the idea of needing to have a conversation around it is frankly offensive even to begin with. Male identity, female identity, trans identity, queer identity, Black identity, whatever. When policing of bodies starts, that's when I'm outa there."

BEAR A-M Rodgers focused on presentation as a way to make transfolk more welcome in any space: "I have never approved of gender-segregated spaces. It is just feeding the internal weakness of the participants. Weakness of so many individuals creates a weak community. If anyone chooses to play in gender segregated space, then they should be sure they are presenting in the gender relevant to that space. A pre-op Transwoman should not expect a woman-only space to be welcoming of her naked penis flopping around, just as a pre-op Transman should realize flopping breasts are not welcome in men-only space. However, if a Trans person is presenting in the specific gender, even if it means binding, tucking, wearing prosthetics, then they should be accepted like any other person of that presented gender. I have been refused admittance to 'women and FTM-only' space due to 'passing' too well, yet only refused admittance to a single men-only space because I refused to send pre-event penis pictures to the organizer."

It will never cease to amaze me how angry questions like this make me. In my opinion, people are people and should be allowed to be where they want to go as long as they are not there to disrupt the experience of others. I think lesbian groups that accept transwomen (because they have cast off their evil male sides) and transmen (because they are really just very butch women) make me the angriest. From my perspective (granted, not a trans perspective, but an equally human one) I would rather be outright rejected from a group/space/event due to who I am, than be accepted because they cannot see or respect who I am. I have personal issues with only space, having spent years of my life showing up in gay bars that did not allow women and other such spaces. I cannot begin to say how anyone else should handle things in this world. If you want to be somewhere, go there. If they don't want you there, you have the choice to ask why and press the issue, or leave and go somewhere where you are welcomed whether truly or falsely. Organizers of events should open their events to people. Members of groups will handle things however they will, and my best hope is for them to be honest.

However, in spite of my own preferences on handling situations where my wife is made uncomfortable by people who cannot see her for who she is, it is not my place to decide how to handle the situation. Having some yahoo refuse her entry into a space she wanted to be in would be far easier for her to deal with than my then being loud and firm about the situation, which may devolve into my hitting them with a chair. I have learned to do my best to not be combative towards people who are unpleasant to her publicly, and allow her to direct how the situation should be handled for her sake. – Ruth, nontrans partner

Ruth's comment about identity refers to the recent situation that some women's groups have found themselves in. Pressured on the outside to allow transwomen to attend, and from the inside to allow transmen who were former lesbians and may still have lesbian partners to continue attending, some groups have created the "women and trans" category in order to bypass the controversy and still keep out the "evil influence", male-identified biomen. This has created a storm of division among transmen, some of whom feel that if you're a man, you don't belong in women's space and should prove your male identity by leaving it, and others who are not yet ready to leave a community that has been their lifeboat for so long. Jackkinrowan comments on this situation:

> One solution has been recently to have genderqueer group where basically everyone is welcome except for cis-men. While I can understand that, at the same time, it makes me sad and feeling like we are failing as a society if cis men cannot be taught to be "good". This also creates a problem when cis-men want to come into the space: some read the gender policy and get it. Some seem to think there are lots of naked women in there and they want to watch. Some seem puzzled that I who look very gender normatively male can go in and am welcomed and they cannot. And of course, I can go in because the community knows me, but how would I prove that I was trans if I was going to a similar group in another city who didn't know me? – Jackkinrowan

The upshot of the argument seems to be that some FTMs will go into any women's space that will let them in, some will avoid those but will go into "women and trans" spaces, and some reject even those because of the assumption that the organizers secretly think that FTMs are "just another kind of woman" and will communicate that attitude to the rest of the crowd. Lee Harrington, E. Nelly, Blaise Garber-Paul and Micah all responded to the question of these spaces and their boundaries, each in different ways. Lee Harrington's take is more mellow and nonjudgmental, while E. Nelly explores practical advice and Blaise explores the idea of how "created space" is affected by gender culture. Micah also brings up the controversial idea that trans people could be allowed into any space that they choose, both men's and women's.

> I feel very odd being part of women's-only spaces, to be honest. I'm a guy most of the time. Legally, socially, emotionally ... why keep inviting me? Other than the fact that I'm nice, which is nice, but curious. But it seems like women's spaces keep being pressured to be "hyper-inclusive" with definitions like "women past, present or future" or "those who feel like they have a place in women's space." Compare this to men's spaces. They're for men. Period.

I personally just ask what the lines are, and engage the organizers in civil and loving conversation around their biases. Ask them where they came from. Oftentimes it was from one trans person behaving badly I have found, or pre-hormone, pre-op/no-op transfolk going hyper-vigilante and causing problems instead of sitting down and talking.

Some gay men get offended by wet pussies. Some gay women get offended by raging hardons. I get it. It's why I have been jokingly referring to myself as a gateway drug as of late. As a cutie gayboy I can play with men and get them OK with alternate bodies and play with cunts without breaking being gay. Playing with straight men, I am a safe way to explore their homoerotic desires while not feeling threatened in their identity either. Dykes can play with me and find a safe way to be with men, and straight women, especially cougars, get to play with pussy without freaking out.

I think, personally, that everyone should take a chill pill. Stop thinking that the rules were put in place just to keep *you* out. Stop thinking rules can never change. Be civil, have conversations, and if it sucks, start your own bloody group. – Lee Harrington

"Only spaces" are a very tricky issue. The intention and the ability to convey the intention must be carefully communicated succinctly as possible. Organizers should be prepared for the onslaught of pissed-off attendees, because regardless of how one communicates, someone will be pissed off. Additionally "only spaces" allow for disenfranchised people to come together and build a micro-community in ways that are meaningful for the attendees. For the most part "only spaces" are not problematic unless the space is created to deliberately offend and keep out certain potential participants because of organizers' bias.

To discuss specific examples: If the intention of the space is to have female-assigned-at-birth people, then the language should clearly communicate that intent and trans guys should be allowed. If the intention is to have women-identified people than that should be stated and trans women should be allowed, but not trans men. If it is a men's only space trans guys should be allowed.

These examples show that organizers should be very clear about the intent of the space and who is welcome and who is not. I fully support women-only spaces but trans women should be allowed in those spaces, and vice versa for men's spaces. I think that to allow trans guys into women's only spaces implies that trans men are not really men and possibly that one cannot have a gender different than their corresponding gender based on assigned sex.

I had an experience where there was going to be a men's area at an event—I asked if trans guys were allowed; they were, so I attended that area. The organizer simply said "men-only" and provided contact information for any questions. In terms of trans folks and members, in the example above I discussed how I dealt with it. I think that is a fine way to address the issue.

Typically trans people think much more about appropriateness of their attendance than the organizers have thought about trans people's appropriateness in attending. Organizers should think about the intent of the space and then be very explicit about who is welcome and who is not. They should also be prepared to get some shit for their decisions, whatever they may be. People get all on edge about separate spaces. It doesn't bother me and I welcome these spaces because the energy is different in a room of all men or all women or all trans guys or all genderqueers. Organizers should consider the trans perspective and also consider how "non-binarily gendered" people might react. Of course you can't please everyone with the chosen language, so a disclaimer is always helpful. But of course some crazy person will be unhappy and throw a fit, and that really can't be avoided, no matter the efforts of the parties involved. – E. Nelly

It depends on the intention of the space. Is it exclusive because it's intention is to protect and heal? Whom is it trying to protect, and from what? How much thought has gone into their declaration of exclusivity?

I was recently involved in organizing a sex and play party that included people of a wide array of bodies and genders and cultural backgrounds. What I learned is that gay men and dykes really do have separate languages for establishing trust and liberating their boundaries. Bathrooms, for example, became a hot topic. Some of the gay men were insistent that they would like to see the bathroom doors removed: they felt that it was liberating for them to remove the social taboo against viewing urination. Transpeople, in particularly, felt that they required the door to protect their bodies from being viewed doing disruptive acts (like a female-bodied person navigating standing up to pee), or simply to preserve their control over who viewed their body. We made a compromise, (one door off, two doors on), but it still brought up significant questions for me.

Creating the architecture of the space, from door policies to coatchecks to changing rooms to the flow of dark corners and dance floors, is the power to construct social interactions and lived cultural norms. It's very different to invite transmen to participate in a gay men's space than it is to invite gay men and transmen to come together to create a new kind of space. I would like to see more spaces that were developed collaboratively.

I like being able to move between the different gendered spaces. I find my ability to move between communities to be an essential part of being trans. I like being able to be integrated into different scenes. I think that if the intention is to create a safe space for a particular tribe, for a particular reason, it should be respected. I have no problem excluding myself from spaces where I would be inappropriate. Spaces that are marked for women only, for example, feel inappropriate to me because I know that there are a multitude of spaces for women and transfolk, so if something is marked just for women then I assume there is a purpose and a lot of thought went into it. Men's only spaces, however, generally read as unreflected exercises in exclusivity. I have an impulse to challenge them. I have an impulse to walk up and request my inclusion, if only to provoke an explanation of *why* they are exclusive.

Perhaps it is my feminist training, but I generally fail to see how my body is actively threatening to men. Nor do I understand how the presence of a non-operative transwomen in womens' space can be construed as an imminent threat, though I can still see the purpose of excluding men. I understand triggers—images or archetypes that reawaken old traumas—but I'm not sure if I'm willing to accept that the triggers of a few are reason enough to exclude our trans sisters (or brothers, as the case may be) from spaces that they desire to participate in.

I do accept that the existence of transfolk, especially naked sexy transfolk, is an implicit challenge to anyone who continues to embrace a fundamentalist orientation to the normativity of gender dichotomy. I can understand how sexy transpeople can be triggering to someone attached to gender binary. Personally, I don't feel inclined to protect binary-embracers. – Blaise Garber-Paul

The discussion gets a bit more interesting when we're discussing genderqueers and others who aren't men or women, trans men in women's spaces, trans women in men's spaces, and so on ... When it comes to trans people, I think key questions ought to be: what policies will most help these spaces to foster queer women's community and decrease risks of gender-motivated and sexual violence? To me, it's pretty clear that welcoming trans people is critical to accomplishing those goals. All trans people, whatever our genders, experience sexism and are at high risk for sexual and gender motivated violence. That sort of targeting happens in all sorts of contexts, including on the street and in play spaces. There's also just no reason to believe that we are any more likely to be violent than non-trans women are. Of course it is also true that many trans people are at times perceived as (non-trans) men and experience some aspects of male privilege as a result and that trans people experience forms of gender-based oppression and violence (transphobia) that non-trans women do not, but there are always going to be people with different experiences of privilege and oppression in these spaces. The ways in and degrees to which people experience sexism is also mediated by their experience of race, disability, class, age, national origin, size, and so on. I think trying to create a homogenous environment would be harmful and pointless; trying to build solidarity in a diverse community of people who do face gender-based oppression seems like the most worthwhile goal. Also, many trans people, including trans women, trans men, genderqueers, and others, have very close ties with women's communities (and in some cases have helped to build them) and often also have queer non-trans women partners. Policing them out of the space creates division and decreases opportunities for building community and having kinky fun with all those who could otherwise find a home in women and trans spaces. Trans men who do not want to be included in these spaces because of conflicts with our identities can self-select our way out of them.

While men's spaces exist, I certainly think all trans people who want to join them should be welcomed. Many trans men, trans women, genderqueers and other trans people have very close ties with queer male communities (and in some cases helped build them), partner with non-trans queer men, and would not want to prohibit sex in their play spaces. Trans people of all genders are also at risk of having to deal with extremely homophobic and/or

transphobic rejection in straight spaces and trans people
of any gender in a men's space are extremely unlikely to
gay bash someone for coming on to them. So again, fun,
safety, and community all seem best served by welcoming
in all trans people. Of course some people will not be
happy about having people they perceive as female and/or
feminine in a men's space. I would suggest that it is not
unusual for people not to be attracted to some people in a
play space and/or to be uncomfortable having members of
a marginalized group (people of color, disabled people, fat
people, poor people, etc.) in a play space—but that that is
never a legitimate reason for excluding those considered
"less desirable." – Micah

The idea that since trans people are a mix of genders, they
should be allowed to go back and forth between men's and women's
space at will upsets a lot of people. When I first heard it proposed a
few years ago, it was met with rejection from men, women, and
transfolk who were identified more with one end of the spectrum. It
has gained ground, however, with genderqueers and more radical
transfolk who identify somewhere in the middle, and have cultural
links to both gay and lesbian spaces—or believe that they ought to.
TransPunk acknowledges the problems of the neither-male-nor-
female-on-any-given-day people, and the struggle for total
inclusivity:

Some FTMs are so queer they don't fit in anywhere
else culturally. I do think we need more queer spaces to
accommodate all the ones who don't fit in anywhere. But
since I am mostly at home in gay male spaces, I do not
consider it my task right now. I am planning to organize a
gay men's BDSM camp that is publicly inclusive of trans
people with a biofag friend to work towards providing
more inclusive communities. I think trans people should
individually find the best way to move in the spaces they
want to move in, and use any strategy that works for them,
without judgment. Passing is as valid as being out. As a
group, though, and as activists we should work towards
the goal of including all trans people on basis of self-
definition. By now I doubt that the gay male community (in
Germany especially) responds well to political arguments.
It works best to show them that FTMs are men on a
personal level, and that they miss out if they exclude us.

> With women, political discussions work better. I feel social
> inclusion of trans people should be the goal, while sexual
> inclusion cannot be forced upon anyone. There will be gay
> men who want biodick of a certain size, just like they only
> want young or thin men. FTMs have to accept that, just
> like other sexual preferences. But there's enough left who
> are open to us. And even if they are not sexually open to us,
> they have to accept us as men or transmen socially.
> – TransPunk

Mik Kinkead casts the problem as one of safe space for
transgendered people: "Oh my, that's like the 12-million-dollar
question! I think both the all-inclusive and the no-inclusivity sides
need to learn how to breathe and release, we also need to learn how
to be respectful of each other. I believe that all people should have
the choice to be in the safest possible sex situation they can choose.
Sometimes that means making very difficult choices; for both trans
men and trans women this often means being in a women's space.
There are a lot of good reasons to segregate space—triggers, trauma,
oppression—but there's also no reason to segregate space if we all
come into the space with the same respect. Quite honestly, if
someone doesn't like another person's genitals or gender
expression ... then don't play with them! We need to allow people
to own their triggers and their experiences. But all sides of this
debate need to understand that anyone playing BDSM is still
discriminated against—all of us are battling puritanical worldviews.
Some of us have more or less ability to engage these issues than
others."

In terms of safety, Micah also pleads for us to consider the
impact of other segregated spaces in the world, and the effect that
they have on trans people, as a way of seeing the importance of
allowing the gender-ambivalent to choose their own spaces and be
welcomes anywhere:

> I think we need to think about our kinky
> communities' policies for sex-segregated spaces in a way
> that will help us when we are navigating sex-segregated
> spaces that frankly matter a lot more. I think about a trans
> man trying to flee his abusive husband who was turned
> away from domestic violence shelters because they were

for "women only"; a trans man who could not get treatment for eating disorders from any programs until finally he agreed to keep his gender a secret; a trans man who held his urine for a full 24 hours in the holding cell of a police precinct because the officers would not believe he was trans and placed him with men; a trans man who was gangraped by other residents in a men's drug treatment facility after he was denied entry into the women's program; a trans man who was placed in a men's prison and held in solitary confinement for his own protection until his mental health deteriorated so severely he attempted suicide; a trans man refused screening for gynecologic cancer at a women's health clinic, and a trans man who was hospitalized in a psychiatric ward after a suicide attempt and whose mental health only worsened when they insisted on treating him as female and his gender identity as a delusion.

The exclusion of trans women from women's spaces is off even more sweeping and at least as damaging—I think of a trans woman gang raped in a men's homeless shelter and then sleeping on the street because she could not get into a women's shelter; a trans woman living on the street after she was kicked out of a women's domestic violence shelter when the director found out she was trans; a trans woman raped, stabbed, and nearly killed in a men's prison; a trans woman placed in a ward with men when she was committed for psychiatric treatment and told she should be "flattered" after one of the other residents began groping her while she slept; a trans woman who could not complete her drug treatment because she was not allowed to participate in the women's therapy group; a trans woman arrested for using the women's restroom in a public park.

While the dynamics of gender-based violence can tend to make women's gender-segregated spaces particularly important for trans people, exclusion from men's spaces can also have similarly violent and life-threatening impact on trans people. Trans people of different genders have also gotten arrested and beaten up for using restrooms and turned away for needed services at sexual health clinics and HIV programs directed toward men who have sex with men. Trans men who are not comfortable getting domestic violence services from women's programs or who are turned away from those programs are left without any options at all if the few victims' services programs for men also turn them away.

Not all trans people think that placement with women in detention is safest for them; there is a lot of violence in women's facilities that can target trans people as well and some trans people have more allies in men's systems. One trans woman incarcerated in a women's prison was placed in isolation because she was assumed to be a security risk to other women and was constantly harassed by guards. She ultimately killed herself. Maybe the same thing would have happened in a men's facility—maybe not—but she almost certainly had no choice in the matter.

People who are running and participating in kinky women's and men's spaces are in many cases the same folks running and participating in some of the other women's and men's spaces in our world. If we can't make it work when it's just for fun, what's going to happen when it's about life or death? Isn't it better to stand up for justice and work on building community and playing together when the stakes are relatively low, to make it easier to do what we need to do when it really counts? Trans people need access to gender segregated spaces— at least while they exist at all—and we need to be able to access them on our own terms. – Micah

On the other hand, Stefanie points out the effect that laws can have on club owners who don't want to get in trouble, and also allows for the problems of overenthusiastic transpeople pushing the issue in ineffective ways:

The situation is made more difficult because of the local laws. I have been to many conventions and each one handles it differently. Usually they mark a bathroom that we can use but over the past few years it has been more open, easier to deal with. Our TG support group goes out every month to a different restaurant and we rarely have any problems. Most of the problems I have seen are mistakes made by the girls, they go into a bathroom as a group and are loud and upset other people ... I also feel many of the rules are made because of one or two people that cause problems. If a group that is mostly biofemale allows TG's but later has a problem with a TG, they stop allowing all the TG's, instead of just the one causing the problem.

Terra Katherine McKeown admits honestly that she was once one of those overenthusiastic people who made things worse instead of better, and has learned painfully from her experience:

> Obviously, I have opinions on this, but I did not handle it in a very good way. I was upset by the attacks against me personally, as well as what I perceived as short-sightedness and privilege on the part of other people. I thought I was calling people out on their shit without really looking at all of mine. I don't think I'm *wrong*, per se, but I definitely I got offended and reactionary and polarized my own point of view ... I personally think that working in the system and not actually addressing the problems of a dominant-group's privilege reinforces their power and actions. On the other hand, I have been in talks with a few kinky queer friends about creating another group in the city that is a queer-focused kink party. While this sounds like lots of fun for me, I think that it's just creating further segregation, as well. I don't want that to happen, but at the same time, I want to be able to play with other queer people and have a social justice model of facilitating a BDSM play space than the privileged one that the local group subscribes to. So I'm not sure what the best way of going about this is, but I'm giving it a lot of thought. – Terra Katherine McKeown

TransPunk admits, "I have also sometimes witnessed disrespectful behavior from trans-identified people towards only spaces. I do think that gay men or women have the right to create their own spaces considering the prevalence of sexism and homophobia all around us. The original motivation is not to exclude trans people in the first place, that is a tragic side effect and should be addressed, but with a respectful understanding for other people's needs as well. I think the discussion has gone a bit off, as straight, mixed places are rarely the target of trans discussions, yet simply being a mixed space does not make it trans-friendly in my experience!"

Some transfolk were clear that they not only completely supported segregated spaces, they were fine with those spaces not including them, even if it meant that they could not attend either, so long as they were honest about what they wanted and why they wanted it. Siobhan Phoenix and Joshua mused on the value of segregated spaces in the face of being transgendered:

> I have a very different feeling when it comes to "only spaces"—I believe it is up to the organizers to determine what that "only" space entails. For example, take the Michigan Women's Music Festival. They make it very clear that it is for "Women Born Women"—that's fine, that's their space to do with what they like. I support it. They shouldn't have to be forced to take women like me into their space, and I don't want to be where I am not wanted. As a staunch libertarian, I will stand up for the rights of anyone to create space they feel is safe for them, and if that does not include me, then that's OK with me. I do appreciate women's space including transmen and transwomen by their definitions. – Siobhan Phoenix

> I think people should be allowed to restrict attendance at events, and I can appreciate the reasons for making an event men-only or women-only. In some cases they've never thought about transgendered people attending, but I think the decision to open up an event needs to be carefully thought through. What is the social and emotional motivation for the gender restriction? Are they relating to each other as people who share a common childhood upbringing, or as people interested in sex with people who have the same type of genitals as they do? Is it important to them to be in the exclusive company of people who share the experience of being socially perceived as this gender, and facing these gender-based expectations? Do they feel they can express themselves more freely when they are not afraid of how people of that other gender will react? Are they uncomfortable with people of the other gender expressing themselves sexually? The group's motivations for single-gender space are going to affect their ability to meaningfully include transgendered people as much as their political stance on transgenderism. Some people are uncomfortable with examining what their reasons are for wanting a single-gender space, and even more uncomfortable examining what their personal emotional criteria are for perceiving a transgendered person as one gender or the other.
> For myself personally, I have been in groups that are trans-only or FTM-only, and I have seen a real difference between how people can interact in those exclusive spaces and ones that are open to non-trans people. I've felt

the same thing in groups that are limited to folks in M/s relationships. We have a certain set of common experiences to build discussion on, without having to back up and re-explain the same old things to people who don't get it. The shared experience provides a foundation for building a sense of community, and a feeling of "us" rather than "us-vs-them". When that sense of community is established, issues where people in the group have differing experiences can provide an opportunity to look at how these different ways of being reflect different aspects of our shared experience, rather than challenging the appropriateness of including those with differing experiences.

The most wonderful thing I've experienced in FTM-only space is that people who are not generally read as male get to have the experience of everyone around them assuming they are male or male-identified. They don't have to ask, or explain, or remind. They aren't assumed to be an ally or someone's partner. This normally invisible part of them is suddenly visible to complete strangers. They don't have to do anything to get people to see it, or worry that they aren't doing enough. It was an amazing experience for me, pre-transition, and I've seen the effect on other FTMs.

Some groups are willing to allow folks who in all respects seem to be the "right" gender for the event, but do not want any of their guests to have to confront any aspect of their trans-ness, or have the person's trans-ness detract from the intent of the group. Transgendered folks who pass well might be comfortable with being included in this way, but many are offended by requests that they keep incongruous parts of their body and personal history concealed. It also requires that someone make the decision about who passes well enough to attend, and who doesn't. I don't think this is a big deal for a private club that routinely screens members and turns away unsuitable applicants for a variety of reasons, but when the only criteria for attendance is looking like you probably have a penis (or a vagina), it is much more difficult to handle well.

A few years back there were some public parties run by a few leather dykes and because of a few prominent dyke-identified FTMs, they decided the parties would be open to "women and transgendered people". However, most of the leather dykes in my local scene prefer private invite-only parties, so only a handful of dyke-identified people showed up. The event organizers were not at all prepared for the majority of the crowd to be older post-transition FTMs and their non-trans wives, looking like average suburban heterosexual couples, and a colorful assortment of young gay-male-identified FTMs. –Joshua

Del poignantly sums up his love-hate relationship with spaces that exclude specific genders, even if they include his:

I have a big "thing" about this, so I warn you up front. I believe very strongly that "only" spaces are important, and valid, and maybe even necessary. I count myself as lucky that I've been able to access gendered space when I needed it, for whatever perceived need it fulfilled. I believe that organizations should maintain the right to declare who they want in their space, and who they don't, and have the freedom and strength to uphold those desires.

I believe that spaces have a requirement, in enforcing their desires, to be crystal clear about who they want in their space. The whys and wherefores are practically immaterial to me; but I want to know when an organization says they run a "women's only" space, what determines a woman in their eyes. Yes, this can get hairy and will almost always piss off someone who feels excluded. I feel the only "fair" way to police the genderedness of your space is to be clear and unapologetic about your gender definitions. More importantly, you need to stick to your guns, all of the time, no exceptions. You can't say that you run a women's-and-trans-accepting space and allow the cisgendered husband of the organizational president to come because "he's practically one of the girls" or whatever. You also can't say that you're trans-accepting, as long as the trans people in question modify their behavior, or have to obey different rules than the rest of your members (like transwomen having to keep their genitals covered if they haven't had bottom surgery). That's not "trans accepting", that's "trans tolerating".

The other half of this coin is that these spaces have to be understanding when trans people, even when they fall within the definitions of what is acceptable in that space, refuse to attend. There should be no cajoling, which almost always ends up making the trans person feel like their identity should remain malleable, maybe moreso than they're comfortable with. You'd think this wouldn't happen, but it happens to me *all the time*. I'm invited to women's only spaces and when I inform them that I don't go to parties that are single-gendered, they continue to tell me how I would be welcome, or find a lot of play partners, or feel completely comfortable there. I try to explain why this causes dysphoria for me, but they don't understand, and instead continue to emphasize that their space is trans-friendly. On the other hand, men's only spaces want nothing to do with me. I have been turned away from men's only play spaces, and denied access to men's only programming. I find that in queer kink community, I am frequently "read" as a butch lesbian, and when I try to identify as transgendered, they admonish me for grabbing for male privilege, and forsaking feminine power.

In my heart, in a perfect world which will probably never exist, I believe that if someone wants to hold a single-gendered space, the definition of that single-genderedness should include people who live most of their life in that gender identity, regardless of surgical or hormonal transition. The issue with that is that it's basically unprovable—ID gender doesn't prove it, and someone's word can be swayed by deep desires to be included for reasons outside of gender identity. It requires someone who may or may not be intimately familiar with someone's gender journey to decide where they are, and the legitimacy of their current identity.

I've personally made the decision to avoid single-gendered spaces, but that doesn't mean you'll never find me in one. I feel guilty about it, though. I can perceive how this sort of decision can be really difficult for trans people to make. I have found that my only real access to sex positive queer space is single-gendered space. I have only attended one queer-identified play party that had no gender rules. I still want to be welcome in queer space, and before I began to identify as third gendered, I never noticed how much LGBT and queer-identified space was so segregated. It makes me sad, and so sometimes I "give in" and attend women's-and-trans-only spaces so I can still feel a part of the queer community. It bothers me to no end.

To promote my own ideals, I've been trying to invite more queer community involvement in "pansexual" organizations. In the past, the word "pansexual" has been synonymous with "heterosexual", but that's no longer the case. More and more gender outlaws are escaping to their non-gendered playspaces, so that they don't feel the need to conform to someone else's gender identities in order to engage in BDSM. I'm hoping that as pansexual orgs see an upswing in attendance from queer communities, they'll address the situations that lead to their bad reputation, and move towards a time where they can corner the market on non-gendered, queer-positive, sex-positive places to play.

The Amazon Promised Land

Ever since the first transwoman got thrown out of the infamous Michigan Women's Music Festival, the battle has raged over whether to allow people who were raised male, and who might still have penises, into women's safe space. Transwomen have been struggling to get into women's space a lot longer than transmen have been pushing their way into men's space, and like FTMs are finding now, this is a method of introducing change that does not square culturally with the group in question. Arguing from a place of privilege and a feeling of entitlement created more bad feelings than progress, and a morass of anger which had to be carefully undone by transwomen who learned, slowly and painfully, how to communicate in women's language in ways that they had never had to learn while living as men.

This also carried over into BDSM women's space, which has actually been somewhat more liberal than similar vanilla spaces. Leatherdykes had a history of being outcasts in the vanilla women's communities, and were more willing to bend for "new women". When the Michigan Women's Music Festival first let in a handful of transgendered women (and Leslie Feinberg) but warned that they could not assure their physical safety in the camp, it was leatherdykes who stood up and offered to be a bodyguard for them. When the time came to negotiate, they were more willing to listen ... but on the other hand, since leather space (unlike the average support group or campout or workshop) is often designed to be specifically sexual, there was an extra layer of safety that had to be assured.

To this day, some leatherwomen's spaces let in transwomen, and some don't. Butterfly Gem wrote: "To exclude someone on the basis of whether they can afford hormones and surgery is classist. Believe me, if I had thousands of dollars, I'd have enough surgery to pass anywhere. But right now I can barely make my rent—should I be punished for that? I'm a woman inside. That should be enough."

Ashley Lynch is a little more conservative in her approach: "People also need to use common sense. If it's a female-only event that is designed to be sex-oriented, then anyone with a penis isn't really going to have a place and is probably just going to cause an undue commotion."

Sable Twilight describes her own experiences, and how far there still is to go, not only with social acceptance, but with the discouraging bugaboo of sexual acceptance:

> Most pansexual organizations are accepting, and most members do make some effort to check pronouns and such. The exception would really be one of the local FemDom groups, which require transsexual women to have had GRS in order to come to the events as dominants. I have found mixed responses in the leather bar scene. While they are sometimes very inviting and friendly, there really is no interest in any sort of scening with trans women, even among gay men who might otherwise scene with cissexual dykes.
>
> Women's spaces though still hold both the greatest frustrations and encouragement. Soon into my transition, I was invited by several women to come to the women's play. These are women I had come to highly respect in the scene. While I was honored to be asked to attend these events, initially I declined. Eventually I did finally show up at one of the events. One of the local dommes that I was good friends with asked if I wanted to scene, since I had come to the event on my own. I did and we had a good scene. Later, however, it seems some of the event participants had an issue with my attendance. This caused a huge uproar over the email lists, and there was a special meeting called to discuss the topic of allowing transsexual women into women's spaces. The owner of the play space, one of the women who had suggested I come previously, decided that only post-op transsexual women would be allowed to attend women's only events in the future. While I knew that it was not simply about me, the attitudes that came out did hurt.
>
> In response, however, the facilitators of the women's events decided they were no longer going to have events at that location as long as such a policy was in place. Many of the women of the community volunteered to host

parties in their own homes, where all female-identified people regardless of full-time or surgical status, were invited. I really commend the women of CO.L.L.A.R. for their very progressive and enlightened attitudes. I do, however, still feel self-conscious and awkward at such events. I don't feel that I can fully engage in some of the play that goes on; that it's okay to play with the other trans women, but I better not try to strike up a scene with any of the cissexual women there. In short, it's okay that I come, but so long as I remember to know my place. – Sable Twilight

Invading Gaytopia

Men-only play space is just as much of an issue for gay FTMs as women's play space is for lesbian-identified MTFs, although the speed with which MTFs tend to leave men's space means that at the moment there is no "men and trans" situation to complicate things even further. While some men's spaces will allow post-transition FTMs, it is a rare one that will allow anything more visibly female than that, and even passing FTMs may feel restricted. TransPunk in Germany says, "I do feel excluded from the easygoing ways bioguys relate to each other. I am usually not part of that orgy or easy flirting or casual sex dynamic." Micah has also been disappointed by his experience being allowed into men's space:

> I've also been in men's spaces where anyone who identifies as male is explicitly welcome. I enjoyed those spaces pretty well, but I had a genderqueer partner at one time who identified quite closely with queer men's communities and wanted to come as well. He was excluded by their policy though—he couldn't say he always identified as male. I realized that I was hesitant to stick up for him because I felt my own acceptance as a trans man was so tenuous in that space, which made me pretty ashamed of myself. I've also noticed in gay male leather bars that some trans guys who pass deliberately keep their distance from trans guys who pass less well, which is pretty sad to me...
>
> Usually I hear people talk about wanting men-only spaces because it is easier to connect with other queer men/find partners; because queer men are less likely to have to deal with hostile, rude, or violent homophobic reactions just for coming on to someone who they think is

hot (and who turns out to be straight); and because a lot of all-gender spaces tend to be pretty straight and tend to have a lot of rules (specifically "no sex" rules) that a lot of queer men are emphatically not interested in following. Those reasons make sense to me. I also hear some other justifications that to me seem pretty related to misogyny— disgust at female bodies or expressions of femininity, irritation with how "touchy" or "paranoid" they perceive women to be about sexual assault, a desire to avoid "female energy," and so on. Given the vast history of spaces that exclude women in order to consolidate male power, those reasons make me pretty uncomfortable. To the extent men's spaces should exist at all, I think we have to be exceedingly cautious about how and why we use them.

Gay men's leather space has its own subculture, aesthetics, and methods for enforcing those boundaries. The latter tends to be very different from the boundary-enforcing of women's space, as FTMs with lesbian pasts have found: bringing up the spectre of political correctness, sensitivity, and the moral value of inclusivity generally doesn't even make a dent. Since this has traditionally been a way to introduce slow change into women's spaces, people whose experience is with that process may find themselves at a loss as to how to create change. The culture itself, while fetishized and idealized by many gay FTMs before and during transition, may be confusing and intimidating when one is actually ensconced in it. Blaise Garber-Paul recounts his cultural dissonance as an FTM in gay male space:

> I never felt explicitly excluded anywhere except gay men's leather space. In pan scenes especially I felt quite at home. I felt like people were curious about me, but respectful of my boundaries (emotional and physical). I never had any trouble finding people who were interested in playing with me. I think, though, that that was mostly due to my exhibitionism and high pain threshold—people were used to seeing me play, when I played I pushed edges which looked exciting, and when I played I had fun, and people were drawn to the laughter and screams. I think being an educator and an organizer also helped, because it gave people a chance to engage with me

intellectually about play in a neutral space. Also, I find that I have the best connections with other people who are intentionally serving the community ... Cruising was easiest in dyke/trans scenes, and in pan scenes. I found that they had similar social organization and etiquette. People meet in educational or munch settings, play at publically announced play parties, and hold each other accountable through leather families and tribes. Sex, at least in NYC, is not part of the expected exchange. It's about the play and only the play. I found it simple to become a known commodity. I rarely had to disclose, because people already knew what they were signing up for. Queer spaces, though rare, are always my favorite because they're based on the premise that you must assume that everyone is genderfucked—no guessing what's between someone's legs or in their heart by what's on their body. There are a few occasional queer sex and play parties which have made me feel very welcome.

Gay men's space was the most difficult for me to feel fully integrated. I spent years with NYboL and never developed any sexual or play relationships out of it. Sex seemed to come before play, or play was relegated to the position of foreplay, rather than main act—which doubly focuses the attention on genitals. Individuals cruise each other at bars or online. Alcohol felt omnipresent. Vagina jokes felt omnipresent (I had to ask my brothers repeatedly not to tell them, at least in front of me and my other female-bodied brothers). I never felt in a position to get personal references or be referred to others for play partners. Men, if interested in me, never made it known. I was too shy to approach people generally. I made some amazing friendships, some of which still survive, but I never felt like I was desired or desirable. It was very difficult to be on the edge looking in, and part of my eventual decision to leave.

I'm not sure if it was me, either my presentation or the energy I was projecting, or the state of the community, but I went to the Eagle recently, after about a year and half absence, and had a very different experience. I found myself almost immediately involved in exactly the kind of bacchanal that I had desired, and had hoped to obtain, when participating in NYboL. I started playing with two boys, who brought in four more, and gathered a little crowd. I'm not sure if it's a repeatable experience, or if I'd want it to be. It did leave me feeling very included though.

> I think one of the most difficult parts about cruising among leathermen is that I do desire to have my genitals recognized and played with. I've met many gay men who have no desire to have their dicks touched at all, who like to suck cock and get fucked, and that's all. Among dykes and straight men there's less vaginophobia. – Blaise Garber-Paul

TransPunk's experience was much more positive, although he also admits a good deal of difficulty:

> The only harsh exclusions I have faced in the BDSM context were from the gay men's community in Germany. They are still far behind; it's only slowly improving through personal contacts. I was forbidden to take part in their camps and clubs pre-transitioning. (There are actually votes on this regarding me in particular.) ... I went to the gay BDSM camp for the first time and I was passing, but I am in the process of outing myself afterwards to anyone who wants to know as I gave my Gay Romeo profile to the group, so now people can check me out and find out.
>
> I find it works better to do away with prejudices if they get to know me first and then find out. Funny enough, during the camp there were two instances of outing to people I befriended there. I showed my tattoo on my chest to a Master/slave couple. Later they told me, they were momentarily dumbstruck by the scar, but that they loved scars and thought it looked great. I told them it was much more prominent before I got the tattoo, and the slave said he thought it was good now: "From afar, you first see the sheep, then the man and then the scar". This is a typical experience of welcoming me as trans implicitly, which I appreciate, as nobody else around us got it who wasn't supposed to. The last day one of my favorite Masters in the camp told me he had heard that a transsexual was supposed to come, but obviously he hadn't. I had to laugh so hard inside and I pointed at myself. He burst out laughing in disbelief and was so happy I was there. It was really cute. So the support is growing. This last guy tellingly was one of the two men of color there and obviously he totally related the exclusion of trans to other exclusions. I often seem to end up with one of the other "queer" queers or gay men marginalized within the community.

Ian MacAlister, a nontrans bisexual man who is partnered to a MTF and has played with FTMs, sent me a long piece containing his advice to FTMs who were beating fruitlessly against the doors of men-only space. He acknowledged that his advice was controversial and would probably upset some people, but his intent was to lay some blunt things out where they could be worked on honestly.

> I have a lot of pretty strong opinions about this, so hold on and try not to be too offended. Or if you are offended, let it make you think about why. I've found that female-originating people who came out of radical political space have a huge amount of resistance around listening

to men's advice on anything. That's understandable, but this subject—men's space—is one where you need to listen respectfully to men, or you'll get nowhere.

I'm very well aware of the problems of FTMs integrating themselves into gay male leather spaces. I have not been in any sexual relationships with FTMs, but I've played with a few and "mentored" them in learning about gay space. I've run into the same problems over and over, especially with FTMs who were active in women's or "college genderqueer" spaces before transition. They don't understand the background context of gay male space, and they come into it with preconceived ideas from women's space, and they try to push them onto the men and become upset when it doesn't fly. Even if they are allowed into men's sexual spaces, they are upset when the men won't just up and have sex with them. They talk about this sexual rejection as if it was a political offense.

When I started talking to FTMs in leather space, I ran into these cultural differences that I didn't understand. Because I'm a geek, I did research. I read material on the politics and history of women's spaces, including women's BDSM spaces. Maybe it's because I'm a guy, but the big thing that stood out for me was that women have a history of deprioritizing sex for community harmony or politics. I am guessing that this is partly because women were and sometimes still are raised with cultural repressions on their sexuality—they are not supposed to make it a big thing in their lives for a lot of pretty negative cultural reasons—and partly because of testosterone. (Actually, talking to FTMs about their hormonal changes solidified that last one for me.) There are strong undertones of "it's not OK to not be attracted to someone for *bad* reasons, like the way that their body is shaped." One is supposed to put one's libidinous feelings aside for doing the right thing, whatever that particular community of women says that is. I wonder about this pressure, given the parallel pressure women get in the outside world to be sexually available, but that's not my problem to figure out.

In (nontrans) male sexual space, that is not going to fly. The libido and all its kinks are prioritized. It's accepted that you get turned on to what you get turned on to. This is not going to change, and I don't think it's evil or wrong. It is what it is. If you want to be in male sexual spaces, you have to accept that. At any rate, coming in as an outsider and telling the biomen in that space that they're doing it wrong is absolutely useless. FTMs need to understand that in order to make change in biomale sexual spaces, the change has to support the hard-on, not tell it that it's not OK with its desires. That's the way it's done here. You can't bring women's culture here and expect it to be accepted. In fact, it plays up the way that you're different and don't belong. If this makes you cringe, maybe this is not the right space for you to be in. I know that a lot of FTMs have this idealized view of gay male sexual space, and sometimes I have to be the one to burst that bubble.

One example of all-male sexual space not being willing to deprioritize sex in favor of politics is that gay men are so reluctant to come to pansexual parties. Being able to have genital sex as part of the public play is really important to them, and most won't go places where they can't have that, and alcohol and poppers as well. I realize that no-genital-play spaces are very comforting to many transgendered people—my girl likes that and so I play with her in nonsexual pan spaces. (I don't take her to gay male spaces because I won't put her in that position.) But it's not my ideal, it's something that I put up with as a gift to my partner. But telling gay men that they ought to sacrifice sex acts they enjoy for the sake of making a pansexual space more "inclusive" is so not going to work. Gay men go to these clubs to have kinky sex. They also go to watch kinky sex, and get turned on. The problem with SM players feeling "violated" by spectators jerking off is never something I've encountered in an all-male space.

In addition, many gay men just don't like female body parts and aren't going to play with people who have them, and that's not seen as a bad thing in that community. Many won't fuck blondes or gym queens or dark-skinned people or old people or people who aren't those things. It's just accepted as the vagaries of the hard-on. There was a study done on gay men some time back on the "ick factor"—I remember reading it. According to that study, a third of gay men are completely icked out by the sight of female secondary sex characteristics. Another third are neutral but not attracted, and the remaining third is primarily gay but will interact happily with female and female-ish bodies on occasion. (Then I guess it slides into bisexual from there.) So an FTM who does not have enough male sexual cues to override their female sexual cues is not going to get laid by most gay men, and is going to gross out some of them. That, too, is not going to change by chiding people and telling them that their reactions are not allowed.

Also, men are raised to be the ones who make the first approaches. Men are used to being rejected. We don't like it, some of us aren't good about it, but we understand that it's perfectly normal to have to approach 50 people and ask them for sex before you get one that says yes. Gay men are used to dealing with sex objects that have good boundaries and say No without hesitation, so we're especially skilled at this. We just do it. I see too many FTMs who stand around waiting to be approached as if they were still girls, or approach one person and then are crushed by the rejection.

So the advice that I have for FTMs who want to get into gay male space is: First, you need to be physically masculine enough to have enough male cues to outweigh female ones. Smell is a big cue for men, so hormones help. Men are often more visual than women, so visual clues help. Sorry, that may not feel fair, but again remember that men have learned to take not being someone's type in stride. Second, be sexually confident in yourself. Be willing to approach a lot of men, and never take rejection seriously. Have good boundaries for when you're approached by someone you don't want. Third, assuming that you are allowed in by whatever policy, come and be social—for months if necessary. Hang around, talk, be one of the guys. Make friends. Don't be hung up on whether you can fuck them. Once you're part of the community, you may become a sexual possibility, but be willing to be patient and let it happen. Fourth, remember that in our little culture, a guy watching you play while jerking off is a compliment. Accept that the hard-on really is the priority there, and that's not necessarily a bad thing. Fifth, don't complain about the sexual politics. It will do no good and you will just piss people off. Sixth, if you really can't stand the subculture, make your own group where the rules are yours! It really comes down to that.

Advice For Same-Sex BDSM Groups

This section was specifically created for same-sex BDSM groups who are struggling with the question of whether or not to let transgendered individuals into their group who did not start out their gender. For this subject, I diverted from my by-trans-for-trans policy and asked for aid from gay men and lesbians who were involved with groups who had done just that. I asked them about their process, and their advice to other groups who were struggling with this issue. I should repeat, again, that I do believe that any group has the right to decide where they are going to draw their lines. Some will draw them in such a way that all transgendered people are excluded. Others will want to include some transgendered individuals but not others, and may struggle with where they feel that it is most fair and useful to all parties to draw them.

Mr. Munter, a long-term nontrans member of a gay male club that opened their doors to FTMs, had a lot of good advice for other clubs who were considering the process. First, he suggested that they personally ask themselves the following questions, to put things into perspective:

+ Would you join a men's only BDSM club if they didn't let men under 18 join? Or only men under 40? Or only men over 50?
+ Would you join a men's only BDSM club if they didn't let people of color join?
+ What if you had to be a practicing Protestant Christian?
+ How do we know who is a man and who is not? Gonads? Driver's license? "Living as a man"? Birth certificate?
+ Who should determine who is a man? A doctor? The Department of Motor Vehicles? The State Department? The board of a BDSM club?
+ Should everyone coming to an event have to drop their pants to prove they have standard male genitals?
+ What about men who are mistaken to be women at birth, raised as women, but have an XY chromosome and develop male traits as an adult?
+ Should a man who has had his genitals removed because of cancer be allowed to join a men's club? Should he be kicked out for that?
+ At what point should a man who chooses to take female hormones be not allowed to join or forced to resign?
+ What about men who have a medical condition that brings about the same results, though not of their choice?

✦ How about guys who take male steroids and develop smaller balls and breasts like women?

✦ How is discrimination against transmen based on the bias that they must act like women different from discrimination against gay men based on the bias that they must act like women?

Beyond this, he also recommends a process by which the management of a men-only club can go about deciding if they want to open their group to FTMs, and if so, how:

> First, for any board, I think a little education is really important. It's hard to have a calm discussion without some perspective on the history of how civil rights are provided over time. Why do we say LGBT? What does that mean? How were gay men treated in the 1920s? 1950s? 1970s? How is that similar to or different from discrimination against transgender men today?
>
> It's also important to perhaps meet some FTM men and get some varying opinions about that experience. For example, I know FTMs who always thought they were men, who discovered they were men, a boy-identified lesbian who became a gay man when he transitioned, women living as men but keeping their female—and often lesbian—identity, and people who want to live in a genderless, gender queer or gender ambiguous life. Where would the line for membership be drawn, and why? FTMs have very different views on this topic as well. One FTM I knew expressed (a possibly transphobic statement) that a change in policy would open the door for all the lesbian/gender ambiguous FTMs to make a political statement by demanding to come to all male events.
>
> Second, I would recommend the board clarify their view on human rights, LGBT rights and transgender rights. What values do individuals hold? What values does the organization hold? It's always difficult for me to respect positions different from mine, but it is important for people to be able to express their feelings on this and have those feelings respected and appreciated. We can all see things differently and still make good decisions together.
>
> Third, how does the membership, participants or broader community feel about this? What discussion has come up before? What has happened when transgender

men have participated? What have you heard from your membership? What leads you to believe your membership may want a particular policy around this issue? It's sad when we have to give up our principles to deal with social pressure, but as leaders of an organization, we need to think about education and a path toward change as well as what's the right thing to do.

I think this lays the foundation for a discussion around how an organization defines being a man or restricts access based on gender. So, perhaps a fourth step is to consider at what point of physical transition would a group consider an FTM, and why? How do you determine a consensus of the group's comfort? Does a man have to have a dick? What about FTMs with phalloplasties? Does a doctor determine who is a man when we are born? Does a doctor determine who is a man when they perform gender changing surgery? Does the Department of Motor Vehicles or the State Department determine who is a man when they issue an ID? Does one have to be "living as a man" to be a man, and if so, what does that mean? Can a person self-identify as a man?

Finally, what sort of policy should the board implement? Would that decision be made on the basis of the comfort of the group members, or a set principle? Would men be allowed to expose their vaginas in public play? Can you expect people to respect this, or do you need a policy of pants-on-only? There are lots of options that we might provide—a smorgasbord of policies, the most liberal one being anyone who does not identify as a woman is welcome to attend. And one option for a board is to make the best decision they can come to now with a commitment to talk about this again in six months or a year or two years to see if education can move the organization toward a better understanding of FTM men.

The problem with this approach is it could take a long time and be used to delay a decision or to keep a more restrictive policy in place. So perhaps to start you need an agreement about a time line. For example, we have a 10 minute meeting, so let's each take a minute to explain what we know about FTMs, how we feel about their rights, and how we think the membership/participants/community feels about this. Out of that, try to pull together a consensus and see what policy we would choose if we could enact one today. If you have an hour, you might spend 10 minutes on each of the first four items and then discuss possible policies for 20 minutes. Perhaps a one day retreat. Perhaps scheduling an educational meeting for step one, and then a separate discussion of steps 2-4 before sitting down to discuss possible policies. But deciding a timeline up front will help keep people getting stuck on step one, saying we need more education and not doing anything. (Or getting stuck at step, 2, 3, or 4 saying we need an agreement before we can move forward.)

Lesbian groups who have allowed transwomen to attend have decided on varying boundaries. Some have go so far as to declare their group "women and trans", meaning, basically, everyone except for male-identified nontrans men. Others have kept it to women's space only, with a legal qualifier—the letter F on one's ID, for example—as the dividing line. Still others allow in anyone who can prove that they are "living as a woman full-time", or in a few cases "identifies as a woman". When asked about the latter case, they stressed that these clubs are private and that all new members are subject to thorough interviews in order to discern if they fit the subject.

At least one group bases its boundaries on members attitudes toward male genitalia, saying:

> This party is open to those that identify as female. It is about you and how you identify.
>
> If you are able to detach your cock and put it away in a drawer, then this party is for you!
>
> If you have a penis that you do not use anymore because you identify as a female and simply wear some sexy panties, you are welcome at this party.
>
> Ergo, if you were born with a penis that you still enjoy using and/or you identify as male, then this party is not for you.

This group makes it clear—as other policies have not, although one would assume that it would be made clear during membership discussions—as to whether genitals that aren't acceptable for that gender should be exposed in that space. (In a word, no.) This is a sensitive subject that is nonetheless one of the first issues that nontrans members may worry about. *Am I going to have to be confronted with genitals of the sort worn by people we are deliberately trying to exclude? What if not seeing those genitals is part of what makes this a safe space for me?* One club organizer who called herself Seychelle said starkly, "The reason that many women are made uncomfortable with male genitals in a sexual space is that they have been so badly treated by people with bodies who are built like that, look that way, and smell that way. Some have serious abuse issues. Some of them are unable to be comfortable about being sexual (and thus vulnerable) in a space with those bodies. Part of the point of this space is the safety issue. BDSM has enough triggers without having to deal with that on top of it."

On the other hand, no one is less thrilled than a transsexual that they don't have the factory-equipped bits that they might want, and to be excluded from genital play for an accident of birth that they are likely even more traumatized about than any nontrans onlookers can feel painfully unfair. Several of the transfolk who do go to same-sex BDSM parties (where they are allowed) fear being thrown out if they expose their ambivalently-seen genitalia; they aren't sure what the policy might be on that matter, but they don't want to test it. To make things more complicated, some parties are less than clear about their policy on the matter. One nontrans woman who organized women-only parties said, "They should know that penises are not going to be well received by most lesbians, so we assume that transwomen will use common sense and keep them in their pants. If they do differently, a dungeon monitor will politely and discreetly come by and ask them to keep that private."

The fact that many transgendered individuals are shy-to-extremely-dysphoric works in their favor; another nontrans party-manager told me confidently, "We've never had this problem. The trans members of our group don't want to expose their genitals." Similarly, "John", a former management member of a gay male club, told me, "We have 3 FTMs here that I know of. So far the issue hasn't come up because they are all bottoms, and while I understand they all suck a mean cock, they don't involve their own genitals, I assume for their own comfort." That may be; dysphoria is a constant haunt of many transfolk. But it's not impossible that the comfort of other members might be haunting them as well.

Seychelle's group goes one step further; she says:

We had many months of discussion on whether to allow or disallow different kinds of transgendered members. We finally decided that we did not want to define male or female. Instead, we tried to define what sort of people would create a safe space for our original women members. For example, a woman who attempted to force herself physically on someone at the party without their verbal consent would not be welcome. Certain kinds of bodies would upset the majority of our members, and thus not be welcome.

For us, it came down to hormones, because our first trans issue was with a butch lesbian who transitioned to male. Once he began to take male hormones, he smelled like a man, and began to very much look like one. We had to ask him to leave. Strange as it may seem, it was the smell that was the real problem. Transgendered women who have been on hormones for a while don't smell like that. (And no, public penises are not allowed.) We have also had to screen for behavioral reasons, making sure that transgendered women understood what kind of behavior was appropriate in that space. Not all of them did. In contrast, a butch lesbian whose behavior was indistinguishable from that of a standard patriarchal male would also not be welcome. We have never had to ban anyone like that, but we do know a few people like that personally.

A club manager has an obligation to her or his members. In the end, it's not what anyone thinks is right or wrong, it has to do with what makes the majority of members comfortable or uncomfortable. They set the tone. They are the ones who were with you from the beginning. Respond to their needs, or you will lose them.

Also, go slow. It is OK to make narrow rules and then broaden them later, when members are used to the first step. Even with our comparatively narrow gate—for which we have been criticized—we do have some transgendered members. To a woman, they are happy with our rules and do not want them broadened. If the majority of the membership thought otherwise, we would think about changing our policy further, but right now the steps we've taken are enough for us.

Another member of a men's group told me: "The vagina thing was a problem at first. Some guys had to get used to it. It helped that the FTMs who joined didn't, well, whip it out at first—they waited until they had been around for a while and were accepted. Then they exposed themselves discreetly. After a while, we just got used to it. Does it make a difference as to who will play with them and how? Of course it does, I won't lie to you. They all have biomale partners who come with them, so they aren't starving, but it does make a difference. I do consider them my brothers, and I would defend them like I would defend any of my brothers in the club, and I have played with one of them ... but not genitally. People want what they want. You have to accept that. You can't force sexual desire. Gay men grew up having sexual desires forced on us. We've had enough of being told that we aren't OK for not wanting vaginas, thanks."

A few same-sex groups were started by transgendered men and women and their partners in order to deal with this problem. SHE, a women's party in California run by transwoman Lilith von Fraumensch, lets any sort of woman come and self-identify. Lilith describes her group this way:

> SHE is a play party at the Center For Sex-Positive Culture in Seattle that is open to all women—cis and trans. The genesis of SHE was in July 2009, when my girlfriend Amber and I were not able to enter a women's play party due to their ID requirements. Bear in mind that not all trans people can update their ID. Some cannot afford to pay the costs of gatekeeping; the bills from therapists, endocrinologists, or lawyers can be a formidable barrier for poor trans people to overcome. Some have conscientious objections to updating their ID—sometimes on libertarian grounds ("Why should the government regulate my gender?") and sometimes on grounds of privilege ("Why should I update my ID when so many others cannot?"). Some risk harm to their families if they update their legal documentation, especially if it impacts their employability and benefits. And for some trans people, legal barriers prevent them from updating their ID at all.

Both Amber and I were distraught at not being permitted admittance, as we had no other opportunities to go to a play party the month prior, and would have none for the month following. Amber, however, took matters one step further—she wrote an open letter to the CSPC explaining at length why it was unfair to have such a policy. This led to an online debate on the subject, and eventually, a proposal. We would launch a play party without the requirement, as a test run for a policy change. Since the only requirement would be that the attendees identify as women, one of our friends suggested a very simple but direct name for the party: SHE.

The first SHE party was in mid-August, 2009, and was a success from the start, drawing more numbers than we expected—and more than the other women's party. By November, the other women's party moved to change its entrance requirements to allow trans people—regardless of gender identification—and genderqueers, as well as cisgendered women. The irony was sublime—we had started as the less restrictive party, and through no fault of ours we had become the more restrictive! But it meant that SHE had become the women's play party at the CSPC—an honor and tribute to our commitment to providing a safe space for all women to explore their sexuality. SHE also was unique in that it was a highly social party, meaning we were not just providing a space—we were building a community.

As of this writing SHE is approaching its one-year anniversary, and looking back, there is very little that I think we would have done differently. We are constantly making adjustments and improvements, to better meet the needs of our community—the community of all women at the CSPC. This party is a critical part of my life, and a source of deep pride. All women—especially trans women—need a space where their womanhood will be recognized and honored, and I can only hope that, given time, the example SHE provides may be followed by future women's play parties.

From Too Little To Too Much

At what point does inclusivity become as oppressive as exclusivity? The idea may make people blink at first, but it's starting to be discussed as a problem. I've bowed out of groups and parties that policed what could be said and done so heavily that I began to feel like I would accidentally be the next one up for a reprimand, no matter what I did. I've always been on the side of the libertines; no matter who has triggers about Nazis, I support the right of that couple over there on the far side of the dungeon to dress up as Nazi and minority-member and gleefully have a scene. As Mik Kinkead pointedly says:

> My partner and I have been to a few BDSM clubs that claim to be trans-friendly, but they generally feel too policed and too "in-crowd" for me to feel comfortable. I also have found that the inclusive BDSM clubs I have been to are so aware of people's triggers that sometimes expressive sexuality ends up not being allowed in case it triggers another club member. Which I can respect. If we are trying to form a community we need to be aware of where everyone in the community is coming from, but I go to a BDSM club to express my sexuality openly and if I can't play how I want with my partner for fear of triggering someone else ... then it seems like there's no point in going! I've heard through the grapevine of BDSM people that less inclusive clubs tend to be more open towards expressing more extreme BDSM activities—but I've yet to go to these clubs as I become nervous about how I would be ID'd by other BDSM club-goers. – Mik Kinkead

Gender Balance and Balancing Genders

While not exactly part of the BDSM demographic, another place where transgendered people have had trouble is in groups that work with sexuality and spirituality in physical ways. Some call themselves "Tantric" groups, with the assumption that what they do is Tantric ritual sex. Some just call themselves "sex-spirit" groups or something along those lines. A good percentage of these groups are merely teaching about the intersections of sexuality and spirituality, usually verbally at the front of the class. The vast majority are heterosexual, with a more recent minority of gay male groups and at least one lesbian group that I know of. While they usually have no clue how to handle issues of positioning and sexual energy for trans people (for which they can be forgiven, because there's been damn little research on the subject), at least people are rarely turned away from the door.

The problem intensifies when the group has hands-on sexual activities, and in some cases, the assumption of full-on sexual activity between participants, perhaps even anonymously. (Some "Tantric" groups set up sex rituals where participants will switch off with each other throughout the ritual, on the idea that anonymous sex will not have the personal baggage that long-term partners might, and transpersonal sexual energy is easier to achieve.) For the groups that are all-male or all-female, the barriers are similar to the problems of the last section. For the other groups, the term "gender balanced" is often used to restrict attendance, meaning an even number of (normally gendered) men and women.

In the BDSM demographic, many people are also beginning to explore the concept of spirituality as intertwined with their special kinds of sexuality. This is leading to some tentative outreach between these groups, and tentative advertising. However, when a "gender balanced Tantric" event advertised on a list inhabited by a lot of kinksters (and a few transfolk), both trans and nontrans began to question the event leader. Where would trans people fit in, of various anatomies? What about people with intermediate gender identities? Would the even be allowed? One nontrans writer of sex books stoutly recommended "…inviting as many transgendered people as you can find, thus making it as balanced as it's possible to get."

The event leader was so taken aback that she didn't even know how to answer those questions. Our existence had not ever occurred to her. She withdrew, and the questions never did get answered … but they've been asked again, since, of other events, and it's only the beginning. (Group leaders in the BDSM demographic can certainly assure them of that.) Ruth, a polyamorous nontrans partner, pointed out that: "If you are asking about spaces where they require one female per one male I can only say that as a poly person as well as someone who is involved with nonstandard gender-identified people, I find the idea patently offensive."

Sex clubs—and especially swing clubs—may also have a "gender balance" policy, although they may not call it that. Joshua muses about the situation:

> If the organizers want "gender balance" because there are activities where everyone is expected partner up in male-female pairs, and switch off occasionally, you need an baseline assumption of interchangeable heterosexuality. Everyone needs to be willing to pair with any person of the opposite gender. So trans inclusion depends on whether the organizers think that most people in attendance would consider the trans person as a potential sexual partner of one gender or the other. If people don't have to switch partners freely, then the issue is similar to the inclusion of having gay men and lesbians. So long as there is someone for everyone to partner with, it can work. However, inclusion might be more difficult in a technique-based class where the structured activities are based on anatomy.
>
> Most attempts at maintaining "gender balance" in a heterosexual sexual space occur because far more men are interested in being there than women, and the more imbalanced the male-female ratio is, the less enjoyable the event is for everyone. (For the men, because their chances of finding a partner are so low, and for the women, because they are swarmed by overly-desperate men.) So there are two main concerns with transgendered people in this type of situation. 1) Regardless of gender balance, the attendees just don't want transgendered people at the event. 2) This decision might allow surplus men to get around the gender restriction by putting on women's clothes. (Unlikely, but that is a common concern.)
>
> I've been to swinger clubs where single women were allowed to attend without restriction, but single men had to be sponsored in by a male-female couple who would be held responsible for the man's behavior. Unless an MTF passed perfectly, I'm fairly certain she'd be considered a "man" for purposes of admission, and would be unlikely to be admitted with a male partner. One SM club I attended encouraged "gender balance" by charging men substantially more than women, and anyone perceived as a "man in drag" was charged halfway between, because a sizable minority of the men attending were generally interested in sex with men in drag.
> – Joshua

To Tell Or Not To Tell

For transgendered people who pass as their preferred gender, or who pass entirely as their birth gender but know that they will have to spring their trans issues on a potential partner before anyone gets naked, disclosure is a nail-biting issue. I remember seeing the problem illustrated graphically in the movie *The Crying Game,* where the sight of a penis on the pretty girl he brought home from the bar makes the male protagonist knock her to the ground and throw up. On an uglier note, some transgendered people have been murdered by dates they brought home from bars and didn't disclose to until they were alone, and the date decided to erase them from existence. (Although to be fair, many such "dates" knew exactly what they were getting, and fully intended to commit murder once they were alone.) Disclosure can be more serious than simply not getting laid. It can be a life-or-death situation.

It can also be something that can get you thrown out of a club, group, or party if it's found out, and some transfolk feel that this is worth the risk. In the end, it's a personal decision based on each person's tolerance for risky behavior, need to belong to a certain community or have (even nongenital) sexual experiences with a particular group of people who might not otherwise want them, closeted status in real life, and willingness to be an educator. Still, it's one of the top ten things that newly-out trans people ask the oldtimers, so it's worth it to know how, when, and why we do it or not.

Some transfolk disclose about their status as soon as possible. This can be a relief to some. E. Nelly says, "I like to just get it out there early before I have anxiety over the disclosure. I never let people get too close before I let them know."

Sejay advises: Be open and upfront about your identity. Further, surprises of the genital kind might be difficult for some folk to swallow (literally & figuratively). Practice safe sex. And, finally, you always have yourself, and you're more important a lover than anyone else.

> I'm honest and up front right off the bat. I let people
> know, this is who I am, if you have a problem, no hard

feelings, I understand. I made the decision early on that I never wanted to be accused of being deceptive about who and what I am. I live my life with a closet free of skeletons and I like it that way. – Ashley Lynch

In person I tend to disclose fairly early in meeting. Mostly because I don't want to be accused of trying to hide something or not being honest up front. – Sable Twilight

I disclose impulsively and opportunistically. I never lie. I occasionally omit. I don't pack. Usually disclosure happens in group conversations, simply sharing my stories generally outs me as trans (for example, I went to a recognizable all-women's college). I prefer to play in a community where I know folk, by the time I know them they know me. In Radical Faerie land I intentionally spend time naked in public space. In cruising situations the dick-handshake generally outs me—men grab for my junk and get a handful of cloth, or step on my crotch while I'm bootblacking and get floor... Sometimes I say things. I've heard some transfolk use lines like "This is getting serious, and I just want you to know that I know that you're a bioguy, and I want you to know that's OK with me." I like that line but I've never used it. Sometimes I'm blunt, and ask them if they like boys with cunts, but only if it fits in naturally into the conversation. – Blaise Garber-Paul

For the past several years I have been so out that disclosing has not been an issue; it was something people knew immediately upon knowing me. I am out at work, active in the GLBT community and on line any profile I have states that I am trans. Recently I have been in a training academy for work for 10 weeks. Here only the people who come from my employer know that I am trans, and I realize that I am so used to everyone knowing that I am uncomfortable when they do not know. I feel sneaky.
– coreyboi

I think I try to preempt disclosure by just being pretty out. I am fairly out in the sense that people in my life know, and if you look at my profile in various places, including on sex areas, I am out as trans. So I try to preempt that. I haven't had a long-time partner since transitioning but most people I have gotten involved with know I am trans and have been part of the community or allies. There are places that I make it a point of disclosing so that the T is not forgotten and we don't become invisible. Other places I realize people know but sometimes forget and I have to remind them. Other places I might not disclose the first time I attend a meeting, but will later if it becomes a regular thing in my life.

The specific wording I use to disclose depends on how much I feel may know or not about the trans community. I will use transgender sometimes if I feel they know little, trans or FTM if I think they'll get that. Queer would be my favorite but I find especially with people who haven't thought about this much, it comes off either as offensive or doesn't have a resonance. Sometimes spelling out "female to male" is the clearest, even though I don't fully endorse it as an identity, and don't consider this a point A to point B kind of journey. – Jackkinrowan

I'm pretty blunt. Because I'm not pursuing surgical or hormonal alteration, I have to be really clear about my gender identity with just about everyone in order to be recognized as my preferred gender. I will admit that I'm sure I've had some casual pick up play partners who thought I was a woman, because our connection was so superficial it never came up. As for legal stuff, I'm still a woman. I admit I am exercising privilege by doing so—I continue to be legally married to my husband, for starters. If a judge or other official asked me directly if I have ever used a masculine identity, masculine pronouns, or the like, I would be completely honest. If I were involved in a hate crime due to my trans status, I would include that in the report. – Del

I disclose that I am transgender to clubs and groups when the subject of gender comes up, or when I think it appropriate to give my point of view that might not have been previously considered. I am fairly open to discussing my transgender status with groups of people. It is more difficult, naturally, when I disclose this information to judges, but it is important to me to let others know even if they do not agree with my lifestyle choices. I want people to know we exist. The hardest people to disclose to are prospective partners, and I usually let them know early on once we begin discussing possibilities of being together sexually. I would rather they know at that point so that our time is not wasted, and so that they will not feel I was keeping something from them. I prefer honesty up front.

– Lord Tom

> Do I have a choice? I don't pass. If I want people to call me my name or use my pronoun, I have to disclose. I know most trans people pass or try to, but for those of us that don't, these questions are sometimes not pertinent.
> – Simon Strikeback

Some of the transfolk that I interviewed—and I myself fall into this camp—are public figures, in the BDSM and/or trans and/or GLBT or other communities. For individuals who have made this choice, disclosing is almost not an issue, as we have to assume that if someone doesn't know now, they will find out very quickly the first time they mention our names. (For me, it's always a bit mind-bending when I meet someone new in a community where I am very out, and they don't yet know and I have to disclose.)

But being a public figure has its own difficulties. Closeted transfolk have asked that I not accompany them or hang out with them too much in the spaces where I travel out and they travel stealth. At least once, a FTM support group that I attended a few times decided to go on a "stealth field trip" where they would go as a group to a gay bathhouse and offer blowjobs to the men attending (or just watch the sex acts). I pointed out that I am well known enough in queer circles that I can't assume that I am ever stealth; someone is always likely to run up and say, "You're Raven Kaldera!" They immediately realized that my presence would "endanger" their field trip—if I'm a known FTM and I'm hanging with this group of short guys, two and two could be put together—and they politely asked that I not attend.

> I do not disclose at cafes, restaurants, folks on the street. In my classes I tend to say something like "as a note, I will occasionally tell stories from when I was a woman, just to let you know, and now let's go on." I acknowledge it then move on, as the classes most of the time are not about my gender, and I don't want the class to get distracted.
> To prospective partners, I just out my different body as soon as it seems that there is a likelihood we will play, assuming that play will involve me naked or topless (scars).

If I will stay closed, I take it on a case-by-case basis. But I am fairly well known in the communities I interact with for the most part, and thus I'm often pre-disclosed by being who I am. At men's bathhouse spaces, I just go nude. Folks figure it out, and they then have the choice as to if they want to play with me or not. – Lee Harrington

My play partners have all been incredibly queer and immediately aware of my gender identity and history. I have a fiery transgender symbol tattooed on my lower arm, and have been a very vocal and public figure in transgender artist spaces in my local area(s) thus making my status very public knowledge so folks have always known what they were getting into. Looking at disclosure to community is a little bit harder for me. I've been burned by queer communities being uncomfortable with the degree to which I've played with my gender. When I was living and presenting as a transmasculine individual, I was pretty immediately recognized as Daddy's *boy* by community members. Now, presenting as a high femme, it is assumed that I am my Daddy's *girl*. I am not a girl, and become pretty frustrated by community assumptions based on the way that I present my gender that I identify differently. There is no reason that a boy can't go to the dungeon wearing a tutu and corset.

As I mentioned previously I only play in queer gender-conscious spaces so I feel pretty confident that if I were to correct assumptions my identity would definitely be respected, but I don't always feel like having to come out and explain my gender journey, or complexity of my present identity to folks. Similarly in the way that I prefer genderqueer pronouns ze/hir which more closely align with my gender identity, it's often just easier to let folks use she/her instead of having to correct them. –Sassafras Lowrey

Other transfolk will disclose quietly to someone that they are going to have sex with, either because nudity will reveal it anyway and it's best to get it over with, or because they need to be treated in a certain way and their unaltered physical body will not necessarily inspire that automatically in a new person of indeterminate experience. The positive side to this is that it prevents *Crying Game*-esque problems; the negative side is that it can quickly spread through a group, especially from people who are freaked out by the disclosure.

Prior to living as a woman full-time, I disclosed to everyone in the BDSM/Leather spaces because I wanted them to use the correct pronouns. These days I only disclose when there is a chance I may play with someone. I pass very well in the outside communities, and even people in the BDSM communities are surprised when and if I disclose, unless they knew me before. Other than if I am going to play with someone—then it is nobody else's business. I am a woman. Period. – Siobhan Phoenix

I disclose to people I will be sexually intimate with more than once, or those individuals who will personally benefit from the knowledge. Ideally I tell a partner before we have sex but have forgotten it was an issue to be discussed until the last moment (or after). Clubs and groups do not need to know so I do not disclose to all, unless of course that club or group is Trans focused and I am demonstrating my membership qualifications. Only once did I disclose to Leather contest judges, but that was during the very first FTM title competition in US. – BEAR A-M Rodgers

I tend to think that since I'm not going to be sleeping with the person or dating the person, it really is none of their business how I handle my personal gender. In the case of pronouns for most people, there is a certain amount of logic to being up-front unless you are prepared to hear the wrong pronoun used repeatedly (or you pass very well). For me though, unless the situation actually requires me to discuss my gender, I simply let people think what they will. I do, however, walk everywhere in skirts and rarely cut my beard, so I'm sure that they are faced with some sort of disclosure automatically. – Lizzie

I think it's an individual thing, in that I decide to disclose with each person/group/jury when I decide to disclose. Sometimes I just forget and am myself, thinking "How can anyone not see me for the genderqueer weirdo I am?" but I am reminded, especially by those people who think I am being "deceitful", that many people don't see me as anything but a woman. Maybe a strange, dykey woman, but a woman nonetheless. – Terra Katherine McKeown

Knowing when to disclose can also mean knowing how much to disclose. Just because you have decided to come out to a group does not mean that you are now obligated to discuss intimate details of your sex life, and just because you have come out to a person you're interested in playing with does not mean that you have to tell them intimate details of your past life. Calmly setting good boundaries is also educational, as it teaches people what is and is not appropriate to ask about. Dax reminds us, "When someone is rude or seems to be asking for the wrong reasons, I reveal less."

Many passing transfolk seem prefer being closeted because it's just so much easier, and it also seems safer as long as it is able to continue. For some of these transsexuals, the fact of their trans status is not a large part of their lives and identity, and they would prefer not to call attention to it unless it was absolutely necessary. Others try out the closet and discover that they prefer being out for reasons of honesty and integrity. Finn in Germany says: "After having lived for over a year as a 'stealth' male, it is a great relief to be in a queer environment within which my trans identity is either openly articulated or silently understood, and is certainly nothing unusual; however, I am aware of what a wonderful privilege this is. The concept of 'disclosure' would previously have given me great anxiety; I would disclose if I felt that it was necessary to either allow a friendship to diminish or to flourish, and if I felt sufficiently secure to offer myself to others as an example of a trans person, being aware that such a revelation can never be reversed. Writing these words, and hopefully participating in similar publications and productions, is my disclosure."

Others may stay closeted until they are well-known in their community, at which time any "outing" may not make too much of a difference because they have enough group support and friends at their back. Far from being an apolitical act, coming out as trans when you're a long-term known quantity can be a very powerful thing. It's a different sort of social shock than the out-and-proud genderqueer on the sidewalk, and while both are useful and necessary, the passing trans individual who comes out after a long period of membership can often get through to people who would have blown off the out genderqueer and never listened to them. TransPunk discusses his situation with waiting to disclose:

> Before transitioning, I had to disclose all the time in order to be read the way I wanted to be read. Now that I'm passing I get to choose, which seems like a huge luxury ... I have made bad experiences in the past with disclosing beforehand to a group of gay men who then get to decide whether I'm allowed to be included. Since then, I take it for granted, exploit the fact that I can pass now, enter their spaces without explicit admission and out myself person by person. I usually tell them it's OK to tell a third party if they do not turn it into bad gossip. That way it spreads a bit more quickly. Sometimes I do tell it right away if I feel it is important people know ... The more I'm integrated the harder it would be for a club or group to exclude me now. So I'm making it public at a point of no return so to speak. Also in Germany, guys are so unfamiliar with transguys that they don't get the subtle hints or signs, e.g. nobody reads my scar as FTM. With more education, this might change over time, as in more queer spaces I am more easily recognized as trans. – TransPunk

Comfort with a greater level of disclosure can come over time, as the individual settles more firmly into their identity. Some choose their level at the beginning and don't change. On the other hand, Micah patiently enumerates all the various choices one can make with this delicate subject:

> I tend only to disclose to prospective partners. I have tried various different approaches.
>
> 1) Never disclosing; staying stealth. Plus: I never need to deal with the awkwardness and potential for transphobia that accompanies disclosure. I am assured that I will get treated like a man without question during the scene. Minus: I am often anxious that I will be "discovered," which distracts me from the fun, and I cannot engage in some of my favorite activities.
>
> 2) Never disclosing; just letting my partner figure it out on their own through their observations of my body. Plus: There are no apologies—I'm letting my prospective partners take responsibility for their own assumptions. Minus: I have to deal with their reaction when I am already

in a pretty vulnerable situation, which can be a bit unpleasant.

3) Disclosing up front in a personal ad. Plus: I get it over with right away and know that anyone who writes me ought to be at least theoretically okay with playing with a trans man. Minus: It seems to distract a lot of guys from everything else in my profile. I get a lot of mail from tranny chasers/fetishizers, some propositions from men who clearly see me as a woman, and a lot of messages asking me obnoxious and invasive questions.

4) Disclosing verbally just before we start to have sex or play. Plus: We get to interact and maybe get to know each other a bit before I share such personal information and they still get the info before it becomes most relevant. Minus: It is often dreadfully awkward timing.

5) Disclosing in an offhanded way as a part of casual conversation. Plus: It is easiest and least awkward for me if I can work my trans experience into a conversation somewhat naturally, rather than setting it up as some momentous announcement likely to precipitate a huge reaction on the part of the prospective partner. I feel like I am maintaining my dignity and sending the right signals to the partner: this is a part of who I am, it is something I am comfortable discussing, and it is not that big a deal. This approach is my current favorite and the one I used with my current boyfriends. Minus: This approach tends to work best in a dating situation as opposed to a casual sex or play situation. Sometimes, there just isn't that much conversation ahead of time to try to slip a disclosure in.

Disclosing is also an act of faith in the future and solidarity with the trans people who have not yet come into the group. If it doesn't get you kicked out (and sometimes even if it does), it may be a way to slowly make social change, and mold the group into a place where gender is less relevant. The decision may well come down to how invested you would like to be, all things considered, any given community. Pick your battles, but don't turn away from them either.

If the person or group of people is important, or you are going to be there a lot of your time and it will play a big role in your life, it is better to tell. If not—often I just skip the embarrassment of telling and explaining, and bear with being misperceived, as long as I can keep myself cold and distanced to those misperceptions. Sometimes telling can also complicate the situation or make it dangerous. Anyway, to tell or not to tell, it's like deciding where it is just water running over and past you, where you don't want to disturb it and get disturbed by the disturbances ... or whether it is the water you are going to drink from and need to make sure is clean. – Vidal Rousso

Epilogue:
Giving Back

For many of us, it was kink that nurtured us, led us into our sexuality even through the darkest doors, and in some cases brought us into communities where Normal wasn't normal, where we could expose our real selves. In return, what is it that we bring to the BDSM demographic? What is our contribution, besides more freaks to ogle or more "local color" to lend atmosphere to the often-contrived weirdness of a venue? I asked my respondents that question, hoping to get a variety of perspectives other than simply "variety", and they did not disappoint me. Some felt that the question privileged our supposed "special perspectives" too much, and that we were really just ordinary people. BEAR A-M Rodgers summed this up by saying: "Transfolk bring the same things to the community table as anyone else, nothing exceptional in my opinion. More Transfolk are screwed up about gender roles and unification than the biogendered folk they claim are inhibiting them. Each group has the same opportunities to learn and then teach, it's how they utilize those opportunities that creates value."

Others felt that we did indeed have special, unique perspectives worth listening to. Rather than send me a questionnaire, Jewel Zingamen sent me a long poem of many verses about her experience with being a trans pervert. With her permission, I have broken it up with a handful of the quotes from the wonderful people who helped to build this book. Just think of it as a verbal collage, seen between the blinking strobe lights on the club stage as that person you were wondering about is performing up there, making you hot, making you think, making you feel.

I am alone in the spotlight
and no one watches me
except the presence that I trust
and who trusts me.
Our eyes meet,
it is time,

> *I drop the leather corset from*
> *the breasts I fought to grow.*

Transfolk can show people that sexual practices of BDSM are often not gender specific, and that sex itself can be an art form through these practices in situations where "traditional" sex/intercourse cannot be performed. – Lord Tom

> *Your hands on me,*
> *reminding me that we agreed to this,*
> *I drop the leather skirt and now*
> *my body is a mermaid,*
> *a winged horse, a cockatrice,*
> *all the other beasts who are*
> *not one thing but many*
> *and therein lies their power.*
> *The eyes are watching now.*

Trans people are usually keenly aware of their lived experience prior to transition and can offer a different perspective of navigating both BDSM and society in general. Trans people can be great teachers on how gender roles and assumptions are outdated, arbitrary, and in some ways irrelevant. They can teach overall how to respect some one's physical differences, but can also give specific teachings on how to deal with differently gendered bodies. I also think that trans people have a unique blend of masculine and feminine energies and bring that energy with them into whatever spaces they enter. – E. Nelly

> *I breathe, center, the cuffs*
> *surround my wrists.*
> *I trust. The blow falls,*
> *then the next, and the next.*
> *The eyes watch, judge,*
> *I do not look at them.*
> *My wings are beating*

Against my horse's back.
I am flying.

I see lots of "play" in BDSM as transgression of various aspects of life; i.e. rape play being consensual, cross dressing (either forced or fetishized or both), racial/cultural/classist stereotypes played out in various roles, age play, etc. When a trans person—especially one who goes outside the gender binary and defines their identity in a third gender, or genderqueer, or the like—comes into the picture, these things become *who they are* or "*real*", rather than "*play*". It causes many of us (including transfolk) to deconstruct gender norms, to deconstruct how we desire gender (as many would say that is what desire is about: the desire for the other and/or same gender), and for many of us, to take "gender" out of "play". – Terra Katherine McKeown

Are you watching,
You who read this now?
Are you wondering?
Does that mean I am wondrous?
Do not look at the horse, the eagle,
the fish, the snake, the other parts –
look at the whole being,
look at my magic, my power
even as I give up that power
and be awed.

If trans people were the ones running BDSM play spaces, just about anyone would feel more comfortable. That's why, in my experience, the disAbled and trans communities have so much in common in sex and play and public displays of sex. – Simon Strikeback

The clamps are butterflies of pain
that perch on my hard-won nipples.
I cry, thrash, you relent

> *after enough time to satisfy you*
> *and off they come*
> *leaving rivulets of agony.*
> *Instead, they go on below.*
> *I forget the eyes that stare*
> *and I weep.*

Both transgenderism and BDSM practices could be regarded as differing elements of the same phenomenon, that of queerness, and so both should be mutually accepting of each other. – Finn

> *Your body against mine,*
> *I am let down from the sky*
> *where I hang in exquisite*
> *state, not pleasure or pain*
> *but something beyond either.*
> *My knees touch the ground*
> *and my forehead is against*
> *your secrets, behind the leather*
> *that is your shield.*
> *You bring me down gently.*

Transfolk in general tend to put a lot more thought into what it means to be of a particular gender—and this seems to give them a lot of insight when dealing with a partner of *any* gender. Based on personal accounts I have read and watched and my observations of my Master's transition, I think that, particularly for those who have transitioned through the use of hormones, there can be a bit of an initial shock at how much a difference biology *can* make—and that there is a very real basis for many of our cultural assumptions and stereotypes of gender-typical behaviour, practices, roles, etcetera. Once they get past that initial shock, however, I find that most transfolk tend to become more aware of how biology *plays into* these roles and practices. I think that men and women who do *not* go through such a transition have a tendency to either believe blindly in stereotypes—or they completely discount the real, physical differences that do exist. – crstlbella

> *I kneel before you,*
> *head between your boots,*
> *until I am back.*
> *Our eyes meet, you smile*
> *and you hand me down the whip.*
> *Privilege comes into my hand*
> *and I rise as you begin*
> *to strip away your armor,*
> *your mask, your safety.*

I think the BDSM community lends itself to folks who are at least in more contact with, if not more aware and celebratory of, diversity in thought and play. The BDSM scene is where I first started using my new (non-gendered) name and coming out as genderqueer … It was a great testing ground too—they let you pick your name for the event, and role play is a commonly accepted form of play; you could be *anybody* (& any *body*) for tonight, this weekend, or you entire life from now on... and it's *perfectly okay* (if not *incredibly fun*) for your identity to change once, twice, or even minute-by-minute. – Sejay

> *Your body is a centaur,*
> *a griffin, a mythic beast*
> *just as mine is—the scars where*
> *sacrifice was made,*
> *the muscles gifted by the needle,*
> *the hips and thighs as*
> *you bare yourself,*
> *piece by piece.*
> *We are both warriors*
> *courageous in walking through fire.*

Transsexuals, having the chance to look at both genders and spending a lot of time wondering about how gender works, can give a lot to the explanation of BDSM mechanisms, why who does what, why who dominates whom and where the urges are coming from, making the porridge of instincts, sexual needs and preferences easier to understand. By just showing that we exist and being among the "normal" population we bring more tolerance, more variety, including sexual variety, more color, more possibilities and ideas of gender play. BDSM is interesting only if it is like life—developing, moving, open, not rigid, settled and closed, and transfolk are like tricksters, whether they want it or not; they are giving a jolt wherever they go. – Vidal Rousso

> *My hands on you,*
> *reminding you that we agreed to this,*
> *that you are safe with me.*
> *The cuffs are still warm*
> *from my hands, my flight.*
> *I buckle you in and*
> *you center, you breathe,*
> *you bear the eyes as well,*
> *we share this ordeal now.*

I think of gender, sex and BDSM as all inherently tangled.

Gender is a system of archetypes. We employ these archetypes, these idealized or stereotyped personality types, when we act out social scripts or perform social rituals. They're like masks, or costumes or puppets that we play out scenes with. The scenes we play out help us make sense of the world around us, in our conscious minds and in our unconscious minds. Sex acts and BDSM acts function as rituals, and these rituals make up the meat of the scripts we play out.

Transpeople disrupt: certain archetypes are expected to have certain anatomy so that they can follow particular scripts that lead to specific (sex/play) rituals. For me, the tension in being trans and having BDSM/sex exchanges lies between the ability to rewrite scripts and invent new rituals, and the desire to fulfill more traditional archetypal roles that my physical body is limited from completing.

I like thinking of myself as a general wrench in the gears of gender. A little spark of disruption. I'd like to think that our presence challenges people's assumptions that we (meaning all people) are intrinsically and simply one gender or the either. I'd like to think we disrupt the idea that there *is* only one gender or the other. I'd love to think that we made it cool for people living more normative constructions to poke their heads out a little and play with their genders. – Blaise-Garber-Paul

Turn it all on its head,
make them all blink,
they know nothing.
I stand proud, their eyes are wide
waiting for that first gasp,
the first blow to fall.
I will take you
where I have been before,
I will make you fly.

About the Author

Raven Kaldera is a Northern Tradition Neo-Pagan shaman, homesteader, astrologer, herbalist, vampire, and intersexual transgendered FTM activist. He is the King of a very small Pagan kingdom, and one of the founders of its current incarnation, the First Kingdom Church of Asphodel. He is the author of far too many books to list here, but any web search will tell you far more than you want to know.

© 2006 Sadie Sez Portraits

Photography

Dedication: Photo of Joshua by Wintersong Tashlin
P.12 photo of Pat Califia
P. 28 photo of TransPunk by Chris Bethke
P. 31 photo of E. Nelly
P. 37 photo of VioletErotica Ita
P. 41 photo of VioletErotica Ita
P. 49 photo of coreyboi by DaddyBear Dave Rubin
P. 50 photo of Jonah
P. 53 photo of coreyboi by DaddyBear Dave Rubin
P. 57 Photos by Christine Kacz Ruse
PP. 58-62 Photos of Sable Twilight
P. 63 Photo of Sable Twilight and sophi
P. 64 Photo of Joshua by Wintersong Tashlin
P. 68 Photo of Lee Harrington in drag by himself
P. 82 Photo of TransPunk by Chris Bethke
P. 88 Photo of Lee Harrington by himself
P. 89 Photo of Lee Harrington by Darrel Victor Lynn
P. 90 Photo of Lee Harrington by himself
P. 91 Photo of Lee Harrington by himself
P. 91 Photo of Lee Harrington by Timothy Burns
P. 92 Photo of Lee Harrington by Emmy Van Ewyk
P. 107 Photo of TransPunk by Chris Bethke
P. 113 Photo of Jennifer Callanan
P. 118 Photo of Drik
P. 126 Photo of E. Nelly
P. 127. Photo of Raven Kaldera and Joshua by Sensuous Sadie
P. 128 Photo of TransPunk by Christ Bethke
P. 142 Photo of crstlbella
P. 144 Photo of TransPunk & partner by slave tom
P. 146 Photo of Sable Twilight
PP. 148-154 Photos of Terra Katherine McKeown
P. 164 Photo of Lord Tom
P. 169 Photo of Joshua by Wintersong Tashlin

P. 172 Photo of VioletErotica Ita
P. 178 Photo of Jennifer Callanan
P. 192 Photo of Ms. Jen
P. 195 Photo of Violet Erotica Ita
PP. 200-205 Photos of Vidal Rousso by Christine Kacz Ruse
P. 214 Photo of BEAR A-M Rodgers
P. 236, 260, 267 Photos of Joshua by Wintersong Tashlin
P. 268 Photo of Raven Kaldera by Sensuous Sadie
Photo directly below of Joshua by Wintersong Tashlin

www.ingramcontent.com/pod-product-compliance
Lightning Source LLC
Chambersburg PA
CBHW020606270326
41927CB00005B/195

9 780982 879405